----------------------------IMAGINATIVE PROGRAMMING IN PROBATION AND PAROLE

by Paul W. Keve

UNIVERSITY OF MINNESOTA PRESS, Minneapolis

4671

PRINTED IN THE UNITED STATES OF AMERICA AT THE
NORTH CENTRAL PUBLISHING CO., ST. PAUL

Library of Congress Catalog Card Number: 67-12966

Second printing 1971

PUBLISHED IN GREAT BRITAIN, INDIA, AND PAKISTAN BY THE OXFORD
UNIVERSITY PRESS, LONDON, BOMBAY, AND KARACHI, AND IN CANADA
BY THE COPP CLARK PUBLISHING CO. LIMITED, TORONTO

Preface

A Minnesota newspaperman was speaking to a corrections conference about the need for bolder experiments in correctional institutions. It so happened that the country's first two-man space flight had occurred a few days earlier. "The success of the recent space flights," he pointed out, "was due in large part to the thorough training the astronauts had on the ground. Every possible aspect of the space mission was first simulated on the ground to condition the men to what they would encounter and have to accomplish in space.

"In the same way we must learn to simulate community living experience for the persons in our prisons so that they may be conditioned for it instead of against it when they are moved back to the outside. If a man has a drinking problem he should have help in learning to handle it instead of being removed completely from all opportunity to develop his control in a real situation. The prison of tomorrow should have a small laboratory-type 'tavern' for experimental purposes where drinks are available just as they are in the community. If an inmate whose resolve is being tested indulges to excess, this would be clearly evident to his fellow prisoners and the staff; so it can be subject to immediate counseling and other action.

"Some men have problems with writing checks, and instead of just removing such people from any chance to handle checks, the prison should have its own inside banking service with checkbooks so men can learn from experience. If a bad check is written this would give urgency and meaning to the immediate counseling and corrective action that could be focused on that problem.

"In the same way, there should be regular social events with women present, giving the prisoners a chance to mingle socially. Again, if a man shows a problem in getting along in mixed social gatherings, this is the safest place for it to appear; this is the place where he should get experience, where guidance is available to help him in handling some of the social relationships he will face on the outside."[1]

This eloquent proposal was naturally received with some amused skepticism by the newspapers, for no matter how sound the basic premise might be, the time has not yet come when we can take quite such bold measures toward the rehabilitation of our clients in the ordinary prison. However, there is also some reason to suspect that the public may be more accepting of innovation than the professional leaders in corrections think they are, and that too often the correctional program administrators are themselves timidly holding back from imaginative improvements in techniques with the excuse that the public is not yet ready for them.

This suspicion is supported by the fact that here and there in the corrections field some creative and radical departures from conventional techniques are being tried and are encountering surprisingly little opposition. At about the time that the remarks quoted above were being made, one of the country's training schools for delinquent boys was starting a major experiment in providing a radical new type of cottage living for the boys, simulating outside living by having the boys earn their own money and pay for all their food, housing, clothing, and recreational activities just as they would on the outside. Probably the most sustained and vigorous public reaction in opposition to any correctional innovation is that attending the opening of a community residential facility for narcotic addicts. But even here the opposition is not to the method, only to the location. The objectors are the neighbors, who have

[1]Walter Eldot, feature editor of the *Duluth Herald and News Tribune*, in remarks to a Minnesota Department of Corrections staff training institute at St. John's University, June 24, 1965.

little or no quarrel with the method but want the facility to be located in some other neighborhood. Other radical departures from the usual correctional programs are receiving enthusiastic moral support and impressive financing from members of the general public. This being true, it becomes daily more regrettable to see probation and parole programs that operate with blinders, that cling to concepts and methods which are based on the instinctive beliefs of an earlier time and which ignore or reject the more sophisticated behavior modification techniques that are available today.

In one semi-urban county of 150,000 population the juvenile court probation office provides to each probationer a list of rules setting forth the punishments for any unexcused failure to report, and also dictating the style of hair for all boys on probation. Haircuts must be "butch or flat-top," and "Hair on the top of the head is not to exceed three-fourths inch in length."

Such probation supervision with ruler and hair clippers is satisfying because of its easy accomplishment of tangible change in the outward appearance of the boy. But elsewhere, corrections workers are recognizing that to force a client to assume the outward façade of conventional living is not the same as making a crucial inner change. So the purpose in this book is to discuss basic techniques for changing people inwardly, with emphasis upon those imaginative new techniques that are beginning to enrich the correctional field. The concern here is not just to describe these programs as they are at the moment, for they will change rapidly as experience dictates. Rather the purpose is to explore the basic principles involved and the lessons learned that will serve as guides for the adapting of such programs to other times and places.

Attention will be focused on field services, not on penal institution programs, though the two — once so clearly distinct — cannot now be entirely separated. More and more there is a blurring of the lines between institutional programs and the field services, for the new group homes, halfway houses, Highfields residences, and the like are programs that bridge the space between the two, linking them in a promising new treatment continuum. Hence, while this account will deal primarily with techniques belonging to the field services, in many instances these cannot be separated from institutional — or at least residential — settings.

We shall be equally concerned with juveniles and adults in the application of probation and parole programs.

IMAGINATIVE PROGRAMMING IN PROBATION AND PAROLE

The reader may be a bit critical of the organization of the material herein, for admittedly the arrangement used is somewhat artificial. Ideally, perhaps, the professional methods of helping clients should be discussed as a whole, if an author's literary skill is equal to such a challenge, for these methods are generic and do not vary in their basic principles from one type of program to another. However, since most readers will be particularly interested in specific types of programs it has seemed most useful to divide the material into categories of programs and methods even though this produces occasional repetition of treatment principles.

It is, then, willingly noted that the classification of material here is contrived and subject to challenge by purists, but its professional soundness should not be less because of the effort to arrange it in the way that is most practical for administrators who must plan social programs like some of these.

In preparing this material actual visits were made to the majority of the programs discussed here. Where names appear in illustrative cases these have been disguised, but the stories are true accounts which are not otherwise altered.

The gathering of these data could not have been accomplished without imposing upon the time of many people who welcomed visits to their offices, spent hours in discussions of their programs, and replied most helpfully to subsequent correspondence. A complete listing of them is impossible but this acknowledgment of their part in the preparation of this book is sincere and grateful.

And, finally, there were still others who believed enough in the value that such a book as this might have, and had faith enough that it could and would be written, to be willing to underwrite the considerable expenses incurred in the data gathering. To these, the trustees of the Archie D. and Bertha H. Walker Foundation, I pay my deep respects and offer most genuine thanks.

P. W. K.

Minneapolis
July 1966

Table of Contents

4671

IMAGINATIVE PROGRAMMING
IN PROBATION AND PAROLE

1

Casework as a Dynamic Method

When Minneapolis, in 1899, hired its first probation officer to work with juveniles, the new officer bought a ledger book and thereafter entrusted to it the full record for all cases placed in his care by the municipal court. In elegant longhand were recorded each child's name, address, age, and offense, and his father's name and occupation. Just one ruled line was allotted for each case and this line had to include, too, the disposition and any special instructions by the court.

During the early weeks that the new officer and the new ledger book were on the job, the record shows that one Otto L——, age fifteen, was before the court for "Disturbing a Religious Meeting." He was placed on probation, and Otto's line in the ledger book concludes with the special order that the judge pronounced in his case, "And see that you behave."

The record gives no clue to what process for the control of Otto's behavior the judge expected to be used, nor do we know how that pioneer probation officer went about the job, or what success he may have had. The chances are that a central part of his technique was a requirement that Otto "report" to him at stated times.

The many men and women who entered the new probation field during the first decade of this century were, of course, without the guidance of any precedents or prior experience in such work, so they took a simple, directive approach to the task of getting each young charge to behave. They developed the system of having the probationer report on regular schedule to the probation office, there to be questioned, admonished, advised, scolded, or praised as circumstances required. It was a highly satisfying system for probation personnel — so much so that it became solidly entrenched in probation practice and has often been a deterrent to the improvement of probation and parole methods. It was satisfying because of its simplicity. It made minimum demands upon the officer's resourcefulness and it had a specific kind of visibility that enabled the officer to prove the volume of his work in terms of the number of office visits per day and per probationer. It offered the comfortable illusion that the "discipline" of having to report to the probation office once a week was good for the child and would somehow encourage the exercise of discipline in other aspects of his living.

One juvenile court judge tells of the reporting process that was followed in his court before he came to the bench. Each probationer was given a card to keep, on which were printed the rules of probation. Around the edge of the card was a continuous row of square blocks — fifty-two of them. The child was on probation for a year and had to report each week, at which time his probation officer would punch a hole in the next block in the row. Each officer had his own punch which made a hole of distinctive shape, thus thwarting any unauthorized punching by boys looking for a shortcut. The final product, the card with fifty-two holes in it, was a satisfying accomplishment for both probationer and probation officer. It was simple, uncomplicated, and concrete. It was irrefutable testimony to a full year of weekly reporting.

But had anything else happened? Had the probationer improved? Had any kind of change occurred? All too slowly the probation and parole field has moved toward acceptance of the idea that the real goal is not outward conformity to an artificial reporting schedule, but rather an inner progress toward maturity. Even today there remains a conflict in approach. A chief probation officer who recognizes the need to accomplish an inner change in clients and who administers his services with that aim in view may still cling to the reporting practice, often with ambivalent feelings about it.

4

CASEWORK AS A DYNAMIC METHOD

In 1942 Helen Pigeon wrote in support of the reporting practice: "For offenders of the aggressive type, both adult and juvenile, regular reporting has a definite value because it symbolizes an authority which demands something from them, keeps them aware of the requirements of their position, and keeps the casework relation alive and moving. It is a necessary measure of discipline." [1] To test the present-day reaction to this, a questionnaire was sent in 1964 to juvenile and adult probation administrators throughout the country which quoted Miss Pigeon's statement and asked two specific questions: Do you agree with the statement? Do you believe that other probation workers today generally agree with the statement? About sixty responses were received, and they clearly reflected conflicting feelings among practitioners concerning the reporting practice. About two-thirds of the respondents expressed themselves as still in agreement with the statement. But a heavy majority, including many of those who agreed with the statement, were of the opinion that other correctional workers are now less convinced of the value of routine reporting.

The questionnaire also invited comments about actual practices in regard to reporting. The reactions ranged all the way from strong insistence on routine reporting to one response indicating that routine reporting was being used in only about 2 percent of the cases in that office and that no probation officer was permitted to have any probationer report routinely without the approval of the case supervisor. But even those who supported Miss Pigeon's stand were inclined to qualify their support with comments about adapting the reporting system differently to individual cases or using it mainly in the initial stages of a case.

It seems clear that most probation officers are coming to recognize that the practice of reporting must be made meaningful by individually focused plans. In this they are moving toward the modern, professional casework interview, which is outwardly similar in procedure to traditional routine reporting. In both the casual observer would see the same thing apparently happening — a probationer walking into a probation officer's office to talk for a few minutes. But there the similarity ends, for one approach is static and the other is dynamic.

In the traditional routine reporting practice there is inherent a concept of simple sequence of cause and effect. Suppose our probationer

[1] Helen D. Pigeon, *Probation and Parole in Theory and Practice* (New York: National Probation Association, 1942), p. 327.

5

is a young married man whose offense was some kind of theft. The sequence would be as follows: the man has a problem (theft); because of this problem he is placed on probation; because he is on probation he must report. In this nicely simple approach to the probation process there is no imperative emphasis on changing whatever it was in the man that led to the problem in the first place. The probationer is permitted to see his reporting as due only to the simple fact of his probation status, rather than to any need for change. He may remain cynical, hostile, antisocial; but as long as he reports regularly and keeps inside the rules he is meeting the expectations of probation. If this continues for the specified period he is discharged as having successfully completed probation even though his aggressive antisocial drives may not have been modified in the least.

Admittedly, this is the bleakest interpretation of the process and does it an injustice which would be protested by probation officers who require routine reporting. Nevertheless, the system of routine reporting allows an easy decline into sterile practice; the example of holes being punched weekly in little cards is but one sign of what an empty ceremony the practice can become. Miss Pigeon was well aware of this problem despite her support of the practice of regular reporting, for she commented that "Too often in the correctional field casework is not productive in [a] positive sense. It is negative, an enforcement of rules and a perfunctory reporting, without goal and without noticeable movement."[2]

By contrast, the casework interview with a skilled professional worker derives from a very different cause and effect concept. Again, for illustration, let us start with the young man with a problem. But here we do not label that problem as theft; instead we see it as being a combination of several more basic problems. He may have, for instance, a health problem with some chronic ailment that causes emotional depression or a degree of incapacity on the job; he may be severely burdened with debts because of poor management; he and his wife may have marital troubles; he may be in a job he dislikes; or he may have any of various long-standing emotional problems.

So here we have a cause and effect sequence which looks like this in the probation officer's mind: the man has a problem (some combination of health, financial, marital, vocational, and emotional difficulties); be-

[2] *Ibid.*, p. 274.

6

cause of this problem, or some portion of it, he is coming to see the probation officer (reporting) regularly to seek solutions.

In this sequence probation does not appear, for the man is not coming in to see his probation officer simply because he is on probation. Instead this is the far more dynamic situation of a man coming to see his probation officer because of a problem he has that they both recognize and that both are working on by means of scheduled conversations in the office. Though probation has been omitted from the chain of cause and effect, it is still present in a different way. It is there as the authoritative device that enables the officer to *require* the client to come in when he would otherwise not respond. Probation is not the *reason* for the reporting. It is only the means for enforcing the office visit.

The distinctions here may seem so subtle as to be unimportant, but the implications have great significance. In the traditional method the simple cause and effect sequence means that for the period of probation the probationer comes in to report and the reporting itself is sufficient. A probation officer with conscience and initiative will, of course, enrich that process in his own ways, but there is nothing that requires the lethargic probation officer to do anything more than keep the reporting schedule in motion. The probation officer whose acknowledged goal is to effect a needed change in the client may also have probationers reporting to him regularly, but he does so only when he sees a clear reason for the reporting — a reason that is individual to the particular case and is far more dynamic than the simple fact that the client is on probation. Furthermore, the officer's assessment of his client's problems may lead to having the client do his "reporting" elsewhere. The probation officer may arrange for a probationer with a health problem to go regularly to a clinic. If the probationer's problem is financial he may be sent to a lawyer for help with bankruptcy proceedings. For a marital problem the probation officer may decide to do the counseling himself, or he may refer the couple to a family counseling agency. For help with job placement the probationer may be sent to a vocational counselor in a public employment service. The probation or parole officer may be doing his best work when he gets someone else to do his work for him.

One example would be the elderly man who arrives on the caseload after a lifetime of lawful conduct but now has been caught in a sexual impropriety with a child. Invariably such a situation suggests a medical problem and the probation officer's job is to see to it that the man's family understands the problem, that they keep him under constant and affectionate supervision, and that medical diagnosis and treatment is obtained. When he has done this and has arranged to keep himself informed about the continuance of supervision and treatment, the officer has met the true demands of the case and it may thereafter be only a meaningless exercise of ceremony to have this probationer report regularly to the office.

(Where probation and parole work is based on the practice of requiring routine reporting, there is likely also to be direct giving of advice and ordering of behavior.) Probationers may be ordered to go to church or to change their haircuts and clothing styles. They may be ordered to stay away from certain people or places and may be told when they may or may not drink beer, own a gun, or buy a car. In contrast to this, many professionally oriented correctional workers will shun the use of direct controls, particularly advice-giving, as much as possible. Instead of issuing orders they prefer to establish a personal relationship through which persuasion can be exercised. Neither approach can be defended as the only useful one. Where a strong relationship can be developed it is by far the most effective way of helping clients, but there is experience to show that simple, direct order-giving has to be the method with some clients who cannot or will not allow themselves to be reached on a personal level. However, too often when we write off some client as unreachable some other worker comes along and with extra patience and a little different approach manages to get a response. One officer found himself with a new probationer who was so uncommunicative that when he came into the office on regular visits he volunteered absolutely no conversation of his own and responded to the officer's attempts at conversation — quite literally — with no more than a monosyllabic grunt. After enduring this frustrating experience several times and making no progress, the officer, in some desperation, asked the probationer if he liked to play ping-pong. The grunt in reply seemed to be a "yes" type of grunt so they went to a nearby facility where they played ping-pong for the rest of that visit time. This went on for three months during which all contacts were ping-pong games. Eventually the officer noticed the unmistakable signs of hostility being expressed in the fierce, hard drives of the ball; then one day the man came in and said, "Let's not

8

play ping-pong today." It was the first time he had spoken so many words to the officer and was the beginning of a relationship that finally permitted this man to talk and search for answers to his problems.

In one office which had probation officers with varying levels of training, the more hopeless cases were assigned to the least trained officers, probably because of a feeling that it was of little use to take the time of more skilled staff for cases that apparently could not be helped. Surprisingly, however, many such cases showed improvement even though the methods used were considered "wrong" by professional personnel. The psychologist in that department observed that "Sometimes the officers imposed their own standards on the probationer, marking out goals for him that were really based on their own aims in life. They directed, gave advice, openly sympathized with or openly criticized and condemned some of the actions of the probationer. . . . They had no understanding of and no curiosity about the more elusive or even obvious pathological elements in their client's behavior. They were concerned only in searching out and addressing themselves to those positives and ego strengths they could see and work with. They were concerned with making that ego function rather than with finding out and dealing with the cause of the ego malfunction. Furthermore, because they sought for these ego strengths, they found their client a more likable and attractive person than if they had addressed themselves primarily to the 'sick' aspects of his personality. This feeling of liking and respect sometimes grew into a mutual admiration society, in which the client looked upon his officer as a father, friend, brother, and confidant as well as a representative of the court." [3]

The obvious conclusion is that the professional probation officer, even as he is committed to developing with most clients a special kind of relationship that will serve as a major treatment tool, must be able to see the occasional appropriateness of acting, instead, as just a friend or as a directly controlling authoritarian.

Conscientious corrections workers have always asked themselves anxiously whether their duty lies more with treatment or with surveillance, or even whether surveillance is a worthy activity for the officer. If the answer to that can be put in simple terms it would be that it is always a

[3] Milford B. Lytle, "The Unpromising Client," *Crime and Delinquency*, Vol. 10, No. 2 (April 1964), p. 133.

better use of a skilled officer's time and is in the long run a better protection to the community for the officer to be engaged in treatment. However, the officer is not compromising his professional stature at all when his diagnostic skill indicates that a certain case is not now treatable by the ordinary means available and that straight surveillance is necessary. With the few such cases there are in each caseload the worker should not feel demeaned in handling them realistically but should be satisfied that his diagnostic skill enabled him to label them reliably, and that his flexibility enables him to work with them optimistically on the chance that after all his diagnosis might have been wrong. Furthermore, in the hands of an imaginative worker surveillance can become a process of building into the client a greater sense of responsibility.

The New York State Division of Parole, which is fully appreciative of good professional techniques, is so cognizant of the need for straight surveillance in some cases that in its New York City office it maintains a unit of men who have full-time assignments of surveillance for selected cases referred to them by other parole officers. The referring officer keeps his continuing responsibility for the case while the surveillance unit assumes the task of checking on the man's activities.

In California the Department of Corrections in 1964 established a Special Service Unit staffed with agents who are trained in police procedures. They work closely with the regular parole agents in maintaining surveillance of parolees who are high risk cases or who may be involved in organized crime. They also conduct investigations of prison escapees and parole absconders, and they serve as an effective liaison between correctional programs and law-enforcement agencies. These Special Service Unit agents are armed and they use cars with two-way radios. The California parole authorities are so far very pleased with this supplementary service.

Thus far in this chapter we have been concerned with enforcement and routine reporting in probation practice versus treatment by relationship. This dichotomy is put in a somewhat different light by some research recently done at the University of Southern California. Through extensive studies of 178 juvenile probationers and 26 probation officers it was possible to describe eight types of probationers and five types of officers in terms of the ways in which probationers relate to probation officers and vice versa. It was demonstrated that certain matchings between these groups tended to foster a high degree of effectiveness while certain other matchings seemed to have negative results.[4]

In general, this research supports Lytle's observation that different types of workers have clearly different capacities for helping clients according to the type of case. This research also, however, shows that the matchings can be systematically structured. It demonstrates that there is a place in probation and parole work for both the worker who functions as a direct, advice-giving enforcer and the one who seeks to use relationship as his primary method.

THE USE OF RELATIONSHIP

Perhaps the first element in the forming of relationship is communication. The rapport we experience when we like another person and feel close to him is usually preceded by a discovery that we can communicate with him in a satisfying way. We say, "He and I talk the same language." The chemistry of relationship is highly complex, but certainly it does not develop easily if communication does not flow effectively and reveal areas of common interests and feelings. Herein lies the first substantial handicap of the average probation or parole officer. With his middle-class, law-abiding background he may find himself faced with a considerable barrier to rapport with a client from a disadvantaged home and neighborhood. The officer may be surprised at the suggestion that he is having difficulty in this respect, for he may suppose that he and his clients are communicating satisfactorily. But the client may be clever at supporting that illusion, when actually the officer's talk and attitudes are exactly what he distrusts, or quite fails to understand. Robert Gover's delightful novel *One Hundred Dollar Misunderstanding* [5] portrays graphically the problem of effective communication between two people who have been raised with totally different values and who, furthermore, have only the faintest realization of the existence of the other's kind of values. The well-bred, middle-class college boy trying his first weekend adventure with a prostitute is completely baffled by the language and the cultural expectations of the teen-aged Negro girl who seems born to her profession. She is no less mys-

[4] Ted Palmer, "Types of Probation Officers and Types of Youth on Probation: Their Views and Interactions" (Unpublished report, Youth Studies Center, University of Southern California, Los Angeles, 1963).
[5] Robert Gover, *One Hundred Dollar Misunderstanding* (New York: Grove Press, 1962).

11

tified by him, and these two young people, both with bright, quick minds, live through their weekend together, each convinced of the complete stupidity of the other.

An interesting experiment in bridging this cultural gap through special communication techniques was tried by Joseph Massimo as a research project for a doctoral dissertation at Harvard. The task was to reach a few hard-core delinquent boys who were dropping out of school and to help them become stable through successful work experience. Making the initial contact in such a way as to minimize the cultural gap was a major part of the experiment. Massimo first got in touch with each boy by telephone — a pay phone. The operator's intrusion on the phone after three minutes served to erase the image the boy might form of the caller sitting in his office. In his conversation with the boy the caller would manage to mispronounce some words and this, too, fostered the image of an ordinary, unpolished sort of person, not too far removed from the boy's own kind of world. The approach then was to offer to help the boy find a job, a proposal which was simple and completely practical. When the boy guardedly accepted the offer of help, the experimenter arranged for them to meet in order to talk about it in detail. The meeting place was chosen entirely according to the boy's own preference and was likely to be a drugstore hangout.

This approach, which ostensibly was concerned only with helping a boy find a job, led naturally, at the boy's own speed, into other areas of personal improvement essential to success in finding and holding work. Comparisons of these boys with similar boys as control cases showed a very satisfactory rate of success in keeping the boys reached by this technique arrest-free. The total process involved in this study goes much beyond this brief description, which is presented here only to demonstrate that the forming of relationship may be facilitated through use of a particularly adapted way of communicating.[6]

Social distance is more of a handicap than the average probation or parole officer usually supposes it to be and more of a special effort to communicate is justified than the officer usually attempts. He ordinarily feels less need to work hard at it than does the worker in a voluntary agency. The corrections worker can simply order his client to come

[6] Joseph L. Massimo and Milton F. Shore, "A Comprehensive, Vocationally Oriented Psychotherapeutic Program for Delinquent Boys," *American Journal of Orthopsychiatry*, Vol. 33, No. 4 (July 1963), pp. 634–642.

in and talk and so is easily deluded into thinking that communication is going on. In other social work settings the effect social distance or strangeness between the worker and his client has had on the extent to which agency help is used has been the object of research. The factors that cause the strangeness are the same that correctional workers confront every day. "Studies of socio-economic characteristics of users and non-users indicate that non-use of help is associated with less occupational skill, less education, and lower socio-economic status in general."[7]

There is no magic bridge for bringing representatives of two cultures closer, though techniques such as that used by Massimo are very helpful. Even such a technique as his is not widely applicable, for a prerequisite is a fine capacity on the part of the worker for personal insight combined with a high degree of genuine knowledge of his client's culture. The word "genuine" is used here to contrast this with the kind of "knowledge" that is made up of subjective impressions and prejudices.

This naturally raises the question of how a corrections worker goes about becoming intimately acquainted with a different cultural world. It is a question that can be answered only by each worker's own experience, though one can say that not even long experience will do the job for a worker who is strongly confirmed in his opinions, inflexible in his attitudes, and content with himself.

At times it will not be possible for the probation or parole officer to appreciate truly the cultural values of all his clients. He can still be effective, however, and the important ingredient here is simple honesty. It is a temptation to say, "I understand just how you feel." But maybe the worker would make more progress toward a strong relationship if he took the more honest course and said quite candidly, "It's hard for me to know how you feel about this, because my experiences have been different from yours; but I'd like to know more about it if you would tell me."

The average probationer or parolee has been lied to copiously much of his life and this has deeply affected his relationship with authoritative persons, for even they have shown a talent for tampering with the truth. In the courtroom the judge commits a young man to a training school or reformatory and, with a wish to put a cheerful aspect on it, he as-

[7] Jona Michael Rosenfeld, "Strangeness between Helper and Client: A Possible Explanation of Non-Use of Available Professional Help," *Social Service Review*, Vol. 38, No. 1 (March 1964), p. 18.

sures the defendant that the institution will teach him a useful trade, or give him psychiatric help, or provide whatever is the object of yearning at the moment. The judge may be wholly well intentioned but the defendant sees him only as a liar when he finds the institution devoid of any psychiatric service or vocational training. Even when the vocational shops are there the judge's assurance is often still a lie, because the inmate on leaving the institution finds that he has been taught an obsolete trade with the use of obsolete equipment and is no more ready to earn his living than when he was sentenced. Or he may get good training in, say, barbering at a reformatory barbershop, but when paroled he finds that the state licensing authority refuses categorically to recognize prison training and so he must start all over at an outside barber college. Here again is reinforcement for his belief that the authoritarian world meets him with a pattern of lies.

The essential untruthfulness of the empty reassurances frequently given by workers to clients is a discouraging aspect of the traditional helping process but at the same time this suggests how very useful can be the reverse — how much the mere practice of rigorous honesty can do to cement a therapeutic relationship. The person who is invariably on guard against the empty (therefore dishonest) assurances of all authoritative people may be startled and won over by the brutally honest bad news given him by a worker. (Wherever ex-offenders have themselves begun to conduct a helping program for other offenders their technique includes an honesty that goes beyond anything that most professional workers are accustomed to. See Chapter 6 for a discussion of this in the Synanon program.)

Some of the better social workers have as much of a problem in this respect as their less able colleagues, for one of the attributes of a good worker is a keen sensitivity to the feelings of others. And sensitivity leads us to want to lift with good news the spirits of a person who has had too much bad news already through most of his life. When the news is bad it hurts us to have to convey it, but the skilled worker knows that there is far more therapy in bad news honestly given than in good news that cannot be fully supported.

Seymore Halleck, writing on the subject of honesty, lists many of the typical ways that professional people lie to their clients, and he presents some of the implications of the idea of strict truthfulness. Do we present a young person with the lie of some form of living-happily-ever-

14

after if only he will conform to conventional adult values? Instead we must draw the picture as it really is. "Adjustment to the adult world is not presented as something that necessarily brings pleasure but rather as a necessary and sometimes unpleasant requisite to survival. At times the worker might even openly discuss conformity as a burden and warn the patient as to some of the dangers of such behavior." [8]

This kind of honesty poses a dilemma for the traditional probation or parole officer who feels he should inculcate in his clients the conventional, middle-class moral values. Any attempt to be moralistic with clients may have the effect of a kind of dishonesty even though the worker at the time is utterly sincere. While in the good and conventional society moral values are prized for their own sake, in a more disadvantaged society values survive only on the basis of what has practical and immediate usefulness. To the well-bred probation officer who abhors stealing simply because it is morally wrong, it may be repugnant to have to appeal to a client to mend his ways for the stark and practical reason that stealing will land him in jail. However, in the context of the client's life experience that is the approach that is meaningful and honest, and so it is the approach that can lead to a helping relationship between officer and client. We have to discover that we are not compromising our moral principles if we make the effort to start where the client is even though it means that "no effort is ever made by the worker to criticize, disparage, or in any way condemn the [client's] antisocial behavior. Rather, it is considered as something the community (rightly or wrongly) will not tolerate if done openly and, most important, as something that *has not served the social or personal needs* of the [client]." [9]

This honest, nonjudgmental acceptance of the client can be the most potent means for developing a relationship through which help can be given to a hostile client. A simple and explicit example of this was the case of Gladys Weber, a young woman who was placed on probation for forgery. She had suffered experiences that lead to severe hostility. She had been severely rejected by her mother and abandoned by her father. Adjudged neglected and placed under the supervision of the welfare department she went through a series of nine foster homes be-

[8] Seymore L. Halleck, "The Impact of Professional Dishonesty on Behavior of Disturbed Adolescents," *Social Work*, Vol. 8, No. 2 (April 1963), p. 54.
[9] *Ibid.*

fore her first commitment to a training school as delinquent. When she came to court at age twenty-six for cashing a series of forged checks she had no home of her own and no one who cared for her, and she was fiercely bitter toward all constituted authority.

The probation officer who carried out the presentence investigation did a good and thorough job, but he did not have the key to winning any friendship with Gladys. She despised him just as she despised all authoritative people, and when the judge placed her on probation her relief at escaping the reformatory was offset by her expectation of having to endure supervision by that probation officer. However, her feeling was recognized and the case was assigned to another officer, Mr. Kelley, for supervision.

When Gladys was introduced to Mr. Kelley that day after the court hearing she was obviously so nervous and apprehensive that he thought it best not to try to talk to her then. He made an appointment for her to come in the next day. Gladys arrived on time for her appointment, dressed in a tight sweater and tight, black toreador pants. She sat at Mr. Kelley's desk in an ungainly, slumped position with her legs straddling the corner of the desk. Her manner was even more unladylike than her appearance and posture. She quickly began to let her new probation officer know how she felt about police and courts. She asked Mr. Kelley if he knew Detective So and So. Yes, he knew him. Gladys' reaction was bitter, blunt, and obscene.

"He don't know from ——!"

She mentioned another detective. Mr. Kelley also knew him. The same bitter obscenity erupted with savage hostility. During that entire conversation nearly every sentence was loaded with four-letter words and hot expressions of resentment.

Here is a challenge of the sort Halleck had in mind when he cautioned us not to criticize, disparage, or condemn antisocial behavior. He was not in the least suggesting that we condone it; rather he was saying that when someone like Gladys speaks feelingly about a world that is extremely real to her, using language which, after all, is the natural language of her particular segment of society, we have to accept the fact that that culture is fully as real and viable for her as ours is for us, and if we cannot accept her as she is at the moment, respecting the life experiences that make her feel as she does, we most certainly will not be able to help her.

Mr. Kelley rocked gently in his swivel chair, calmly puffing his pipe and listening with real, but detached interest. He was careful to show no reaction to the profanity and obscenity. He made no sign of enjoying or approving it but neither did he show any shock or disapproval. He gave no hint of reaction to the clothing or the unladylike posture either, but in an unobtrusive way kept his demeanor toward Gladys the same natural, casual manner that he would accord a true lady. He focused entirely on the completely practical problems that faced Gladys. She needed a job and she needed help with budgeting so she could make the restitution that the court had ordered. Mr. Kelley helped with suggestions on both. A schedule of weekly visits in the office was set up, with a mutual understanding of the practical purpose of these.

For the first several weeks the hostile, indecent language continued, but to a steadily decreasing extent. During her second month on probation Gladys was informed by Mr. Kelley that he would be taking his vacation soon. She was instantly on edge again, fearing that the hated probation officer she had first dealt with would substitute. But Mr. Kelley blandly suggested, "Suppose we both take a vacation. Suppose you just skip the reporting while I'm gone."

"You mean you trust me?"

"Any reason why I shouldn't?"

So the reporting was suspended for three weeks and after that it became still more evident that the bitter language was abating. The tight pants were now replaced by skirts and blouses even though Mr. Kelley had never said a word about dress. By now Gladys had got a job as a clerk in a small department store, where the manager did not know of her probation status. One day Mr. Kelley had a postcard from Gladys, saying that she could not "visit" him that week because she was in the hospital for an emergency operation. As soon as he had a chance he went to the hospital to call on her. It was not a matter of checking up on a probationer, but only the sort of cheer-up visit that any friend would make to a hospital patient. This was another milestone in the formation of the relationship, for Gladys was surprised and impressed by the new experience of having someone from the authoritative world go out of his way to do a purely friendly act toward her.

On her job Gladys did well and the manager began putting her at the cashier's post. She reported gleefully to Mr. Kelley about this and told him the boss wondered how she could be so perceptive in spotting probable bad checks. Gladys was highly amused that *she* should be put in charge of the money and should be watching for check passers. One day, though, her boss himself took a check that later bounced and then Gladys was worried. She promptly called Mr. Kelley to tell him that the boss would be coming down to the police department to look at mug shots of known check passers to see if he could recognize the person who had given him the check. Gladys knew that her own picture was in that collection and the boss would be sure to see it.

Mr. Kelley told her he would see what he could do and would let her know. He visited the police inspector and explained the situation. The inspector was willing to cooperate, so Mr. Kelley was able to call Gladys back and tell her not to worry, for the picture would be temporarily removed from the collection.

After another few weeks Gladys called to say, with obvious excitement, that she was in school. Her boss was so impressed with her as to think she might develop into a buyer, so he had encouraged her to take courses in merchandising — at his expense.

Gladys was released from probation after one year, with excellent progress. Her good feeling about probation was evident as she continued to come in to see Mr. Kelley occasionally after her discharge. Her language, clothing, and demeanor were feminine and respectable. It is too much to say that her hostility was gone, but it had subsided considerably and was no longer a crippling factor in her relationships with people.

THE USE OF PRACTICAL HELP AS AN AID TO RELATIONSHIP

Mr. Kelley's success with Gladys illustrates how the probation officer can sometimes effectively play the role of fixer. The word does have negative connotations, of course, relating to graft and payoffs. However, it is used here strictly in the positive sense of a person who is able to give a fully legitimate and needed bit of help to a recipient not in a position to help himself in the particular instance. Everyone needs a fixer from time to time and we have only to look at our own experiences to realize this. A suburbanite, Mr. A, has trouble with his sewer clogging and faces a major repair bill. But he has a neighbor, Mr. B, who is a handyman and can either help Mr. A or tell him how he can fix it for himself. Later, when Mr. B is trying to get tickets for a big league game that is already sold out he finds that Mr. A has just the kind of contacts needed to get two tickets. So each man enjoys the chance to do a practical favor, and in turn is appreciative of getting help when he needs it from a friend who has skill or knowledge or influence which is needed at the moment.

If the ordinary, well-adjusted, and competent person needs and appreciates an occasional fixer, certainly the average probationer or parolee has even more need. In-service training for caseworkers has always emphasized that we should avoid doing everything for the client, should avoid encouraging dependency. The caseworker should not go out and find a job for the client, for instance, but should help him learn how to find his own. Without denying any of this we can still say that a potent factor in the process of developing an effective relationship is the readiness to be a fixer when the client occasionally needs something done that is important to him and that he cannot do for himself. Whether or not Gladys' picture being in the file of check passers would have caused her to lose her job, it was a severe threat to her peace of mind at the moment. It was a problem that she herself was helpless to do anything about, and so it presented a splendid opportunity for the probation officer to act as a fixer and in so doing to strengthen the relationship.

There are some situations in which a period of constant practical help on nearly a daily basis may be needed and, in fact, there has been more than a little experimentation with this kind of intensive, pragmatic therapy. It is proving especially appropriate with drug addiction cases (see Chapter 6), and it was a primary feature of the approach tried by Massimo, who was dealing with boys pathetically ill-equipped to cope with their own practical necessities. "Motility and action were emphasized. The therapist had no central office and made frequent field trips when necessary. In essence, the therapist entered all areas of the adolescent's life. Job finding, court appearances, pleasure trips, driving lessons when appropriate, locating and obtaining a car, arranging for a dentist appointment, going for glasses, shopping for clothes with a first pay check, opening a bank account and other activities require this maximum commitment." [10]

The utilization of such techniques points up the importance of the personal qualities of the probation or parole officer. A most reliable sense of perspective and self-understanding is essential if the officer is going to become an active ingredient in his client's life and still know

[10] Massimo and Shore, in *American Journal of Orthopsychiatry*, p. 636.

exactly where to stop. He must be able to recognize the point beyond which he is no longer properly helping with problems the client can't handle and instead is beginning to relieve him of responsibility for tasks he could assume himself. Providing a person with a specific piece of assistance is a sound casework process when the help is clearly needed, but an unhealthy condition develops as soon as the helper goes a little beyond actual need and begins to foster dependency or dilute the client's sense of responsibility. With this in mind the professionally trained worker should recognize that the giving of practical help is not unworthy of his professional status, though there is a tendency to feel that casework skill must be something more profound than "helping someone get a job, be readmitted to school, find a place to live or establish eligibility for welfare, medical treatment, etc." However, "These and other concrete services are what many probationers need more than insight. When we attach to these practical services the dignity and importance they deserve, our probation staff will function more freely, without the guilt feelings they are now expressing." [11]

A simple example occurred in the case of a New York City parolee of limited intelligence whose parole officer had found him a job as an elevator operator in a large hotel. After a few days the bell captain called the officer to complain that he would have to fire the parolee. The officer hurried over to the hotel to see what the problem was and found that his man was refusing to cooperate with the regulations on uniforms. The elevator operator's uniforms required black socks and the parolee insisted on wearing white socks. He and the bell captain had reached an impasse over the issue. The parole officer, with immense patience, sat and talked with his parolee and succeeded in learning the reason for the white socks. The man explained that when he was a boy his mother had told him solemnly that socks with dye would be bad for the feet and so he should always wear white socks only. He had never questioned his mother's advice on this, even now in the face of losing a job. The parole officer's solution was to get a pair of the uniform black socks and ask the parolee to put them on over his white socks. That did it. The parolee was content with white socks next to his skin and the bell captain was content with black socks showing. There was nothing profound about the process, but it was good casework.

[11] John A. Wallace, "A Fresh Look at Old Probation Standards," *Crime and Delinquency*, Vol. 10, No. 2 (April 1964), p. 126.

Related to this is the technique of selecting simple and practical goals for both probationer and probation officer to work toward. In the California research on types of probation officers and types of probationers, this was a concept that emerged when effective kinds of interaction were studied. "Also among the recurring themes would be a working together of officer and youngster of fairly concrete, situational problems, in which progress is not difficult to discern. Together with this, however, would be the placing of a considerable measure of initiative with the youngster, but not without a readiness, on the part of the officer, to at times provide support and encouragement, structuring or interpretation, for the purpose of allaying anxieties associated with feelings of helplessness, hostility, isolation, guilt, or rejection." [12]

Too often we have frustrated our clients by describing goals in vague terms: "The length of time you will be on probation (parole) depends on how much you improve your attitudes." The client is likely to feel a sense of futility in reaching a goal that is so vague and expressed so entirely in terms of the officer's frame of reference. A simple, objectively stated goal can be far more effective. For example an officer and his juvenile client may sit down together and decide jointly how much improvement the boy could make in his grades in each subject at school. That then becomes a goal that is crystal clear and, furthermore, has extra appeal for the boy because of his own participation in establishing it.

In the course of any one probation case there can be many goals, and success in reaching them will be more likely if they are simple and explicit, and if they have some meaning for the client as well as for the worker. Success will also be greater if there is some system of immediate reward for goals reached. This can take many forms, but in general the effective reward is whatever succeeds in enhancing the client's sense of status among his friends or otherwise building his own self-esteem. If there is a good relationship with the probation officer a prompt and warmly enthusiastic word of praise from that officer may be as effective as anything, especially if it is pronounced in the presence of a parent, a teacher, the judge, or friends. But the praise and the feeling accompanying it must be utterly genuine.

Rewards also can take more specific and concrete form. In one experiment boys were taken for rides through their home neighborhoods

[12] Palmer, unpublished report, p. 26.

in a rented Cadillac convertible. This worked well for these boys, who had little or no chance to ride in such cars and lived in New York City where such transportation was not common to their neighborhoods. Even actual gifts can be used if the office has any funds for such a purpose. Young people especially have a tremendous need to be acceptable in appearance to their peers. A new pair of shoes, new jacket, new skirt, may have tremendous meaning to some of our young clients. The use of such rewards is viewed uneasily by many people as being hardly different from bribery, and, admittedly, the line between an acceptable reward for accomplishment and a bribe to secure such accomplishment can be indistinct. But a professionally competent person should have little trouble in keeping the distinction clear.

In normal, acceptable social functioning, rewards most often take the form of wages paid for work done. This is completely honorable if the work is honest production. We frown on it only if it is some form of "busy work." The other major form of reward is found in the various kinds of recognition given for quality performance. These include testimonial dinners, certificates of appreciation, the invoking of certain Latin words like *magna cum laude*, the pinning of ribbons or medals on military jackets, the placing of a gummed silver star after a fourth-grader's name on a list on a school bulletin board.

The reason these practices exist is simply that they work! They do encourage people to achieve desired goals, and they are not considered bribery. We might discern a taint of bribery if a youngster is told, "If you will stop stealing hubcaps I'll buy you a new motor bike." But if a goal is set of no delinquent activities for a specified period of time, and the youngster makes good on it, then no question of bribery arises if he is complimented warmly on the accomplishment and unexpectedly rewarded with a gift that carries token value rather than substantial and disproportionate intrinsic value. Some simple but basic data have emerged in recent years about patterns of learning. Whether dogs, monkeys, pigeons, or people are involved, behavior can be modified by causing some kind of discomfort every time unwanted behavior occurs and giving some kind of prompt reward every time desirable behavior occurs. In corrections we have made copious use of the punishment part of this process but have failed to develop the extensive possibilities of rewards for behavior we wish to encourage.

With many of our delinquents we need first to provide them with opportunities to be nondelinquent [13] and then devise appropriate systems of rewards for improved behavior.

EXPLOITING CRISES

Closely akin to the exploiting, on occasion, of a client's need for practical help is the exploiting of some of the threatening kinds of crises that frequently embroil our clients. Here again the officer must do a delicate balancing act between opposing considerations. It is a great temptation, for instance, for the officer to want to act as his client's protector against such things as police "harassment." But pick-ups and interrogations of known offenders are standard practices that they have to learn to live with, and the probation or parole officer would do better to help his client adjust to these events than to shield him from them.

Nevertheless, these crises sometimes offer superb opportunities for accomplishing improved attitudes. The parolee who comes from an institution with a hostile resentment of any more controls in his life may soften his attitudes and be ready to use help only when he finds at some point that he has run into real trouble and might be back in the "joint" if it were not for the efficient and uncondescending help of his parole officer.

This happened, for example, to a parolee named Carl who had served a sentence for carnal knowledge. He looked like a nearly impossible case at the time of the first parole contact. He was divorced, had no family and no friends. He was a drifter, an army deserter, and at age thirty-seven he had been in at least three penal institutions. To his parole officer he expressed resentment of everything and made constant unrealistic demands. On one occasion the parole officer happened to see Carl drinking beer in a bar (which for this parolee was not a parole violation) and so he sat down beside him for a moment with a cheery, "How's the beer?" Carl's bitter response was, "It was fine until you sat down here!" This kind of attitude permeated all his activities and he lost his first job because of his surly approach to everything.

The event that changed the course of the case occurred after Carl had been on parole for three months. He lived in an area not too far from the penitentiary from which he had been paroled. It was discovered that somehow liquor was occasionally being smuggled into the in-

[13] Richard A. Cloward and Lloyd E. Ohlin, *Delinquency and Opportunity* (Glencoe, Ill.: Free Press, 1960), pp. 173–177.

23

stitution through the prison farm. When a bottle was intercepted and traced to two inmate farm workers they explained that Carl had driven by the farm and had dropped it off for them at a point along the road. The warden called loudly for Carl's arrest and return to the prison as a parole violator. Despite Carl's hostile and uncooperative behavior the parole officer was doubtful that the allegations were true. In fact, there was some reason to think that Carl's sour personality was the reason his former associates in the prison were so willing to pick him as the one to blame for the smuggling. Carl denied the charge, admitting only that he had driven by the farm; nothing had been dropped off, he insisted.

The parole officer picked up Carl and arranged to obtain a lie-detector test for him. The test was made and it fully supported his story. The parole board consequently followed the recommendation of the officer and declined to revoke parole. It was this crisis and the way that it was handled that started a change in Carl. He not only became far more accepting of the officer from that point on, but also showed an improved attitude generally. Here again, a man needed a fixer and his parole officer exploited that need and gave the parolee a new feeling about other people.

This kind of point should not be made, however, without noting that an opposite kind of action can on occasion serve just as effectively to cement a relationship. That is, a relationship can be enhanced by cracking the whip when disciplinary action is deserved, even as it is enhanced by giving protection when punishment is not deserved, as in Carl's case. The officer is sometimes confronted by the immature client who has never been adequately controlled by his ineffective parents, so now even as an adult he still is petulantly looking for the control his behavior seems to be defying. The perceptive officer who finds this kind of a client testing him constantly with persistent, borderline infractions of rules will often discover that the judicious use of a weekend in jail, or some other such disciplinary measure, changes the whole climate of the case. There is such a thing as punitive action taken in a nonpunitive spirit for the purpose of convincing a client that people are truly concerned about him and that in his probation or parole supervision there will be, along with unwavering helpfulness, a strong, dependable, and fair enforcement of his responsibilities. The client's discovery of this can give him a sense of comfort and security that results in a surprising improvement in adjustment.[14]

THE USE OF AUTHORITY

The exercise of authority by the corrections worker is an art. It can be badly abused and can cause severe new damage in an already damaged person, but if it is used with a skillful blend of realism and sensitivity it can be a valuable rehabilitative tool. It is often misused both by those people who are professionally trained and by those who have no special preparation for the job. The finely educated professional too often shuns the authoritative role as too crude, and the untrained worker often wields authority comfortably and freely but with little appreciation of the expertise needed for applying it with some finesse.

The officer must be ready to use his authority fully when the occasion demands, but the most effective kind of authority he carries comes not so much from the law that backs him up as from his stature as a strong helping person. He attains this stature largely through the skill that he does in fact have, but also through conducting himself in a manner that is different from the usual social relationships. In ordinary social contacts there is free exchange between two people. I tell you my experiences, my fears, my problems, my pleasure; you reciprocate by telling me yours. That reciprocity is a function of friendship. But in the professional relationship reciprocity is curtailed if not eliminated. The patient tells the doctor in detail of his pains. The doctor does not tell of his in return; in fact, he tells very little of himself personally. The probationer's personal life is subject to scrutiny by the probation officer, but the officer does not bare his own personal life to the probationer. Traditionally it has been a primary tenet of proper casework practice that this professional aloofness must be maintained, and this has been both a virtue and a liability in social work. While it has contributed to the "professional" character of the work, it has also sometimes contributed to the appearance of coldness in social workers. The most effective worker is one who recognizes that he can be reserved in regard to information about his personal self but can still give generously of personal warmth and love. He will present a better image of strength if it is unblurred by exposure of his own personal life, but to have maximum impact on

[14] Paul W. Keve, "Jail Can Be Useful," *N.P.P.A. News*, Vol. 35, No. 5 (November 1956), p. 1.

the client he must be convincingly genuine in his affection for people.

A central fact of the probation and parole officer's work is his authoritative status, but if his professional discipline is well augmented by basic human qualities of affectionate and sensitive feeling for people the invoking of raw legal authority will be less needed. The "big stick" should be used with decisiveness whenever it is the only measure that will serve the purpose of therapy or control, but the artistry is in having the wisdom and the personal security to leave the big stick on the shelf when it is not needed. "The fact that a therapist must be in a superior position and take charge in therapy is obvious when one considers how impossible the situation would be if he did not. A patient views the therapist as an authority who can help him, and should the therapist behave in an inadequate way the patient will go elsewhere. However, it does not necessarily follow that the therapist makes an issue of being in charge, because, after all, he is dealing with people who are peculiarly sensitive in this area. The therapist assumes a position of obvious advantage in the interchange and claims the right to set rules for the relationship, while at the same time treating his superior position lightly and perhaps even denying it." [15]

A professional worker in a voluntary agency may *suggest* a course of action to a client. In a correctional agency the worker has the authority to *order* a course of action, and the mistake we often make is to give orders instead of suggestions only because we do have this authority. An example is the manner in which home visits are made. If an ordinary man and his wife are going to make a brief social call on some friends they do the courteous thing and prepare the way with a phone call first. But the same man, acting as a probation officer, may not suppose that he should bother with such social niceties, so he stops in at his client's home unannounced whenever he chooses.

When the officer does make these unannounced visits he has honest reasons for the practice. He sees it as essential to get a look at the home and its family as they really are. He also sees gross inconvenience for himself if he must call first every time he wants to visit. Partly, however, he is just assuming that because he has the authority to order the home to admit him at unannounced times he should proceed to use that authority as a matter of course. Yet his authoritative privileges need to be

[15] Jay Haley, *Strategies of Psychotherapy* (New York: Grune and Stratton, 1963).

used in a way that serves the treatment process, not just his own convenience. Our clients often are people who have been among the community's downtrodden. They have become much too accustomed to being the ones who receive the least respect and who have the fewest opportunities. One of the elements in treatment is the fostering of a higher degree of self-respect and pride. The probation or parole officer, consequently, is working against his own treatment efforts whenever he accords his client less courtesy than he would use toward other people.

The specific application of this idea will have several possible variations: (1) The officer may make arrangements to see his client for all the regular contacts at the client's home, with these being at scheduled times agreed upon in advance. This meets the demands of social courtesy if the client has had the opportunity to suggest the schedule that would suit himself and his family best. In the long run the officer will still get the effect of a true look at the home because gradually he becomes a familiar figure and the family relaxes and makes less and less effort to present an artificial appearance. (2) The officer who covers a wide rural area will have to give his clients some kind of notice of his coming if for no other reason than to be certain to see them when he arrives. He cannot afford to make another fifty-mile trip the next day to see one person. (3) The officer may have cases where, for some particular reason, he must make occasional unannounced visits to the home. At the outset he should say to the family, "I am going to have to drop in on you from time to time as part of my responsibility. I will be coming about ―― times per month and the purpose will be to ――. Is there any time or day of the week that would suit you best, or any time that would not be convenient for you?" (4) Sometimes the officer may have a case that is beyond rehabilitative help and calls for aggressive surveillance. In this instance concern for protection of the community is paramount and frequent unannounced check-up visits may be called for. Even here, however, the officer should in the beginning explain the practical necessity of this to the client, letting him know also that a different handling of his case can be instituted if the client shows by his conduct that vigorous surveillance is no longer needed. (5) Even in those cases where no home visits are being made without prior announcement, the officer may find himself in the vicinity of the home one day and feel that it would be well to take that opportunity to drop in for a chat. He can still

27

do the courteous thing by explaining at the door the unusual nature of the visit and asking if it would be convenient for him to come in.

Admittedly these practices may annoy those people who think that we already are coddling our parolees and probationers. But nothing said here is intended to discourage the decisive use of authority, no matter how heavy-handed, when it is necessary to control a dangerous client and protect the community. For the client who is not dangerous, giving him all the courteous consideration that the probation or parole situation permits actually serves a useful function in treatment by encouraging him to see himself as a normal, self-respecting, and respected social being. This approach may seem to be inviting clients to take advantage of the officer, but if this happens it is only because the officer has himself confused courtesy with weakness. The skilled officer will make clear to the client decisively and firmly what procedures are to be followed, but then will let him suggest any modification of the procedures that does not interfere with the essential purposes of the probation or parole process. It might seem to a client that this is weakness on the officer's part, but if so he will soon test the officer in other ways and there will be ample opportunity to demonstrate the authoritative strength in the position, without resorting to discourtesy. To argue for courtesy toward probationers or parolees does not reflect merely a liking for the social amenities, it should be stressed, but — more important — a recognition of the practical value of courtesy in the correction of people with problems of social adjustment.

Though these principles may seem of minor importance they actually are basic in the treatment process, for anything that helps the client accept authority is helping him mature. Authoritative controls permeate our daily living to such an extent that we have little consciousness of them. A person cannot get into his car and drive it away from the curb without accepting the authority that requires him to have a driver's license on his person. He is authoritatively restricted to driving on the right side of the street, at a certain speed, making his turns in a certain prescribed way in response to certain signals and after giving certain signals himself. We accept these controls and a thousand more every day because we have a general belief in the benign and practical quality of the authority that controls us. When we consider how we face authoritative controls at every turn in our lives, we realize how unfit for successful functioning is the person who is at odds with authority.

The damaged view of authority our clients have must be countered with a constructive example of authority as they deal with us, and every little error we commit in using authority unfeelingly, dishonestly, or weakly adds to the problem and reduces our effectiveness in treatment.

Dale Hardman has described the use of authority with fine perceptivity in one of the most significant articles available on the subject. He emphasizes that we must, above all, define for the probationer or parolee exactly what our authority is:

I will make crystal clear, in defining my role, where my authority begins and ends, and I will consistently function within these limits. I will avoid veiled threats, bluffing, or any behavior that might be so interpreted, since this clouds, rather than clarifies my limits. This rule will eliminate a vast amount of testing by the client.

I will further clarify which decisions are mine to make and which the client must make . . .

Once I have made a decision, I will steadfastly resist all client efforts to alter my decision by threats, tantrums, seduction, illness, etc. I will just as steadfastly defend his right to make his decisions and stand by them. By the same token, if a client shows me rational evidence that I have made a hasty or unwise decision, I will alter it and will tell him so. Common terms which authority-conflicted persons use to describe authority are "arbitrary, inconsistent, and unfair." For this reason I must demonstrate that authority can be considerate, consistent and fair.[16]

This statement reflects an old and respected casework technique of telling the client what to expect in some future course of action. If some treatment plan is being started and it is likely that in the course of it the client will pass through stages of depression, anxiety, frustration, or anger before he reaches a condition of improvement, this should be discussed with the client. When he then reaches a point of frustration or discouragement the fact that his worker had accurately predicted it makes the condition more tolerable, enhances the client's confidence in the worker, and makes him more likely to stay with the treatment plan.

ENHANCING SELF-ESTEEM

The authoritative stance of the probation officer can work either to enhance or to depress the client's self-esteem, depending on certain in-

[16] Dale Hardman, "The Function of the Probation Officer," *Federal Probation*, Vol. 24, No. 3 (September 1960), p. 7.

tangible qualities in the way it is applied. Certainly the building of self-esteem is one of the most important aspects of rehabilitation. Persons who have been rejected, who have forever been on the receiving end of help given by stronger persons, who have never had the experience of being complimented by anyone for anything — these are persons who have no sense of self-worth and so no motivation to work at the goals the probation officer sets for them.

Unfortunately, many a probation office has been operated in ways that have served to defeat the rehabilitative process. The probation or parole organization that tolerates dirt, noise, and confusion in its offices and that permits people to be herded impersonally through its reception areas is saying, in effect, that these clients are of little worth, otherwise they would be treated with more dignity and privacy. A probation or parole officer may be doing a good job back at his desk but his work may be undermined by a bored receptionist who treats clients in a peremptory and condescending way and who talks loudly with each visitor without regard to the listening ears of the others in the waiting room. If the officer hopes to build self-esteem in his client and convince him that people in authority genuinely care about him he must be sure that all the others associated with the agency are reflecting the same concern.

Self-esteem is composed of highly personal elements, including matters of personal appearance, an area in which feelings are often delicately balanced. In the Preface was mentioned the juvenile court that requires all boys to have their hair cut no more than three-fourths of an inch in length. Conceivably this requirement could be defended on the grounds that a boy with a neat haircut will be more readily accepted by middle-class adults, and this will contribute to his self-esteem. But a worthy goal must be reached by worthy means, or it will not, in a true sense, be reached at all. A conventional haircut is a worthy goal for the probationer, but a peremptory order is not a worthy means of attaining it.

Styles of hair and clothing give identity to a group. The dignified, cultured, and responsible segment of the community will have its own way of dressing, and the persons who see themselves as rejects of the conventional social group will have theirs. Special hair and clothing styles serve to give the delinquent boy a sense of belonging to some social group at the same time that he is showing defiance of the group that is rejecting him. If he must give up his identifying haircut only because an authoritative person from the "squares" has peremptorily ordered him to do so, he feels that this imperious rejection of his haircut (his badge of membership in his social group) is just further rejection of himself and his social world.

The unskilled, insensitive worker will get that unconventional haircut changed, but he will do it in a dictatorial way that engenders more hostility and increases the distance between the boy and the person who is supposed to get close to him to help him. The skilled, sensitive worker will also get a more acceptable haircut, but by accepting the boy instead of rejecting him. That is, he will be saying, in effect, "Come on into my part of the social world — we like you and want you; and a different kind of haircut will help to make you one of us."

The legal purist will argue properly that we have no moral right to force middle-class standards of grooming upon a person just because some misdeed of his has put us in an authoritative position over him. With equal validity the behavioral scientist will argue that we will accomplish genuine change for the better only when the client moves to the desired behavior with some interest and willingness on his own part, rather than resentfully under duress. If the boy is going to give up willingly an objectionable style of grooming in favor of another style, he will have to be persuaded of the greater rewards in doing so. When he recognizes that the middle-class world will reward him with an acceptance that is more satisfying than the acceptance of his delinquent peers, he will pay the price in the kind of appearance required.

The probation officer who orders a boy or girl from a culturally desolate family to dress or behave in certain ways is only one more person among the many who have bossed this child around for reasons related only to their own biases and convenience. But a probation officer who takes a genuine interest in the child will find less directive but more effective methods. A very practical approach is called for. A boy may want to get a job. If he is satisfied that his probation officer is honestly and sensibly trying to help him attain this practical goal, he is ready to tolerate the suggestion that an employer is not going to give him a chance unless his haircut is modified a little. The officer may have to give him much encouragement and support in this seemingly simple matter because it cannot be taken for granted that this boy can just walk into a barbershop and casually get an ordinary haircut. He may not know what shop to visit or what words to say. But when he does make a move to do something about his hair, the officer's job is to follow the supportive encouragement with rewarding praise. The youngster is very much in need of acceptance and any tiny improvement of appearance or behavior should be the signal for a warm and pleased response from the officer.

This need for acceptance is often of particular importance with adult women clients. Typical in a female caseload is the woman who is dispirited and unimpressed with her role as a woman. She sees femininity mainly in terms of casual invitations to bed. As a developing girl she did not have the kind of complimentary attention that could teach her to be pleased with her femininity for its own sake. In a more normal home and society a girl will receive an occasional cheerful comment from an unselfish male—"How nice you look today." Or simply, "That dress is mighty purty." The process of making a girl happy to be female is so very simple, and also so very, very important. When the girl or woman for whom that process has not taken place comes onto the caseload, we find that she does not know how to be feminine and is hostile toward a world that rejects her for this failure.

For a person like this the very active cultivation of self-esteem will be the heart of the casework process. If she is too heavy, every pound of weight she diets off should call for a word of praise. In the most sympathetic, supportive, and practical manner she should have suggestions about shoes, stockings, hemlines, color combinations, hairstyles; most important of all she must receive *genuine* compliments for every sign of improvement. If the effective men in her life — father, husband, brother, son, employer — are unappreciative, it may be that the officer can help them to see how important it is for them to contribute too.

Either a male or a female worker can handle this job, with some individual exceptions, of course; but if a female officer is dealing with this kind of female client, an essential part of the worker's technique will be her own grooming. It may seem peculiar to classify the worker's personal grooming as a part of her casework technique, but the validity of this concept becomes clearly apparent when we see how our female clients, especially teen-age girls, instinctively respond positively to a caseworker who is truly attractive. This does not mean that a requirement for all female probation or parole officers should be natural beauty. In fact, the woman who is less than beautiful but makes the most of her limited assets with exquisite grooming may be the most effective worker. The woman who assumes a casework job with girls must believe in her own feminine self enough to keep her weight under control, her hair in attractive order, and her clothes in tasteful style, and to show a zestful sparkle in her approach to the job.

It should not be assumed that haircuts and good grooming are being set forth here as the main concern of the caseworker in probation or parole. The haircut does have much significance because of its meaning to the client himself and to people whose acceptance or rejection of him is crucial. But it has deserved this much space only because the technique advocated here for dealing with it is illustrative of the technique of dealing with many of the other social characteristics which officers have to try to control or modify in clients.

FOSTERING RESPONSIBILITY

The development of a mature sense of responsibility is twin to the development of a mature acceptance of authority. The rationalizations in which offenders indulge to excuse their crimes constitute elaborate evasions of responsibility. With this in mind leaders in the correctional field are showing a growing concern about dealing with the offender as he is, here and now. The new presentence investigation manual for the federal courts cautions against overly extensive inquiries into the defendant's distant past. "In conducting the investigation and in writing the presentence report, the probation officer should be primarily concerned with how the defendant thinks, feels, and reacts *today*. He starts with the defendant as he finds him — as of this moment — and includes in his report no more from the past than what is believed essential to help the court understand the defendant as he is *today*."[17]

A principal exponent of the practical concern with the client as he is at the moment is Dr. William Glasser, who advocates what he calls "reality therapy." Glasser, a psychiatrist working with delinquents, argues that no matter what obscure factors in the past have acted to cause a person's defects of today, the problem we now face is essentially the same from case to case: we must help the client develop a sense of responsibility. He discounts the probing of the client's early

[17] *The Presentence Investigation Report* (Publication No. 103, Administrative Office of the United States Courts, Division of Probation, Washington, D.C., 1965), p. 2.

history and argues that attempts to give the offender an understanding of the reasons for his personality distortions only provide him with an excuse for continuing to be that way. His view is that most antisocial conduct can be construed and treated as an avoidance of responsibility.

Because of his readiness to use detention and training school commitments to bring the irresponsible person to an awareness of realities, Glasser is viewed by certain observers as punitive in approach. However, he is emphatic in insisting that while punishment has its uses, it is of no avail without the presence of deeply humane qualities. "No one, delinquent or not, can become responsible without some warm human involvement with a strong mature person who cares about him. . . . The reality therapist has to assume that in the life of the young offender no one was close enough to enable him to feel worthwhile enough to take responsibility for himself." [18]

Glasser has put his own label on the concept, but this view of the helping process is fairly widespread. It is inherent in much that has been said in the foregoing pages about the stating of moral concepts in the most simple and practical terms. Nor is the emphasis upon the client's own responsibility contradicted by the foregoing remarks about giving practical help to the client. It has not been suggested here that the probation officer should do things for his client which the client can do for himself. It has been argued instead that rapport with the client can be increased and the officer's stature in his client's eyes can be enhanced by the officer's ability to do things helpful to the client which the latter cannot do for himself.

There are times, however, when it seems legitimate to interpret that concept somewhat broadly. In one case, for instance, a probation officer working with an older teen-ager found the boy to be so immature (irresponsible) that he would not get up in time to go to work in the morning. This officer happened to have a demonstration caseload of just fifteen cases, so he had the time to give the problem concentrated attention. He personally went to the boy's home every morning, roused him from bed, and stayed with him until he ate his breakfast and got to his job — on time. After some days of this the boy got the idea that it had to be done and as soon as he showed enough responsibility to get up without being prodded the officer discontinued his morning visits. This kind

[18] William Glasser, "Reality Therapy," *Crime and Delinquency*, Vol. 10, No. 2 (April 1964), p. 139.

of help to a grossly immature person is no different from that given by a father to a small child learning to walk. He holds the child's hand, guides his direction, and gives balance and support; but he withdraws his support as soon as the child can walk by himself.

The alert officer will find many opportunities to help his clients, adult or juvenile, exercise their own responsible decision-making abilities. One adult probationer came in to see his probation officer and asked for permission to borrow money and buy a car. The request was an impractical one for this particular client. The probation officer surprised him by getting up from his swivel chair behind the desk and asking the client to move to that seat. The officer then sat in the side chair where the client had been. "Now let's say you're the probation officer and I'm a probationer asking for permission to buy a car. You know what my finances are at the moment and you have the responsibility to see to it that I do the right thing. So, how about it? Can I buy the car?"

This, of course, is a technique that could backfire, but, as in this case, if the officer knows his client and has the knack to carry off role reversal effectively, this can work well as a lesson in responsibility for the client. The probationer in this case rose to the occasion and told his probation officer the reasons why permission could not be granted. When he left he had his answer and he himself had formulated it.

2

Special Casework Approaches

The correctional field has long regarded social work training uneasily as a kind of book learning that is somehow not quite practical or realistic enough for dealing with the criminal world. But in all honesty we must ask ourselves whether this has reflected an accurate evaluation of the deficiencies of social work or a resistance to *any* kind of graduate academic preparation. Corrections was for decades the province of practitioners and administrators who performed on the basis of experience unmodified by special education, and it is only human for such personnel to resist any trends that seem to emphasize qualifications they do not have. Inexorably, though, as salaries improve and as more is learned about the dynamics of human behavior, there is more emphasis in corrections upon graduate education; and while advanced work in any one of the behavioral sciences is acceptable in various locales, the master's degree in social work is steadily gaining acceptance as the most generally useful academic qualification for persons who administer correctional programs or deal directly with clients.

The field of social work education has lately begun to recognize its responsibility to corrections and in the last few years has made impressive efforts to strengthen its usefulness to prospective correctional officers. In 1960 the Council on Social Work Education established a Corrections Project which over the next five years succeeded in increasing greatly the number of faculty members in schools of social work who had practical experience in corrections, in adding substantially to the teaching materials in social work drawn from correctional settings, and in multiplying the number of field work placements by schools of social work in correctional agencies. The final outcome of the Corrections Project was an interim committee which planned and established the present Joint Commission on Correctional Manpower and Training, a three-year program authorized by Congress to improve all aspects of personnel selection and training for corrections.

While the field of social work is thus assuming increased responsibility in training for corrections, it does not yet have the capability of supplying the demand for workers. The enrollment of students in graduate social work increases each year, but the jobs in corrections increase at an even faster rate. This is the ostensible reason why many correctional agencies still do not require more than the B.A. degree; but in some instances the lack of an aggressive agency effort to recruit personnel with graduate social work training betrays a lack of real conviction about its worth.

There is a widely accepted argument that where graduate education can be made a qualification for probation and parole personnel it is social work that is the most appropriate field. Graduate studies in sociology or criminology provide relevant informational courses. But probation and parole officers cannot be satisfied just with having knowledge about social problems; they must in addition have a technical skill in attacking such problems. The social work curriculum is ordinarily the only one that provides training in the techniques of directly helping individuals.

This is not to say that social work training is a sine qua non, or that all persons with social work training are suitable for corrections work. There is no magic in such training that will make a good corrections worker out of a poor one. But a person who is naturally endowed with qualities of personality that make for a good probation or parole officer will be a still more effective officer if his natural abilities are sharpened by social work training.

It is from this point of view that this book has been written. It will be assumed here that social work methods belong to probation and parole.

37

If a corrections officer is sensitive to human needs and feelings, if he is competent and effective in helping his clients, he is performing as a social worker whatever his education. But if, in addition to having these qualities, he can obtain social work training, he will exploit still more fully the opportunities he has for improving the social functioning of his clients.

This is true even though sometimes the person who has acquired formal social work education assumes that casework is an explicitly defined method fraught with psychiatrically oriented concepts and limited to the format that was used in his academic training. This is sometimes an impediment to the social work science as it offers itself to corrections. The practitioner who avoids using, in a situation of the moment, a simple, practical, earthy technique on the grounds that it is not proper casework method does a disservice to himself, his client, and the profession. The more mature and secure social worker will see that any process that is genuinely helpful to a client is worthy of professional regard. In fact, the social work profession will not be progressive unless its practitioners can be innovative and are able to venture into processes that represent new and resourceful applications of the basic principles taught in school.

So here the term "casework" is being used in a very broad sense, even including such a situation as one in which a worker might elect to administer a spanking to a small boy client. This can be casework if properly done. It will in fact require a good degree of casework skill, and it should not be attempted at all unless the worker does have the skill to determine the proper time, the proper place, the proper mood for such a measure, and to administer this kind of correction with both the objectivity and the love that make it a truly professional procedure. Casework, then, is seen here as the use of any humane and unselfish process that truly helps an individual client; any corrections practitioner, whatever his training, can employ it with professional pride.

With an eye to subsequent chapters it should be mentioned that the social group work method will be approached with the same broad outlook as casework.

DIFFERENTIATION OF CASELOADS

As one means of making casework a little more efficient and effective there have lately been new refinements of systems for differentiating caseloads, providing various kinds of specialties, or adapting casework techniques to varieties of cases. It might be a matter of selecting some cases to be worked with intensively by a caseworker, while other cases have more casual attention on over-sized caseloads. Or it might be a matter of assigning to a certain worker a caseload composed exclusively of one type of case. When this is tried some kind of screening system for classifying cases is called for.

The simplest use of differential criteria is as old as probation and parole themselves — the division of cases by sex and age. In the United States it has to a large extent been taken for granted that we separate males and females into different caseloads, and we also customarily separate adult and juvenile cases. Depending upon the locale, there may also be separation by race. Some of these conventional differentiations have been meaningless and even unwise. To a certain extent, for instance, separation by sex is sensible and useful, but sometimes it is adhered to when it is so impractical that the persistence of such separation can be due only to habit or prudery.

Admittedly there are extra cautions to be observed by a person working with clients of the opposite sex, but with intelligent alertness to the dangers a worker can handle cases of both sexes with minimum risk. In fact, when rigid segregation of cases is practiced the client who needs and would respond more quickly to a worker of the other sex is denied the special benefit he would have from such a relationship. Also, in state-level organizations the practice of segregating by sex greatly and unnecessarily increases administrative costs since it results in two parallel systems of agents covering the same territory. Where the area includes extensive rural districts this represents a travel cost per case which cannot be justified in relation to the minimal risk there is in the integrated caseload. There have been years of experience with integrated caseloads, especially in the small, locally autonomous offices where there is no choice but to have the one probation officer handle cases of both sexes. When on occasion it appears unwise for a male officer to work with a certain female case that officer can ordinarily find a local female welfare worker or a competent volunteer to whom he can delegate the direct casework while he remains as consultant and the person with the ultimate responsibility.

It is evident that flexibility is desirable. We must adapt both to administrative considerations and also to case considerations. Where we have an easy choice, as in an office with a number of workers of both sexes in one location, probably most of the cases should go to a worker of the same sex, but we should be quick to recognize that a certain small boy will respond best to a woman who can give him the maternal attention he needs, while a certain girl will respond best to an authoritative, strong man.

One of the more unusual forms of caseload differentiation is separation by religion. This is a rarity except in New York City where for many years it was traditional to hire probation officers for juvenile work according to whether they were Jewish, Catholic, or Protestant, and then to assign cases to them accordingly. The reasons for this were largely historical and have no importance in this discussion.[1]

Differentiation by certain broad problem categories is being practiced now in some offices that have a large enough volume to permit this. As an example, the New York City office of the New York Division of Parole has classified cases by level of intelligence. One unit of parole officers is assigned entirely to cases of retarded parolees while another unit works with gifted parolees. Narcotics cases also have the attention of a special parole unit (see Chapter 6).

Differentiation by Objective Criteria. One of the most extensive efforts to differentiate adult caseloads has been in California where the Base Expectancy Scoring Method was developed to predict probable parole success. By means of this predictive device parolees in certain districts have been grouped in caseloads according to whether they are high, medium, or low risk cases. It has been hoped that whether or not this results in more effective rehabilitative efforts, there will be, at least, greater economy in the operation of the corrections program by identifying those inmates who can safely be paroled early and by providing the parole officers with a means of differentiating between cases which have to be worked with closely and cases which may be given minimal attention.

The device is based on a check list of twelve items that seem to have predictive value: (1) arrest-free period of five or more consecutive years, (2) no history of any opiate use, (3) few jail commitments (none, one, two), (4) current offense not checks or burglary, (5) no family criminal record, (6) no alcohol involvement, (7) not first ar-

[1] Alfred J. Kahn, *A Court for Children* (New York: Columbia University Press, 1953), p. 300.

rested for auto theft, (8) six or more consecutive months for one employer, (9) no aliases, (10) first imprisonment under this serial number, (11) favorable living arrangement, (12) few prior arrests (none, one, two).

These items are weighted variously and the scores for each subject are added to produce his total "raw score." By use of a table the raw score is converted to a percentile rank which indicates the risk level. Persons in the upper 30 percent are considered low risk and may be placed in large caseloads with minimum supervision. The high risk cases are those in the lower 30 percent and must be subject to close supervision on small caseloads. The remaining cases are the middle expectancy cases and considered amenable to active helping processes on caseloads of conventional size.

A check list is started for each man sentenced to a prison term as he arrives at the institution in which he is incarcerated. The presentence report from the committing court is utilized in assigning scores as well as information obtained directly from the inmate.

This procedural means of predicting the probable success of the parolee was understandably greeted with skepticism by people who believed that it could not match the reliability of an experienced parole officer's subjective judgment. However, some research in which the two methods were compared showed that the scoring device was fully as reliable as the judgment of any experienced person. At the same time the proponents recognize that the scoring device cannot consider all the factors that are pertinent to classification of cases. No matter how reliable it is in identifying those cases, for instance, in which new arrests are unlikely, it will not single out the cases that do need and will respond to casework help with personal problems even though possible new criminal activity is not the issue. The scoring method, consequently, is useful as an initial classification device, but must be supplemented by a more subjective refinement of it for each case, when the parole agent considers emotional, marital, employment, or other factors.

There also may be movement from one classification to another as the character of a case changes over time. A murder case may be classified for minimum parole supervision on the basis that there is very little likelihood of new arrests. However, after a number of years in prison such a parolee will need active help during his first few weeks on parole, so he is likely to be scheduled for intensive supervision at first and then for minimum supervision as soon as his situation seems to be stabilized.

Even though this technique has been in use for a number of years it must still be regarded as very new, with much of its potential as yet unproven. High risk cases have been placed in caseloads of no more than thirty parolees and in some instances as few as fifteen each. Low risk cases have experimentally been granted early parole and have been placed in caseloads with as many as one hundred cases and with scheduled contacts only every three months. The research that has accompanied this program has shown that low risk cases handled in this way have been fully as successful as similar cases that had more attention under conventional handling. The higher risk cases seem to be more successful, too, in this over-all program, which California refers to as its Special Intensive Parole Unit project. However, the research findings are not at all conclusive. In one twenty-four-month period, for instance, the high risk cases that were handled in intensive caseloads had a 49.6 percent return to prison, while the similar cases in conventional caseloads had a 51.9 percent return.[2] This is a nearly negligible difference and there are variations in the results according to geographical region, time periods, and various other factors. Nevertheless, the research findings in general do give evidence that there is greater effectiveness in the reduced caseloads.

The Base Expectancy Scoring Method is not reported in complete detail here because, while the general principle is fully appropriate for use elsewhere, the specific structure of the device should probably not be considered exportable as it is. It was developed with particular relevance to California, and any other correctional organization would be more certain to be satisfied if it develops its own. As a guide to others regarding the principle of the scoring method California offers the following "Recipe for Base Expectancies":

1. Select a representative sample for study.
2. Define "favorable" and "unfavorable" parole adjustment for the purpose of the study.
3. Collect information which might be related to parole outcomes. This must be sufficiently available, accurate, reliable, and valid for the specific purpose of parole outcome prediction.

[2] Joan Havel and Elaine Sulka, "Special Intensive Parole Unit, Phase Three" (Research Report No. 3, Research Division, California Department of Corrections, March 1962), p. 12.

4. Measure the relationship of each item of information with every other item, including the outcome.

5. Mix well (add a little algebra and a lot of arithmetic, preferably with help of electronic computer). [A footnote here elaborates: "Complete a multiple linear regression analysis."]

6. Result is an equation for Base Expectancy raw score calculation. It tells which items are best predictors and how they should be weighted.

7. Proof of the pudding is in how well the method of assigning scores works when tested on other samples.[3]

Differentiation by Maturity Levels. While the adult cases described above are classified according to mathematical processing of standard objective criteria, there is another process which, for juveniles, attempts to classify cases by subjectively observed evidence of the child's level of maturity. The Base Expectancy Scoring Method is hardly useful for juveniles, since most of the items in it deal with actual life experiences or patterns that ordinarily would be meaningful only with adults. In classifying children the progress of the maturing process is the important consideration and in California's Community Treatment Project an elaborate and sophisticated classification plan has been developed. This divides the children into three main groups — high maturity, middle maturity, and low maturity cases.[4] These in turn are subdivided into nine classifications altogether. Once the cases are classified they are worked with in small caseloads of no more than twelve each and the worker is especially selected for his personal interest and adeptness in handling the particular type of child that is assigned to him.

The Community Treatment Project is located in two cities, Stockton and Sacramento, and takes its cases from the California Youth Authority. These are boys and girls who have been committed to the state as delinquent by the juvenile courts in these two cities and sent to a reception center. Certain of them are then assigned to the Community Treatment Project, which means that they return to the community again, but under this specialized program of supervision. Other cases, not so assigned, are handled conventionally and are observed as control cases. The state is financing the project and a National Institute

[3] Don M. Gottfredson and Jack A. Bonds, "Systematic Study of Experience as an Aid to Decisions" (Research Report No. 2, Research Division, California Department of Corrections, December 1961), p. 3.

[4] Marguerite Q. Grant and Martin Warren, "Alternates to Institutionalization," *Children*, Vol. 10, No. 4 (July–August 1963), pp. 147–152.

of Mental Health grant is financing the very thorough research that accompanies it.

This, too, is a project that attempts to determine how many more offenders can safely be left in the community, avoiding costly expansion of institutions, but it also attempts to demonstrate what further gains may be achieved by differentiating types of personality problems and matching these with differentiated treatment methods. For instance, the low maturity child is defined in the project as a youngster who has almost no control over his emotions and so is completely self-centered and impulsive. He sees other people only in terms of givers or withholders, and tends to suppose that all his troubles are the direct result of the arbitrary and hostile actions of other people. He has no understanding of his own emotions and no awareness that his emotions and activities affect what happens to him. With this type of child there must be a long and patient process of teaching him to recognize his own emotions and to discover what effect they have on other people. It may take six months to a year just to accomplish this much, and during this time the worker (in the Community Treatment Project he is called a community agent) has much to do in pacifying those who suffer under the impact of the child's disturbance. Such children are constantly damaging every situation they enter, so the agent must regularly give sympathy, help, and interpretation to teachers, police, and others. Nevertheless, the low maturity cases seem to show the best success rate.

The three major maturity levels are further divided into subtypes according to whether the children are characteristically passive, aggressive, neurotic, anxious, manipulating, conforming, or show certain combinations of these. Probably the least success in this program has been achieved with a psychopathic, manipulating subtype of the middle maturity children. These are children who avoid forming relationships and have no anxieties that lead them to desire change. They are inveterate con artists who manage to get by with much of their own brand of mischief when on regular parole. In the Community Treatment Project, however, they are under such close supervision that they get caught more readily and so the research tends to show a greater rate of failure for children of this type in the project than for the same type in the conventional program as control cases. By contrast, some of the subtypes are showing substantially fewer arrests or failures among the project children than among the control cases. In one two-year period, for instance, a middle maturity subtype showed a 29 percent failure rate among the experimentals while the conventionally handled controls showed a 46 percent failure rate.[5]

These differences from subtype to subtype point up a persuasive argument advanced in behalf of the differential treatment of cases. One finding has been that the treatment methods which work for one type of child may have no effect or even a reverse effect on another type. In the same way a particular staff member will be successful with one kind of child and not at all with another. The conventional, undifferentiated caseload tends to hide these effects. "Thus, by lumping together all subjects, the beneficial effects of a treatment program on some subjects, together with the detrimental effects of the same treatment on other subjects, may each mask and cancel out the other."[6]

As an illustration of the need for differential handling, Marguerite Q. Warren cites the following: If psychological testing before and after a period of treatment shows that an unsocialized, aggressive, and impulsive child — one subtype of immature child — has gained in self-control, this is a healthy trend. However, the same test results would be considered an unhealthy trend if obtained from a more mature but rigidly neurotic child.[7]

If different techniques are to be used with different types of children, an agency's staff must work in a setting which allows great flexibility of operation and which offers the easy development of a variety of activities. In Stockton, for instance, the Community Treatment Project offices are in a store-front, one-story building that has a reception area and waiting room in front; behind these are offices, and then space for a schoolroom, craft shop, and general recreation area. The children are encouraged to come to this center often and much of the work with them is planned so that they will have to be there on the premises frequently. The agent sees his cases with a frequency that amounts to almost daily contacts in some instances. As the children work at crafts, play ping-pong, or just hang around, the agent has opportunities to ob-

[5] Community Treatment Project Research Report No. 5, State of California, Department of the Youth Authority, February 1964, p. 14.

[6] Marguerite Q. Warren, "Implications of a Typology of Delinquents for Measures of Behavior Change: A Plea for Complexity" (Paper delivered at the Annual Convention of the Council for Exceptional Children, Portland, Oregon, April 23, 1965), p. 3.

[7] Ibid., pp. 4, 5.

serve the progress each is making and he can talk to the boy or girl when issues of the moment make the youngster ready to talk.

In addition to frequent one-to-one talks, the agent uses group methods. He may form about half of his caseload into a group and may meet with them twice a week. They will sometimes have discussions and sometimes go riding or try some other recreational activity. The agent has a budget for such program incidentals as popcorn. In some of the groups of low maturity children the role-playing techniques are found to be useful. Many of the agents also hold regular group meetings with parents.

The enormous advantage of this kind of program is not only in the low caseloads that allow frequency of contact with the child, but also in the almost daily opportunity to see the boy or girl in natural activities and relationships. The problems the child has show themselves in the social situations at the center, so the agent is able to observe a child's defects in social functioning and to evaluate any progress he makes. This means, too, that the agent can be ready at any time to refine the treatment process according to the observations made of actual behavior. The worker in the Community Treatment Project is, further, given great freedom of choice of treatment devices and supported by the project's administration with the necessary practical aids to the methods he may want to employ. Foster homes are also used in some cases, and detention is a part of therapy when necessary. Sometimes detention is the only way at the moment to convince a child that someone really cares, and cares enough about what happens to him to go to the trouble of locking him up for a day or two.

The center, as was mentioned, has a classroom, and this completes a picture that is rather foreign to most probation and parole personnel. We ordinarily proceed on the assumption that a probation or parole service provides only casework service, and this in a restricted sense which excludes any services that might be found elsewhere in the community. And certainly school is one of these. Yet, here is a type of probation program that acts to provide whatever services the child needs — not only school, but recreation and a wide range of social experiences. The staff at the center includes a full-time teacher, and at any one time several of the children under the supervision of the center will be in his classroom regularly every day. These have been expelled from school or are such school problems that they would damage both the school and themselves by staying in it. Because the general environment at the center is a supportive and comfortable one for the child he is better able to use the school experience here. The teacher can gear his approach fully to the needs of these special problem children instead of having to give major attention to a classroom full of more normal children.

In respect to the child's other social needs, the program operates on the assumption that for maximum effect on these volatile cases the community agent must himself be involved with the child in many of his activities so that he can shape these to the child's particular needs — and this means having these social experiences centered on the project's premises.

This is a costly program as compared with conventional probation, but it still is a money-saver to the extent that it serves as an alternate to institutional care. The quoting of cost figures is risky because of their constant fluctuations, but it is sufficient here to say that the cost per month to supervise one case in the Community Treatment Project generally stays below $200, while care for the same person in an institution would be about $350. Research so far seems to show very satisfactory results from this type of program. A study of wards who had been released to the community from the project for a period of fifteen months, compared with a control group of similar size and the same release period, showed that the project cases had a 28.4 percent failure rate, while the control cases had a 42.4 percent failure rate.[8]

This is also a demonstration of the value of having a competent research project operating with such a program. When case classifications become so finely differentiated it is essential for research to validate the distinctions both in the types of cases and in the type of treatment approach for each. In the Community Treatment Project the research team has made great progress in developing a "treatment model," a manual which defines in detail the definitive characteristics of each type of child, the means of treatment for each, and the type of worker who will be most successful with each.

Though this chapter is intended as a discussion of casework it is already obvious that group work is not to be neatly separated from it. The Community Treatment Project, for instance, could be discussed

[8] Marguerite Q. Warren, "An Experiment in Alternatives to Incarceration for Delinquent Youth," in *Correction in the Community — Alternatives to Incarceration* (Monograph No. 4, Board of Corrections, California, June 1964), p. 46.

under either a casework or a group work heading, and this fact is indicative of what is happening generally in the social work field. Though we have always thought of social agencies as being either group work or casework agencies, there is now a pronounced movement toward a flexible combination of the two methods in any one agency. Individual social workers, too, are beginning to employ both methods; and schools of social work are beginning to give all students training in both rather than assuming that the student will exclusively work in one or the other. This is a very welcome and inevitable development.

Differentiation of Goals. The very broad attack on the child's problems that is characteristic of the Community Treatment Project should not be seen as incompatible with the idea of a precise and limited concept of casework goals. With disturbed, immature, and hostile children the goal must be stated in broad terms: to teach these children how to live successfully with other people. That could be called a single goal, although to accomplish it these children must be guided for a while in all the kinds of social contacts they have. So even with the single goal there is a fairly total involvement of the helping process in the child's life.

With some other cases, however, and particularly with older clients, the helping process should be more narrowly applied. It would be hard to dispute the virtue of the probation or parole officer's wish to be helpful in a broad sense, but we could argue that if a more specific focus is established for the helping process it might lead to more efficiency. With some cases, for instance, a broad-scale attack on all facets of the client's problem may be wasteful. Nevertheless, too often the probation officer addresses himself indiscriminately to all manifestations of the client's problem, responding crisis by crisis, applying casework help to the difficulty of the moment, whatever it is.

A better technique might be to determine in the beginning just what single goal is both important and reasonably attainable. This should be discussed with the client and his acceptance of the goal obtained so that both worker and client have an agreed-upon, realistic goal to work toward. Periodic discussions then have a focal point and dynamic purpose. For some especially intractable client the goal may have to be one which is grossly elemental, such as staying out of jail for one whole year. If this has been something a particular client has not been able to accomplish before he may now be tired enough of jail to be interested in some effort that would result in a full year's holiday from it. He might have a fairly interested reaction to the probation or parole officer who would propose to work with him on this one idea and not bother him about matters that are unrelated to it. This would give a clear focus to the weekly casework interviews. A starting point, for instance, would be some reminiscences about the client's former jail commitments, analyzing them one by one to define and understand the factors that led to each. Perhaps in this way a pattern of defective behavior will become apparent to the client and gradually the retrospective view could be converted to a prospective view, with discussion of how he will handle himself in future situations like those that have led him to trouble in the past.

The focus which starts out as an extremely narrow one is soon discovered to be much wider than might have been supposed. Just considering how to stay out of jail inevitably leads to an appraisal of a wide area of a man's affairs. But the technique is to begin with the one specific area of discussion that the client has accepted and move out from there only as fast and as far as the client, seeing the connection of new topics with the primary goal, is ready to move.

It may be a bit painful at times to maintain this single kind of purpose with determination. The client's grocer is demanding that the officer make the client pay his grocery bill; his wife asks that the client be told to stop swearing at the kids; his employer wishes the man would not show up for work so late, or so sleepy, or so dirty, etc. All these are issues that any probation officer is usually ready to take up with a client because of his own ingrained feeling that right is right and probationers or parolees should learn to know right from wrong. However, if a specific and limited goal has been agreed upon with the client then other goals have to be shelved for the time being if they do not impinge on the primary one. If it has been seen, in analysis of former jailings, that poor regard for employers' rules has led to trouble in the past, then the officer has a legitimate route to a discussion of this employer's complaint. On the other hand, if the presenting problem is not related to the primary one we then have to say quite honestly to whoever is complaining about the client that the only way we can help at the moment is to support the complainant in taking whatever measures he himself would use if the man were not under any supervision. Actually this is not nearly as much of a withdrawal from the problem as it may sound, for this technique may serve to involve the officer rather than detach him. The possible involvement would start when the officer tells his client quite simply and candidly, "Your employer called me and asked me to get after you about being late to work all the time. But since that isn't a part of the problem we are working on I told him that that problem is up to you and him to work out." The client at this point may be anxious enough about the employment situation to draw the officer into the problem. This then means that, notwithstanding the original narrow focus, the officer is helping the client on a broad basis after all, and the help has far more impact because the client himself is asking for it instead of holding to his hostile rebellion against the officer's intrusion in his life. If this metamorphosis occurs it is likely to have been substantially aided by the trust engendered because of the officer's complete faithfulness to his original agreement with the probationer.

There is even therapy for the worker himself in the concept of limited goals. It can be constantly frustrating to want to make general improvement in all clients and to be always falling short. The adoption of highly specific and limited goals can give the worker a clearer, more satisfying sense of purpose and possibly a better sense of achievement. Even if he does not actually achieve more in this way, he does come closer to achieving the attainable goals he has set. He has also provided himself with a measuring device to appraise the eventual progress of the client.

Jacob Chwast, in an article on the subject, comments that, "Practically speaking, treatment of the offender must often be immediate and in small doses. Holding the line may well save the fort. It can keep the patient a patient rather than a dropout or failure. Indeed, since so many variables affecting the delinquent's life are beyond the compass of the therapist, holding the line until normal processes of maturation take over seems valid and realistic." [9]

Reaching Unreachable Cases. In considering the differentiation of case types we have to come finally to certain kinds of clients who have a characteristic maladjustment that at once makes them highly needful of professional help and at the same time intrinsically repelled by the very idea of it. These are the older delinquents who are deeply hostile, who have been emotionally hurt by such conditions as parental rejection, who are sensitive about their emotional needs and stoutly defensive

[9] Jacob Chwast, "A Small Goal Is Big Enough," *Crime and Delinquency*, Vol. 9, No. 2 (April 1963), p. 162.

against emotional entanglements. They are also heavily committed to a delinquent culture in which their status would be badly damaged if they consorted with anyone wearing any variation of a therapist label.

While such a boy supposedly could develop a relationship with a therapist and profit by it, it is almost nothing but an academic exercise to say so, because the boy would never tolerate the initial contacts that might lead to such help. Contempt for authoritative and doctor-type people is inherent in his most basic values.

Some novel techniques have been experimented with for reaching such boys. Charles W. Slack, particularly, has tried a method that avoids the doctor-patient situation and in its place uses what he calls the experimenter-subject relationship.[10] In the context of the boy's experience this would be most akin to the employer-employee relationship. This technique is best known through an adaptation of it by Ralph R. Schwitzgebel in his "Street Corner Research" program.[11]

Slack's thesis is that while this type of boy will not go to anyone who is ostensibly in a helping role, he will go to someone who is simply an employer. An employer is not seen as being concerned with what his employee is as long as the job gets done. This means he is relatively non-threatening. An employer pays money for work done. This makes the situation rewarding. Both factors together make the situation acceptable to the delinquent and his peers. There is likely to be status gain for them instead of status loss in getting a job, particularly if it is easy and pays cash each day.

So in this kind of technique the therapist assumes an employer's role. He reaches selected hard-core delinquents with an approach similar to that which Massimo has used (see page 12 above); he offers them work, referring to himself candidly as an "experimenter" who is in need of "subjects" for experimentation.

The technique Schwitzgebel developed was to present himself in this way to boys (sometimes also girls) whom he would contact in their natural haunts in high delinquency areas. He explained that he was studying delinquency and the best way to know what delinquents do and how they think was to get the delinquents themselves to tell him.

[10] Charles W. Slack, "Experimenter-Subject Psychotherapy: A New Method of Introducing Intensive Office Treatment for Unreachable Cases," *Mental Hygiene*, Vol. 44, No. 2 (April 1960), pp. 238–256.

[11] Ralph R. Schwitzgebel, *Street Corner Research* (Cambridge, Mass.: Harvard University Press, 1964).

So he would pay qualified delinquents to act as experts at perhaps $1.50 or $2.00 per hour.

The work the boys perform can be in various forms as long as it is true work concerned with inquiry into delinquency. Slack used extensive experimentation with psychological tests as one activity. Schwitzgebel built his process around use of tape recording. The subject comes to the experimenter's office and is asked just to sit and talk into a tape recorder, telling all that he can think of about delinquents, their activities, their ways of thinking, etc. At the end of the hour the promised payment is made in cash, and an appointment is made for the next session. What happens, to describe the process in an oversimplified way, is that the subject cannot talk about delinquency except in terms of his own involvement in it, and as he does this over a period of many sessions it is necessary for him to reach deeper and deeper into his own feelings to keep the sessions productive. The ultimate result is self-examination and development of insight.

A supplementary process is the development of relationship with the experimenter. Essential to this is the fact that the experimenter maintains every aspect of the disinterested employer's role with complete faithfulness. He has no connection with police or courts; he maintains an academic laboratory atmosphere around him (Schwitzgebel operates on or near the campus of Harvard University with which he is associated); he remains detached and objective regarding the delinquencies being discussed, making no effort to moralize or control the subject's activities. The experimenter also maintains a character of complete dependability. He never presents himself as anything the slightest bit different from what he really is, and he makes cash payment strictly as promised. These are the kinds of conditions that are requisite to forming relationships with this type of delinquent.

This process provides opportunity to affect behavior fairly directly in some respects. The most common example is in teaching the boys to appreciate time schedules. In the beginning they usually come for their appointments at any time other than the appointed hour. The modification of this behavior depends on the experimenter's being willing at first to use them at whatever time they come, and without reprimand for coming at the wrong hour — or even on the wrong day. At first simple rewards are provided for the boy having arrived at all. Candy or fruit may be on hand for him to have. As he continues coming he is rewarded with words of praise for any improvement in his time schedul-ing. He may also be rewarded for especially good production in any particular session. The reward for this may be an extra fifty cents or a dollar for that day's work.

In this kind of treatment approach the cases that move along success-fully often show a typical pattern of progress. The subject is at first cautious: the content of his talk will be noncommittal, factual recount-ings of experiences that do not involve much sensitive or risky material. As he feels more secure in the experimenter's presence he will begin to let his hostility show itself in bitter complaints about authoritative peo-ple and institutions, particularly the police. This may be followed by a depressed period and if all goes well the subject will finally reach a point of generally improved outlook and adjustment.

In the beginning of any case the experimenter will tell the subject that the process may help, or at least change him. The subject does not see this as his reason for participating, however. What attracts him is that it is a job with pay. Later, he does begin to recognize that some-thing is happening to him and begins to use the experience as more than a job. He may want to hang around the offices and assist with other work there, and eventually he may openly admit that the process has been helpful to him and needs to be continued for that reason. At this point he can discontinue being paid and may return regularly for the sort of therapy sessions that he would have scorned a few months earlier.

The research that has been done shows encouraging results. Schwitz-gebel reports that in respect to a small number of experimental "em-ployees" compared over a three-year period with a control group the program "was effective in reducing, by almost one-half, the expected number of arrests and months of incarceration of male adolescents with extensive records of delinquent behavior." [12]

It has yet to be discovered whether such a technique, in essentially this form, can be utilized in a probation or parole setting. The fact of its being entirely independent of any authoritative agency has been con-sidered one of the most effective elements, and supposedly the tech-nique would be inoperative, or at least badly handicapped, if it were handled by persons connected with a court or parole system. It can be theorized that an agency might set up a remote office on a university

[12] Ralph R. Schwitzgebel, "Delinquents with Tape Recorders," *New Society* (Lon-don), January 31, 1963.

campus or in a neighborhood house where such a program could operate, serving clients of the agency, under the direction and support of the agency, but otherwise with as much independence of the agency as possible. This has yet to be given any systematic trial, but it is worth extensive experimentation on the basis of the experiences with this kind of approach in detached settings so far.

INTENSIVE SUPERVISION

Much of the experimentation that has gone on with the aim of improving probation or parole effectiveness has been done with variations of so-called intensive supervision. The term has many different meanings. One of the most noted experiments was the Saginaw Project which operated in Saginaw County, Michigan, from 1957 to 1960. It involved the state-administered adult probation service in that county. This project did not attempt intensive case handling in the sense of very low caseloads of fifteen or so, but it was an effort to show what could be accomplished with caseloads kept to the generally recognized standard of no more than fifty units (each case carried for supervision in any one month being one unit, and each investigation five units), and with increased professional qualifications for the staff. When the project was initiated the staff was enlarged to permit a reduction of caseloads to only about half what they had previously been. The added staff members had been trained in social work and the other staff members were encouraged to take further professional training.

At the same time the Saginaw court undertook to use probation much more liberally. During the project's three years there was a 7 percent increase in the use of probation as compared with the control period, the three years immediately preceding 1957. This probation-use rate was 18 percent higher than the state average.[13]

There was a substantially increased amount of work with the total family environment of each probationer. Sometimes this meant regular interviews with a wife or other family member. Where the work with other family members was not on a regular basis it often had to be established quickly and intensively when some family crisis put heavy stress on the probationer. The staff gave close attention to employment and work adjustment. Vocational training was arranged and urged

[13] John B. Martin, "The Saginaw Project," *Crime and Delinquency*, Vol. 6, No. 4 (October 1960), p. 362.

wherever appropriate. Help with job finding was persistent. "Activities of the officers along this line ranged from some pressure on those who could find jobs if they wanted to, to actually locating jobs for those who couldn't find them. . . . The officers' belief in the importance of work was expressed in terms of the probationers' own eventual satisfaction. This fits into the modern conception of probation case-work as a method of helping the probationer function more satisfactorily for his own benefit, and for the benefit of the community. Indeed, unless the probationer's way of life is satisfactory to him, he will always have to be coerced into behavior satisfactory to society, and surveillance of his conduct can never cease."[14]

An evaluation of the project indicates that despite the increased use of probation the failure rate was reduced. During the three years of the control period 32.2 percent of the probation cases failed and were sentenced. During the experimental period this was reduced to 17.4 percent. The effect of this in dollars and cents was computed as $296,560 saved in imprisonment costs; $78,594 saved through reduction of welfare costs; and $49,280 saved by avoidance of parole costs. So the total saving to the state, accomplished over three years in just the one county, was $424,434.[15]

The Saginaw Project was different from most attempts at intensive supervision because of its having included all cases in a given county probation office. This is also a reason why it did not attempt to bring the caseloads down to less than the fifty units recognized as generally desirable. The very small caseload with extremely close supervision is appropriate only for selective referral of cases. It would not be an economical procedure if applied to the full range of cases in any office.

A current example of a program that does use selective referral of cases to very small caseloads is the Community Delinquency Control Project which is operated in the Oakland and Los Angeles areas. We have already seen how some juveniles from Stockton and Sacramento who are committed to the California Youth Authority are assigned to the Community Treatment Project instead of being routed to institutions. In the two localities now served by the Community Delinquency

[14] Eleanor Cranefield, in *The Saginaw Probation Demonstration Project* (Printed report of the Michigan Crime and Delinquency Council, 1963), p. 42.
[15] *Saving People and Money: A Pioneer Michigan Experiment in Probation* (Printed report of the Michigan Crime and Delinquency Council, 1963), p. 6.

Control Project it has also become possible, since April 1964, to refer certain wards back to the community under intensive supervision. Agents of the Youth Authority handle these cases on a special basis for a period of about eight months, after which the ward is transferred to regular parole supervision just as if he were being released from a regular institutional facility.

Because these wards (boys only) are being returned to the community almost immediately after the local courts saw fit to send them away, presumably to institutions, considerable care must be exercised in the selection of cases. Accordingly, boys who have committed serious offenses involving bodily harm are excluded from the project, and excluded also are any boys to whose prompt return to society the community would strongly object.

The two units of this project are staffed adequately to handle one hundred boys each on caseloads of only fifteen for each agent. The agent uses a variety of approaches, including group counseling, recreational activities, and intensive individual counseling in every aspect of the client's activities. The staff in each unit includes a part-time school tutor and psychiatric consultants. Here again is the concept of intervention in a client's life on a broad and intensive basis, providing a range of services that in most probation and parole settings would be left to other community resources.

Authorities in California are enthusiastic about the results of this project so far, even though it is too soon for the evaluation process to provide reliable data on its success.

An interesting example of intensive supervision applied to the juvenile parole setting was a prerelease and aftercare project operated at the Alabama Boys Industrial School. This three-year project was begun in 1961 when two professional social workers were added to the institution's staff for the purpose of carrying out the project. In this experiment boys were included in the project only if they were from the Birmingham area where the institution is located, and if they were not major psychiatric cases.

An encouraging aspect of this project was the integration of institutional and aftercare treatment. When the child's home is at a considerable distance from the institution it is, of course, difficult, approaching impossible, to make the institutional experience and the aftercare supervision one continuous process. But even where geography does not complicate the situation we have far too often allowed institutional treatment and community treatment to be so completely separate that treatment effectiveness is lost.

In the Alabama project the cases were selected far in advance of parole and the work with them was continuous as they later left to go home. A control group of similar boys was set up for research purposes. While the project boys were in the institution the casework staff saw them more often than the other boys, arranged home visits whenever these seemed therapeutically helpful, and worked with special effort to prepare them for jobs and to find work for them. Efforts were especially intensive at the point of actual return to the home. "Very possibly the key to the superior performance of the project boys is the effectiveness of the project staff in combating community rejection of the boy, whether the rejection is reflected in the attitude of parents, school principals, potential employers, or by the court." [16] It was recognized that families of boys in the institution tend to forget the boys' future needs and so plan insufficiently for their eventual return. The project staff tried to overcome this by regular contacts with the homes of the boys. The whole range of community resources was very actively exploited. There was cultivation of the public schools, specialized social agencies, and the state employment service. With the intensive kind of attention given to the project boys it was found feasible to release them after somewhat shorter stays in the institution than the other boys. Even so, they adjusted better in the community, as they had in the institution. In counting up the number of boys who got into further difficulty with any law-enforcing agency within twelve months after release it was found that 86 percent of the non-project boys, but only 34 percent of the project boys, got into such trouble.[17]

To a large extent, the projects that attempt "intensive supervision" are not so much concerned with novel methods as with just having more time to be more thorough about doing the things that have always been considered part of the probation officer's standard repertoire. While the Community Treatment Project in California is certainly a form of intensive supervision, it is unusual in including some treatment methods that are different from the usual probation practices. A comment of

[16] *Evaluation of the Pre-Release and Aftercare Project of the Alabama Boys Industrial School* (Printed report of the National Council on Crime and Delinquency, September 1964), p. 7.
[17] *Ibid.*, p. 8.

the worker who developed the intensive casework service at the juvenile court in Cleveland describes the more typical situation: ". . . the intensive service is *not* characterized by any one distinctive type of activity. Anything we have attempted might just as well have been tried by some members of the harassed regular probation staff and no doubt at times has been."[18]

When a system like this is inaugurated within a regular probation or parole service it is accompanied by various administrative and procedural problems. Ordinarily it handles cases referred from regular caseloads as being in need of intensive help. The administrator has the problem of determining what kind of cases shall be referred, how to encourage staff members to make referrals despite their feelings that such an action might imply that they are not quite competent to handle their own difficult cases, and then how to handle in one caseload cases coming from all parts of the county. The practical problems involved affect the criteria for selection. Practical considerations require, for instance, that a youngster be mature enough to come by himself to the office, so that the intensive service worker does not have to travel about the whole county so much. Otherwise the criteria call for boys who are likely to be probation failures but whose families are potentially strong enough to use help. The practice in Cleveland has been to have office appointments with the boys very frequently, sometimes as often as daily when the case is in turmoil, and then less frequently as the situation stabilizes. No appointments are on a regular schedule but are set one at a time. "The distinctive feature of the intensive program has been not so much the uniqueness of its approaches as the relative depth and subsequent exploitation of them — careful advance planning, adequate time for crucial interviews, thoughtful summaries, etc."[19] The intensive supervision program in Cleveland has been in use now for five years and, while there has been no research with it, it is being continued on the basis of a sense of satisfaction about its apparent special usefulness. Two trained social workers are handling this service with caseloads of twenty each.

Experiments in intensive supervision have been carried out in far more instances than need be reported here, and almost invariably the results seem to justify the extra cost of such service. Nevertheless it is

[18] Edward S. Newman, "An Experiment in Intensive Probation with Boys," *Crime and Delinquency,* Vol. 8, No. 2 (April 1962), p. 155.
[19] *Ibid.,* p. 156.

rare that political support is gained for extending the intensive service. Nor should it be extended to *all* probation or parole cases. The experiments with the differentiating of cases will make the intensive supervision idea truly appropriate when we eventually are able to select with accuracy those cases that especially need and will productively respond to intensive work.

ADJUNCTS TO THE CASEWORK PROCESS

There are many special techniques that various courts or parole systems have utilized to supplement the casework process. These are found in infinite variety and many of them cannot be said to be either good or bad except in relation to the particular circumstances in which they are operating or to the personalities of the persons directing them. Only a few will be mentioned here to suggest some of the possibilities, and these are the ones that usually are subsidiary to the casework process instead of being themselves major techniques such as those discussed in Chapter 4.

The preparation of a client for a job, or even for just more satisfying social living, often calls for encouraging the client to get more education. An effort to do this for probationers with severely limited education was tried by the Supreme Court Probation Department in Brooklyn, New York, with the use of programmed learning. "Teaching machines," which are not actually machines at all, were used by the probation office to stimulate an interest in education on the part of young adult probationers who were badly deficient in basic education and who were consequently doing poorly in finding adequate employment.

The programmed learning materials typically present the learner with an extensive series of questions or problems. Each one is viewed through a cut-out window in a covering card. The learner writes down his answer through another cut-out window and then moves the question sheet to reveal the proper answer which he can compare with his own answer. This device of rewarding the learner immediately by revealing to him the correct answer, which, usually, will be the same as his answer, derives from the same theory of learning that led to the use of immediate rewards in the programs of Slack and Schwitzgebel already described.

The first question, or frame, in any one subject series is easy enough for nearly anyone to answer. The next one is hardly less easy, and in the progress to harder questions the materials are so designed that the answering of the simpler questions guides the learner by logical stages to the answers to the harder ones. He is encouraged, consequently, by his continuing success and the reward of immediate confirmation of his correctness each time. It is a technique especially well suited to probation office clients. One helpful aspect of it, for instance, is the fact that the learner works alone at it. The typical probation office client is fearful of failure and especially fearful of having other people see him fail. A teacher standing over him, watching his mistakes, can be unnerving for him, so he can much more easily accept a teaching process that lets him work in privacy where no one need see his mistakes.

In the Brooklyn program a number of probationers were selected to meet with a probation officer one evening per week. They were provided with sets of programmed learning materials, each man having free choice of whatever topic appealed to him. He would work at it during the first half of the meeting and could also take the material with him to work on at home. During the second half of each meeting the staff either would conduct group discussions or would assist individuals with any special learning problems. To provide the necessary motivation toward learning, the probation office each week paid the probationer one penny for each frame completed since the previous week. If a man worked at home on this he could go through several hundred frames in a week's time and would have several dollars coming to him when he reported to the Thursday evening meeting.

The Brooklyn experiment was terminated when the funds for it, provided by a foundation, were expended. It was felt that it had good potential for stimulating academic progress for some men, but it was found necessary to modify the original plan to include more personal involvement with each individual. Even with the cash payments there was insufficient motivation on the part of the probationers unless individual supportive counseling was provided. An interesting aftermath of this project has been the development of a booklet on *How to Get a Job*, and another on the rules of probation, both done in the format of programmed learning.

A technique that deserves to be much less rare than it is as a treatment adjunct in corrections is psychodrama. Its rarity no doubt is mainly due to the dearth of professional persons who are skilled in its use.

One court that made use of this method was the Montgomery County (Maryland) juvenile court which, for about three years, used the services of a psychiatrist to involve a number of juveniles and their parents in family psychodrama sessions two to three times a week.[20]

By this method one youngster as the protagonist and several others as auxiliary actors work together in a very active dramatization of significant, emotionally charged episodes from their own lives before an audience of parents, caseworkers, etc. It is considered a useful technique especially with neurotics and persons with character disorders, but relatively less useful with psychotics. The typical session may start with the sort of discussion that is usual in any group discussion process, customarily centering on problems of immediate and mutual interest, though in an experienced psychodrama group there is generally a more rapid movement toward emotional involvement. At any point in the discussion the therapist may interject the suggestion that the experience being referred to in the discussion be acted out.

More often, it will probably be less spontaneous than this, as the therapist may set up an episode to be acted out, based on background material suggested in past discussions. He may assemble several of the group members to act as the various participants (auxiliaries) and will coach them briefly on the general action. However, the protagonist is briefed very little if at all. Specific lines and direction are left entirely for the actors to improvise; in fact, this is the critical element in the technique. The persons acting the various parts must be free to respond as their emotions lead them, giving a revealing and significant glimpse of feelings that otherwise do not easily find expression.

There is seldom need for any props other than the simplest furniture, but it is helpful to have a stage and to let the audience area be darkened. Even though the actors are aware that their parents are sitting and watching they may be less restrained by their presence if the audience is set apart to this extent.

Actors are encouraged to let their feelings erupt as they wish and they usually get quite excited. Even rude, vituperative, and physically assaultive behavior, within reasonable limits, is expected if it is appropriate to the episode and its mood. It might be a boy remembering the way

[20] Michael M. Miller, "Psychodrama in the Treatment Program of a Juvenile Court," *Journal of Criminal Law, Criminology and Police Science*, Vol. 50, No. 5 (January–February 1960), p. 453.

his parents handled a disciplinary situation, or some other episode in the history of that family. With the parents present and watching, the action may call for an argument between an actor-parent and child, and with astonishing quickness the actors enter the parts and become caught up in the emotional mood the episode invokes.

The therapist may abruptly stop the action at any point and set the actors or the group to analyzing the dynamics of it immediately while the interplay is starkly fresh in their minds. The technique has a dramatic impact that can hardly be matched by any usual counseling technique. It might be impossible to sit across a desk from a father and try to tell him what effect his domineering rigidity has on his son; but when that father sees an acted-out episode with himself being played by his son in an uninhibited and emotional release of feelings, no one has to tell the father the significance of what he is seeing. It is then just a matter of going on with discussion to help the group members clarify and digest the feelings that have been evoked and consider the meaning and application of the new view they have had of themselves. For the youngsters, too, there is revelation, for when a son sees some background family episode acted out he may grasp, as he never could have otherwise, some of the reasons why his parents handle themselves as they do.

A major purpose of the method is direct treatment, but it should be evident that psychodrama is also highly useful as a diagnostic device that reveals underlying family dynamics and adds to the therapist's understanding and hence effectiveness in helping the family.

A practice which is not primarily an aid to treatment, but which deserves mention as supportive of it, is fee charging for probation services. Fee charging is common enough in other social agencies, even in governmentally provided services. Families of patients in state mental hospitals are often asked to pay part of the cost; and fee charging in adoption and family counseling services is quite general. But when the state imposes a service upon a person against his will it has not been a usual practice to charge for it. So probation, parole, and prison costs have traditionally been borne entirely by government.

Lately there has been some limited experimenting with charging daily fees to parents of delinquent children being held in detention, and now there are experiments with charging fees to adult probationers to cover the cost of their probation supervision.

The Wichita County (Texas) Probation Department has been charging fees to adult probationers since 1963. It is authorized to collect up to $10 per month and it tries to charge some fee in every case even though it may later have to waive the fee in hardship cases. No objective appraisal of the effects of fee charging has been attempted anywhere, but the staff in Wichita County believes that the probation officers feel a greater sense of responsibility toward their clients when the service is being paid for, and that the fee payments give the officer more opportunity to help some probationers learn responsible budget management. Some of the probationers are financially unable to pay and others fail to pay because of strong hostility to the idea, but about 50 percent of the clients pay their fees reliably and the staff believes that these are the ones that show the best attitudinal change. What is not known is whether either one is the cause of the other.

Another advantage of the fee system is the political one of its effect on the budgeting process. With nearly two-thirds of the cost of probation services being met by fees collected in Wichita County there seems to be greater willingness on the part of the county commissioners to appropriate funds for an adequate probation staff.

In Kanawha County, West Virginia, the Probation Department instituted a fee-charging plan in 1955, and with a caseload of about 425 it collects approximately $15,000 per year. The procedure is to set a one-time fee instead of monthly fees during the full period of probation. This may be in any amount up to $150. Though there is only this one fixed amount for the entire period of probation, the probationer may pay it in monthly installments. This staff, too, feels that it has been a useful tool in counseling with probationers.

In Denver the Adult Probation Department of the district court regularly charges each probationer a fee which, in felony cases, is the flat amount of $50. The fee can be waived in severe hardship cases, and in all cases it can be paid in weekly amounts. During 1964, $52,200 was collected from 1,500 probationers.

The practice of fee charging raises the question of whether probation may be revoked for refusal or failure to pay the fee even though the client's behavior otherwise is acceptable. This in turn raises the possibility of what would essentially be imprisonment for indebtedness. The officers who work with fee-charging plans seem to have little basis for concern about this since their experience is that in nearly all cases where a fee is charged there is a good record of payment.

3

The Group Work Method

After half a century of always working with clients on a one-to-one basis, probation and parole practitioners have discovered group work and are experimenting with it in a wide variety of forms and structures. Some are elaborately devised and others informal and even accidentally engendered. There have been instances of probation officers trying to develop group methods in an effort to save time, or to offset large caseloads by the labor-saving device of seeing several probationers together instead of one by one. Usually this does not have the desired effect on the officer's schedule, for although there has been some experience that shows a saving of work in the sense of more accomplished, the general experience is that group work may be even more demanding of time than casework with individual clients and it may easily be more demanding of the emotional energy of the worker.

Actually, group work introduces certain chores for the worker not involved in a casework approach. Clients must be selected for the group and must be assembled with regard to the personality types that will work together successfully in a group. Much preparation of clients is needed for the group experience. A meeting place must be found — and not just any old place will do. A time each week must be found when the group members can all come; and sometimes even transportation has to be arranged. With all these logistical problems, it is still a uniquely rewarding experience, for it can give the worker a sense of action, of case movement, that at times can be quite exhilarating. If it is less time-consuming than casework it is so only in the sense that, if all goes well, group work can, for some cases, accomplish greater or more rapid progress than casework would for an equal amount of time and effort. In the group work process there is not the time lapse while a relationship builds up as is usual in casework.

There is no more magic in group work than in casework, but we are finding that the supplementing of one technique by the other is more richly effective in treatment than either technique by itself.

In Minnesota the Department of Corrections conducted a research project with its group work among parolees, seeking to test several hypotheses. The findings are interesting and significant:

Hypothesis 1: The group method of supervision reduces recidivism. When viewed in terms of months-per-man completed on parole without revocation, the Experimental Group had a significantly higher "success ratio" than did either of the control groups.

Hypothesis 2: The group method permits more intensive and extensive parole supervision and the smallest investment of money and time. Each member of the Experimental Group received three hours of supervision per month; the parolee supervised under "normal" practice received approximately two hours. The group leader was able to supervise ten men in four hours per month (including travel time); to supervise ten men on a one-to-one basis usually requires approximately thirty hours. Transportation costs were reduced substantially because the parole agent had to travel to only one location rather than make ten separate visits. The extensive number of topics discussed in group sessions and the opportunity for all members to express their own viewpoints freely created a dimension of individual involvement not usually experienced in the traditional agent-parolee dialogue.

Hypothesis 3: Permitting controlled associations among parolees has no inherent negative effects. Waiving the rule prohibiting association among parolees, for purposes of this experiment, produced no difficulty whatsoever.[1]

ADMINISTRATIVE ARRANGEMENTS

Group work is met with resistance nearly everywhere when it is first introduced. It is typical that the probation or parole officer will be

[1] Nathan Gary Mandel and William H. Parsonage, "An Experiment in Adult 'Group-Parole' Supervision," *Crime and Delinquency*, Vol. 11, No. 4 (October 1965), pp. 324–325.

skeptical of it and unenthusiastic about becoming involved in it. A California parole officer who later became sold on the value of the group technique wrote about his initial reaction: "When, by administrative decision, the writer was directed to establish a group from his own caseload, he had serious misgivings about doing so. He saw himself primarily (in view of his previous experience in the honor camps) as a non-directive counselor. He was blocked by the apparent incongruity between the two roles he was expected to play: the first, authoritarian, and the second, permissive. Actually, it must be confessed that the formation of the group was delayed for several weeks while he attempted to resolve his own conflict regarding these seemingly opposing roles he must play. With the interest and advice of two members of the administrative staff he was able to work out a rationale for combining the roles, and thereafter proceeded to develop the group." [2]

Often the casework staff will look at the proposed group work as a frill, as frosting on the cake. The comment will be made that, after all, casework is *the* function of the agency and casework cannot be sacrificed in order to experiment with frills. Even so, a few agencies are realizing that a probation or parole agency's staple function should be couched in more basic terms — to help people and protect the community — and any process that furthers this intent is a proper one whether it is casework, group work, community organization, or even just surveillance and enforcement. The first prerequisite for bringing a resistive staff to a happy use of this broad social work approach is the genuine, active support of the agency administrator. Without such support from the top no such new concept or technique has a chance.

There is no easy way to bring group work practice into a correctional casework agency, but some good experience is accumulating. The most usual approach is to encourage certain of the regular probation or parole officers to select a few individuals from their caseloads and start meeting with them in groups while still carrying the bulk of the caseload in the conventional manner. Another approach is to let the regular casework staff carry their cases as usual while a trained group worker is added to the staff to specialize in group work by forming groups from cases referred to him from the regular caseloads. The first

[2] Gordon H. Stafford, "Group Counseling with Parolees from County Honor Camps," in *Explorations in the Use of Group Counseling in the County Correctional Program*, edited by Norman Fenton (Palo Alto, Calif.: Pacific Books, 1962), p. 152.

method has the advantage of not requiring cases to be transferred from one worker to another, and it provides for a more general infusion of the method through the total agency caseload. It has the disadvantage of requiring a considerable effort in persuading caseworkers to try this technique, and it requires a substantial amount of training for those staff members who do decide to use it. As with many such issues, the best choice in the long run is likely to be a combination of the two. The specialized group worker will, finally, serve most usefully to entice the caseworkers into experimenting with the group process and then will be available to give them consultation if he personally and professionally has their confidence.

This is important because group work can be an unsettling idea to the uninitiated, and the person who must advocate and teach it needs to be comfortably acceptable in the face of the caseworkers' anxieties. The typical worker who has a B.A. degree and no graduate-level specialized training gets accustomed fairly quickly and easily to the handling of cases on a one-by-one basis. The dynamics of interaction between him and the client can be kept relatively uncomplicated, or at least not too threatening. With his mantle of authority he can ordinarily deal with his manipulative and hostile clients when they present themselves just one at a time. And when he becomes experienced, and has had good supervision, he can learn, too, how to handle the hostile client with skill and understanding, rather than just by pulling his rank and issuing peremptory orders. But when a group of such clients is confronting the worker they gain courage in each other's presence to let their hostility show more freely, and the worker may find it crackling about his head like lightning. The feelings that he could handle in the one-to-one situation may suddenly seem to overwhelm him in the group situation and leave him shaken to his roots. If he has been accustomed to being treated with the outward signs of respect, and sees this as being important in his relationships with the client, he will be deeply repelled by a group work philosophy that allows clients in a group to lash at his agency with profane expressions of cynical resentment. Sooner or later he has to discover that if the group experience is going to be effective it will have to permit the expression of anger so that the source of that anger can be examined and treated. But this will be a jarring experience for many people who may not have the inner serenity and sense of security to permit such hostile expression. Or perhaps, instead, the worker has picked several clients who are not articulate, who do not strike sparks with each other, and so he goes home afterward with deep discouragement because he could get no real discussion going, could engender no useful interchange and no sense of group feeling among the several individuals.

These are the sorts of reasons why the average worker needs some close, supportive supervision when he tries the group work technique. The administrator who encourages his casework staff to try working with groups without giving them some specific training will find that they move into the group work process with reluctance and that they either discontinue it after experimentation, or else continue it with uncertainty, aimlessness, and lack of satisfaction.

STAFF TRAINING

If the casework staff is composed of persons with graduate training in social work they will be able to move fairly confidently toward the group work process, but will still need supportive supervision in it if their training was in casework rather than group work. Persons with the master's degree in social group work are increasingly looking toward opportunities to conduct for agency staffs intensive indoctrination programs in group work that deals with emotional disturbances, and their training is highly appropriate to this type of professional supervisory program. In some agencies consultative and supervisory service is furnished by a psychologist and this is satisfactory if his training has included an emphasis in group work. Either a social group worker or a psychologist may be good in giving supportive supervision and either may be poor, according to the individual's personal qualities and the emphasis in his training.

For persons without specialized training there are various ways that this extra help can be given. It is useful, of course, to allow the worker to attend an institute, conference, or summer course on the subject. This is a splendid start but is not enough by itself. The learning process must continue on an intensive basis when the worker later begins to handle groups. He runs into situations that are surprising and challenging and offer magnificent opportunities for learning *if* he has access to a supervisor who can help him analyze the event and consider the ways that it should have been handled. So it is well for the administration of an agency to find some way that a group work specialist can be made available for continuing consultation if there is to be assurance that the group work program will thrive.

In one probation office (the county court of Philadelphia) use, after surprisingly thorough training, of the regular juvenile court probation officers for supplementary group work has been tried. These officers are expected to become a part of a discussion group themselves first, and under the direction of the psychologist who is responsible for the training they pursue the same sort of personal examination that they are later to handle with clients. It is a remarkable effort at training in depth, for the worker not only must enter wholly into the sharing of feelings in a group with his colleagues, but must continue this training for six months to two years before he is considered ready to direct groups himself. This training is given, of course, while he is occupied full time with a caseload, so the group work training is just an hour and one-half a week. Up to ten probation officers will be in the training discussion group at the start but there is a considerable reduction in its size as time goes on, for many of these probation officers find it difficult to tolerate this kind of shared personal examination with their colleagues and they drop out.

In view of the experience of other offices it would seem that this training plan requires staff time and effort that are out of proportion to the realistic requirements of the situation. Admittedly, two years of training is desirable for this demanding kind of leadership, but it should be a well-rounded training with supportive studies in related subjects. Furthermore, no matter how thorough an experience is gained with a group of one's colleagues, the trainee may be left without even his first sight of a group process involving clients. For most people, effective training should include actual supervised experience in handling groups. For this reason a better plan seems to be one used in Sacramento where it was, again, the staff psychologist who was responsible for instructing the probation officers in group work methods. In this case, however, the officers were given preliminary orientation to the group process in class sessions held for two hours per day through ten consecutive workdays. After that the officers proceeded to select cases and start their groups. Once the groups were meeting regularly a system of individual consultation was arranged for the staff. Each officer spent an hour with the psychologist for each hour spent in leading a group. This permitted intensive analysis of what happened in the meeting and how the officer handled it, which was considered the really effective part of the training. With both the group work and the continuing training under way, this office, too, turned to the use of group discussions for the staff. Once a week the psychologist conducted a small staff group discussion, but contrary to the Philadelphia training process, this staff group followed the rule that the discussions could cover any subjects except the administration of the department and intimate personal matters that were not voluntarily brought up by the person concerned. To all appearances the staff group discussion works better as an experience that comes *after* the members have actually gotten into the task of leading groups and their interest in the process has become more solidly based.

Another device for staff training is the use of a co-leader. A group that has been meeting long enough to develop a group feeling can easily tolerate a trainee who sits in to observe the experienced leader. In fact, much experience has shown the value of having co-leaders for a group as the standard procedure. This presents a splendid opportunity for a training situation in which the experienced leader carries the responsibility for the group process while the trainee is present and participating as much as possible as a co-leader, with the two then holding an evaluative discussion together after the meeting.

Continued training when the new leader is conducting group sessions by himself is effectively accomplished by means of tape recordings of the meetings. These can be useful even when the supervisor has been present in the meeting, for the trainee, in listening later to his handling of the group, is sometimes surprised to hear himself saying certain things, or saying them in a way he had not been aware of at the time. This can contribute much to his self-understanding in areas that affect his rapport with the group.

In Los Angeles the state parole agents have a cooperative group practice and training arrangement that is unique in some respects. The plan is a joint arrangement between the several parole officers who work as one unit under a common supervisor. Each of the officers has eight to a dozen men from his caseload whom he sees as a group once a week. All the officers in the unit meet with their groups on the same evening, in the same building. On that evening there are four distinct stages of the process.

The first starts about suppertime and is referred to as "sensitivity training." The several officers, their supervisor, and a psychologist adviser meet together shortly after the close of regular office hours. They bring their sandwiches and coffee and spend about an hour and a half in discussion of group techniques. It may be a general discussion concerned with sharpening their talents as group leaders or it may be discussion of specific matters that will be handled in the groups that evening. One parole agent, for instance, may mention what he intends to do with his group or a certain parolee in the group. The staff unit then discusses the ways to handle the proposed discussion most effectively, with the psychologist giving technical advice. By seven o'clock the parolees arrive and the officers go off to assemble with them for an hour and a half in small group discussions in various assigned rooms in the building. The next step is an unusual one. After these small group discussions the parolees and staff convene in one large room for a one-hour group discussion that involves all fifty or sixty parolees, the five officers, the supervisor, and the psychologist. The discussion in this large group is ordinarily a continuation of one of the small group discussions. When the large group discussion is over and the parolees have gone home the staff unit again sits down for another hour of discussion to analyze, while it is fresh in their minds, the success or the errors in their evening's work.

Altogether it makes a long day. The large discussion period is a feature that is characteristic of California agencies where correctional leaders have been impressed with the therapeutic community concepts of Maxwell Jones. Most group work devotees have been convinced that the small cohesive group is best, since it gives more opportunity for participation by every group member and, in fact, forces the involvement of each one. Jones agrees with this but advocates the use at the same time of large groups which he considers to have a value of their own. "The whole atmosphere tends to be more emotionally charged than in the small therapeutic groups, where there is much greater cohesiveness and a better opportunity to work through a situation with gain in insight. The large discussion group is more permissive in the sense that, as one of a large crowd of patients, the individual is in less direct contact with the doctor, and is more ready to reproduce his own particular emotional patterns."[3]

Whether or not the large group is included in the evening's sequence,

[3] Maxwell Jones, *The Therapeutic Community* (New York: Basic Books, 1953), p. 56.

the format is a useful one. By having all meetings on the same evening an ideal opportunity is presented for sharpening staff skills and giving mutual support through the pre-meeting and post-meeting discussions.

A group discussion, like a casework interview, can be held with any of several purposes in mind. It may be set up with a specific purpose of considering a problem of one group member and coming to an action regarding it. Or it may be an open, undirected talk-fest with no more immediate purpose than giving the group members a needed socializing experience. It may be focused on an educational topic for the simple increase of knowledge in some particular sphere. Or it may be a sharing of intimate feelings, a discussion in depth which aims at basic changes in attitudes through the client's increased understanding of himself.

These widely varying forms of the group process call for varying degrees of professional skill, and we consequently see a range of practice, from groups conducted by untrained lay citizen volunteers to groups under the leadership of such professionals as specially trained psychiatrists. However, these two extremes account for the smaller part of total group work efforts; quite properly, most group work in corrections is being done by the professional probation or parole worker with a B.A. degree plus a graduate degree or some in-service training.

Though the novice may approach the task of group leadership with the uneasy assumption that group work skill is something elusive and profound, actually the essence of it is found in the attributes of simplicity and honesty, and the device of constantly requiring that answers be reached through discussion by the group rather than through pronouncements by the leader. But still it usually requires training, experience, and courage to pursue a simple and honest course in dealing with groups. It is too easy to assume that skill is something that has a devious quality about it, that it is an artfully esoteric way of handling people. This may also include the assumption that the delinquent group would almost categorically resist a direct, forthright approach from the authoritative person, so they must be reached by indirect (skillful) means.

Not so.

It is true enough that neither in casework nor in group work can we address a hostile or skeptical person or group and just flatly say, "Now remember, if you are going to avoid trouble in the future you must do so and so." Our words would be wasted on cynical ears. But suppose instead we sit down with a group of delinquent boys and start out by saying, "All of you guys have been arrested two or more times in the last year; as a result you're all on probation — which you'd rather not be. What we're going to discuss is the question of how to keep from getting arrested any more." What could be more simple, direct, and honest than that? And that is the skilled approach. It does not bluntly set one cultural concept against another. Instead it starts with what is common concern in both cultures. The boys as well as the leader can agree on the desirability of avoiding arrest. And yet it does not compromise or dissemble regarding the intention of the leader or his value base.

Along with the concepts of simplicity and honesty the group worker must also keep in mind the principle that his goal is for decisions or conclusions to be enunciated by the group — not by the leader. The element that is unique about group work is that client is listening to client; client is interacting with client; client is being influenced by client. This is totally different from the idea that you get a group together just so more people can listen at one time to the advice of the leader. The probation or parole officer using group work must recognize that delinquents, young or old, are predisposed to listen more receptively to fellow delinquents than to the authoritative person, and that with some guidance they have a capacity to find their own path to improvement.

So by pointing the boys in the direction of finding ways to avoid arrest the leader has set in motion the process of having them find their own answers. It will take them hours to find the answers that he could formulate for them in a minute, but the answer they find for themselves will stick, whereas the answer pronounced by the leader would hardly even be heard.

A common problem the group leader in corrections faces is the expression of hostility. This is particularly true when he has a group of men or women who have been recently paroled or who are preparing for parole. The hostility they feel will show itself in the group process in a predictable pattern of development. The members of the newly formed group start out cautiously, saying little, or talking on neutral, bland topics. As they become more secure with the leader, they test him with expressions of hostility that at first are safely directed at remote objects such as the parole board, the governor, the system, or other persons or offices that are fairly well out of range. The group next will shift its attack to more immediate objects, and then the parole officer, as group leader, may find himself being bitterly criticized. Also attacked are other staff members, the rules of parole, employers, etc.[4]

It appears that these stages have to be worked through in the typical group before the members come into the more mature final stage of looking at themselves. Overlying these steps in the process will also be a tendency of the group members to indulge in a superficial discussion of group and personal problems in an effort to satisfy the leader and more quickly gain whatever favors they hope for him to give. Probationers or parolees are adept at sensing the kind of answers and expressed attitudes that authoritative personnel like to hear. They will almost instinctively mouth the phrases that the group leader is encouraging them to use, so that the discussion may have a fine sound to it, though actually it is quite spurious. A sign of group maturation is the giving up of these empty recitations in favor of a more genuine probing for underlying feelings.

The difficult stage for the leader to endure is, of course, the second one, which subjects the leader to criticism that can be downright vituperative at times. The officer who has been accustomed to expecting the forms of respect from his clients will at least be uncomfortable with this development, and may at that point abruptly reject the technique altogether. Actually it is not necessary for the officer to endure meekly, like a sitting duck, any purely splenetic goading that might be aimed at him. The skilled leader can maintain the kind of demeanor that says that such attacks are out of order. If he is competent in this the group itself will do its own policing, for while these are people with hostility, they are also anxious people who do not want to see things get out of hand. At the same time the leader's skill must enable him to recognize and tolerate the more therapeutic hostile expressions. A profane speech of bitter complaint and personal criticism might actually be an honest attempt to express a problem and ask for a solution — expressed in the vernacular which is altogether natural to the voicing of intense feelings in this client's cultural setting.

At this point in the group process the leader's job is to help the group to an increased or new sense of comfort with, and confidence in him, the parole officer. This will be accomplished if the barbs of the group

---

[4] Fenton, editor, *Explorations in the Use of Group Counseling in the County Correctional Program*, p. 78.

are met with a cool, unruffled, and objective reaction on the leader's part. If the group is criticizing him for making a mistake, and if they really can make a case for its having been a mistake, the officer will gain, not lose, by freely admitting the error.

If the group is complaining about any of the many problems of being on probation or parole — the nuisance of being checked on; the nuisance of reporting; the injustices of discrimination against the man with a record; the unreasonableness of the rules — the officer is losing no status with them in letting the complaints flow. He will, instead, gain status by letting them talk and by turning their questions back to them. If he does pronounce some decision it is desirable although not necessary that the clients be able to see the rightness of the leader's stand. But it is important that they see that he himself is convinced of its rightness in terms of an honest concern for them and subject to a willingness on his part to hear and consider their views. Forthrightly he must avoid being shaken by their attacks and must constantly insist that they find most of their own answers. His attitude should seem to say, "Sure it's tough; but what's the practical, sensible thing you're going to do about it?"

With such a stance the officer avoids being their punching bag and instead is another human being joined with them in a practical search for the answers to their problems. The officer, as group discussion leader, has to remind himself that to a large extent a critical and rebellious quality in a group may be a necessary ingredient in the effectiveness of the technique. Consider, for instance, how it would be if a new group of parolees were told by the parole officer in some detail how the group is expected to conduct itself. Suppose he designates himself as chairman and then not only describes what topics will be discussed but also enunciates the rules: speak only on being recognized by the chair, use no profanity, limit each comment to only two minutes, to name a few possibilities. With such an approach the officer may have a fairly comfortable, well-behaved, but bored group. These men are accustomed to rules. They know all about how to adapt to them in their own ways and they can relax on finding themselves on this kind of familiar ground. But not much that is therapeutic will be happening. On the other hand, an open, unstructured situation will be anxiety-provoking for them. Invite them to a group discussion and present them with no chairman, no rules, no discussion topic. In such a situation they no longer have the familiar touchstones or crystal-clear criteria of behavior to conform to or circumvent. They are forced to their own resources in finding rules of conduct and relationships in the group. It is this condition and not the former one that has potential for promoting growth.

But growth is an uncomfortable experience and it comes at an uneven rate. Group members groping with the no-rules freedom of such a method will go too far at times, will become intemperate and abusive as they experiment with letting their feelings go. But this is true of any experiential learning process and if the officer remains consistent in his handling, and keeps the group facing its own responsibility for finding answers, the group members will gradually learn how to control themselves through controlling the more difficult ones among them. The uncertain or insecure leader will want to insist on controlled and respectful talk, but the skilled leader will know that the free flow even of bitterly rebellious talk from some group member presents the group with immediate problems of how to get along with that person, and in solving such problems therapy is begun.

The leader will also have to resist the temptation to indulge in preachments. This is one of the harder lessons to learn, for the average leader will want to give earnest cautionary advice when he finds his group members continuing their delinquent plans and practices. He is not expected to ignore such things as planning of projected new offenses that he may overhear, but neither should he plunge into a direct assault on all the practices that seem to be characteristic of his delinquent group. If improvements can be made by the group itself in its own time such progress will be far more real. In one discussion group of older teen-age probationers the leader was well aware that most of the boys carried switchblade knives. He made no effort either to suggest or to insist on any change in this practice. It was not long before the boys themselves found a way to bring up the subject in a discussion where they watched warily to see what the leader's reaction would be. The leader pushed the question back to them and helped them discuss the issue as objectively as possible. No final conclusions were reached and no instructions given. The effect of this sort of handling is subtle and may be discovered later, if at all, in unexpected little ways. In this case it was a few weeks later when someone brought the boys a watermelon during their regular discussion meeting that the leader learned how effective his work had been. He was amused and pleased to discover that they had no way to cut the melon. Nobody had a knife.

A welcome and highly useful by-product of the discussions is the improved relationship the clients seem to develop with the leader, notwithstanding any harsh words that fly about in the group discussions. Officers find that probationers or parolees who are members of a discussion group more quickly develop a good working rapport with the officer, making the casework contacts more effective. The group setting exposes the officer to the clients in a social setting and gives them a chance to see him as a normal, human sort of person, rather than just as an authoritative controller of the clients' destinies.

The Minnesota research cited earlier also pointed up this aspect of the value of group work. A fifth hypothesis in this study was that "subjecting the parole agent's activities to the collective scrutiny of his clients reduces the social distance between the agent and the parolee." The researchers report: "Tape recordings of group sessions clearly show the decreasing reticence of group members to question the group leader's decisions and the agent-parolee relationship. Social distance was reduced as members and leader came to know each other better and developed feelings of mutual respect, understanding, and concern. Interaction between agent and group helped the agent develop clearer insights into the needs of the parolee." [5]

THE CO-LEADER

The leader who is moving with uncertainty and difficulty in handling a hostile group may find it helpful to use a co-leader. In fact, as indicated above, the practice of regularly conducting groups with two leaders seems to have special usefulness, particularly in women's or children's groups. Experience with this in California correctional settings,[6] the Minneapolis juvenile court, and the New Orleans juvenile court [7] indicates that a man and a woman working together as co-leaders provide an extra stimulus to discussion and arouse a new kind of interest on the part of group members. The two leaders give more of a family quality to the setting and tend to provoke areas of discussion that are less likely with one leader. Questions about sex may be elicited by the presence of male and female leaders, but at the same time their presence

[5] Mandel and Parsonage, in *Crime and Delinquency*, p. 325.
[6] Fenton, editor, *Explorations in the Use of Group Counseling in the County Correctional Program*, p. 80.
[7] John Wall, Jr., "Group Treatment of Adolescent Males in a Juvenile Court Setting," *Federal Probation*, Vol. 21, No. 2 (June 1957), pp. 18–22.

tends to be a healthy influence on keeping the conversation at a more seemly level than might be true if people of only one sex were present.

The more certain advantage, however, is the practical one that two people accomplish more than a single leader does. During the meeting certain subtle asides or covert reactions might not be caught by the leader who is involved in the discussion at the moment, while the other leader will see and note these significant items. Also, during the meeting the two leaders may disagree about some issue the group has raised and may have to discuss it briefly between the two of them. For many clients it is a fresh and useful experience to observe how these two adults handle their difference of opinion with friendly but objective discussion; and also to see the evidence of the leaders' maturity in the way they relate to each other just as person to person at the same time that they relate appropriately as male and female.

After the meeting the two leaders have the advantage of being able to discuss the dynamics of the discussion just completed by comparing their separate observations and their separate diagnostic impressions. This post-meeting analysis affords an opportunity for introducing one more device that involves and helps the clients: to admit the clients themselves to the "debriefing" session. This helps to solve the problem of the gulf existing between the intention of the social worker and the client's skeptical view of that intention. The client has all too often been schooled in a cynical view of authoritative people and automatically discounts a heavy percentage of what they say. It is not unlike the average person's discounting of the slickly presented television commercial. He knows that everything about it is selfishly and commercially inspired, and so he may put very little faith in it. But he would be encouraged to have much more faith in the same product if it should happen to make a straight news report. If a reporter with no bias has reason to present a news story involving the success of the product, the reader is far more impressed. This same sort of psychology is at work when group members are allowed to listen to an analysis of their meeting, conducted just as if they were not present.

At the California Institution for Men at Chino this technique is used in connection with some of the large daily group meetings at which several staff members are present. After the meeting the staff members return to their offices for a discussion of what happened within the group. Nothing is said about group members coming to this post-meeting discussion but it is tacitly understood that they are free to come if they want to. What happens is that the two or three members who were most hotly involved in the discussion will have some anxiety about the staff view of the action and will want to hear the staff's analysis. With no invitation given or requested and with no attention being paid to them, they go along to the staff conference room and sit outside the small staff circle, against the wall, while the staff discusses the session just completed without taking any apparent notice of the men.

In Minneapolis, group workers with the juvenile court have been trying a variation of the same device. The two co-leaders of a girls' group were using a room for their group discussions that happened to have an adjoining observation room with one-way glass between the two rooms. The girls knew that the two leaders stayed awhile after each meeting to discuss what had happened. After the girls became rather mature in their group experience, the leaders invited them to go behind the window and observe and listen to the post-meeting discussion between the co-leaders. In this way, though no one was fooling anyone, the girls were given the illusion of listening in on persons who were unaware of their presence. The theory was that some of the comments made by the leaders would have more impact in this context, but that whether or not this would be so, the girls would be presented with a reinforced image of the probation officer as a person whose discussion of them showed an impressive specialized knowledge and skill and who was genuinely interested in them far beyond the attention that the officer's salary could be expected to buy. This technique gives every indication of being highly successful in cementing the relationships between the leaders and the girls.

In this kind of process, though the discussion should be no less genuine than if the girls were not there, good judgment must be used by the leaders in the way that diagnostic material is discussed. It is not a matter of withholding diagnostic material but rather of using care in word choice. Some diagnostic words can be quite frightening, or at least confusing, to uninitiated persons. Just as bad as words that confuse would be words that conceal because of their strangeness. Use of some unfamiliar words may have an ominous sound to a group member who imagines the worst about a word that is unfamiliar to him. Clinical discussion in front of the group should be kept within the limits of a simple and common vocabulary.

GROUP ORGANIZATION

In organizing a discussion group the agency is presented with the question of whether to operate it as an open-end group or a closed group. In the former the group is kept going permanently, with new members added as other members drop out. With the closed group the group members are kept together until the group's purpose is accomplished, then discontinued completely. The most highly developed use of the open-end group is in the Highfields programs (see Chapter 5) and in some of the halfway houses (see Chapter 8). In these settings the participants are meeting almost daily and developing a group culture that needs to be preserved by the unbroken continuation of the group. The frequency of the meetings also means that a new member is quickly assimilated and does not present the problem that he does in a group that meets only weekly.

In probation and parole settings the closed group is the most common. Such groups, meeting usually just once a week, have to make the most of the limited time they have. A new member being introduced to such a group is a "foreign object" at first; he may be an annoyance to the other members and may alter the pattern of group interaction. The delaying effect this can have on the progress the group is making is a principal reason why probation and parole officers usually prefer the closed group.

One variation on the pattern is sometimes tried when the agency has several staff members working with groups at the same time. In Minneapolis, for instance, the Department of Court Services had several adult groups in which the members were talking about their adjustment to the many problems of being divorced. As the groups approached a natural point of termination a new group was formed by one or two people from each of the original groups. This was by invitation to those who were interested in moving on to a group experience in which they would study their own personal adjustments in greater depth. By this point they had become experienced and comfortable in the group process and even though they suddenly moved into a new group they could do so with a minimum of lost motion.

The novice group leader may be apprehensive about how to introduce suitable topics for discussion. The answer is simply to let the group introduce its own. In a corrections setting the group members would not be there if they did not have problems, and ordinarily these problems are close enough to the surface to be verbalized with a minimum of prodding. It should not be assumed that the discussion has to involve only issues of deep and profound import. Discussion of deep-lying feelings will occur only in a mature group that first has practiced and gained comfort in many, many discussions of simple, practical everyday kinds of problems.

An example of the simplicity of these discussions comes from a group of six girls. They were seventeen and eighteen years old and in the group was one girl who had recently been married. During one meeting a girl asked the leader (who was the probation officer for the whole group) if she would be allowed to move out from home and live by herself. She had got a job just a week before as a clerk in a variety store, and now her father was saying that she should pay rent at home. She had immediately decided that if she had to pay rent she would rather move out and have a furnished room of her own.

In this case the probation officer had ample reason to refuse the request but instead of answering and arguing her point of view she tossed the question right back to the group. The married girl tended to discourage the idea with comments about how expensive it is to move out on your own. The other girls, though, were all bending in the other direction and saying that Sally should be allowed to try it if she wanted to. The leader directed their concern to the practical financial aspects of the question and on the blackboard she listed the expenses that the group members suggested. Sally's monthly pay was set down and then the group struggled to compute probable expenses. They argued with Sally about her low estimate on what a furnished room would cost. They thought of all the things she would have to buy — food, bus fare, laundry, dry cleaning, soap, shampoo, hairspray, toilet paper, cosmetics, toothpaste, etc., etc. Sally argued for low estimates on all the items because of her eagerness to win her point. When the total was figured for a month's expenses there was a margin of reserve income, but the other girls were sobered by the unconvincing estimates that made this possible. It was obvious that it would have to be a spartan life. Sally's figure of sixteen cents daily for lunch, for instance, had them worried. They were seeing the bleakness of her idea of just a hot dog and a grape soda for lunch every day.

When they went on to list what Sally's expenses and margin of reserve would be if instead she remained at home, the contrast between the two plans was enough to make the girls shake their heads over Sally's proposal. Their initial, instinctive support of her request changed into remarks about the obvious advantages of staying at home awhile yet. It would not be accurate to say that Sally was convinced, but she was impressed, and she accepted the unanimous view of her peers to the extent of dropping the issue.

As the situation originally arose the leader might well have been tempted to answer Sally's question directly, explaining to her why she could not be permitted to leave home right now. If she had done so she would probably have left Sally unconvinced of the fairness of the decision and Sally would have had all but one of the other girls on her side and supporting her feelings of injustice. However, by turning the question to the group and suggesting their line of inquiry, the right decision was found and Sally was influenced more effectively.

It is of great importance, however, that the leader not allow this technique to trap him because of some less than honest element in his approach to the issue in question. The leader for this girls' group could not have turned the question over to the girls with the spoken assurance that the decision would wholly be up to them. This can be done only when the leader is prepared to take the risk of some quite unexpected outcome. Also, the responsibility for making a recommendation can be given to a group only when the group can also be given all the facts pertinent to the issue. If the question had been affected by highly private facts about Sally's home situation that could not be shared with the girls the leader would have been dealing dishonestly with the the girls if she had invited them to recommend action on the basis of incomplete information.

The leader who commits himself to the principle of having the group members make their own decisions within the limits of their capability has to learn to remember this when it comes to some of the smaller decisions that may seem unimportant. He may say to his group, "This room is a little small for us so next time we'll meet in room A down the hall." He might be entirely sensible in this decision but he will be a better group leader if he will say instead, "Room A down the hall is available now and it's a larger room. Do you think you'd like to change to it for meetings after this? We can go and look at it if you want to."

Or some professional colleague may want to sit in on a group meeting some time and the leader may feel that the group process would not be hampered by the observer and that it would be quite all right. But his reply should be that he will take it up with the group. So at the next meeting he tells the group about his colleague who wants to visit; tells who he is and the nature of his interest, and gives the group full freedom to say whether they want to invite him or not.

This would seem to be the most picayune of issues but the real test of a leader's sincerity is seen in these little things. He may be trying to build the group's sense of responsibility and of self-worth by having the members make their own decisions, and this will not be at all hard to remember in respect to the more weighty matters. But if he forgets and ignores the principle when the issue is seemingly trivial the group feels the denial of the leader's stated purpose. In the same way, when the leader leaves it to the group to decide whether the room shall be changed or a visitor invited, the group feels it as a very concrete reaffirmation of the honesty of the leader's announced principles.

HONESTY AS A TECHNIQUE

Utter honesty in dealing with the group includes a willingness on the part of the leader to let the group find its own decisions, rather than the expectation of manipulating them into finding and backing the decision the leader has already made in his own mind. It is legitimate, and even expected, that he will give subtle guidance to the direction of their discussion, but it must be guidance without subterfuge and must not promise more decision-making authority to the group than the leader is prepared to sustain.

An illustration of the consequences of well-intended dishonesty may be seen in a group discussion of parolees in which the parole officer was attempting to accomplish group censure of one member. This parolee, whom we might call Carlo, had been out of prison only a few weeks, was living with his wife and working steadily. However, the job did not pay much and Carlo and his wife had different ideas of what money was for. A day or two before this group meeting the parole officer had talked with Carlo's wife and had heard a fulsome account of Carlo's irresponsible use of the house money. The wife had been highly effective in convincing the parole officer of her view of the problem, the main item of which was that Carlo had just bought a car without first clearing this with the officer. The wife was complaining that it was unneeded and that after car payments were made there simply would not be enough money left for household expenses. The officer did not have a chance to see Carlo after that but, full of the wife's convincing complaint, he decided to bring it up at the meeting and let the group discipline Carlo. His goal was to accomplish a decision that Carlo would have to sell the car immediately.

The trap that this group leader set for himself and then walked right into was that he arranged a session that could be successful for him only if it led to one particular outcome; he was lulled into an overconfident expectation of that outcome by the view of it in his own mind, not realizing that the group would be getting a different view.

As the group convened, the parole officer brought up the subject of Carlo's new acquisition and its extravagance in relation to the family finances. But this was the first time he had confronted Carlo on the subject and he had underestimated the parolee's capacity for self-defense. Carlo's wife was not present to tell her side of the story and the officer could not relay it to the group with her effectiveness. Carlo produced a spirited and convincing defense, bringing up arguments in his favor that were unexpected and, hence, not easily countered by the parole officer. Furthermore, his audience was stacked in his favor. Every member of the group was a man on parole with the same problems and desires as Carlo had. No woman was in the group to give the wife's view. So the officer's effort to get group censure of Carlo backfired as the men gave Carlo complete support and went so far as to make strong comments about how unreasonable his wife obviously was, even suggesting that it was high time he should leave her.

This is the sort of situation that calls for flexibility on the part of the parole officer. The problem he was faced with here might be met by inviting the wife to come to the meeting too. Why not? Or an occasional meeting with all the wives present could be tried. And a bit of refreshment at the end of the meeting would be just the thing.

In another such instance a parole officer was trying to break up an association between parolee A and parolee B. The former had been on parole for a long time, had become very well stabilized, was financially successful, and was developing a satisfying home life. B was a long-time friend of A, and although he was making a satisfactory adjustment he was not capable of the degree of success that A enjoyed. The two men started out associating together very closely as personal friends and B had continued the association with frequent long visits to A's home, attempting to share all his spare-time activities with A. But as A grew more successful, his interests turned more to his own family, and he was increasingly oppressed by B's parasitical friendship.

When eventually A earnestly implored the parole officer to get B "off my back," at the same time stipulating, "But whatever you do, don't tell him I said anything about it," the parole officer decided to bring it to the group of which B was a member. He was trying to say to the group that for various reasons the association between the two men was not good for B and the group should support the parole officer in requesting B to stop seeing A. But though the officer tried to give some reasons why the association should break up, he could not tell the real precipitating reason for bringing up the issue, and the stated reasons sounded as unconvincing to the men as they deserved to sound. Under the circumstances, it was understandable that the group did not support the officer. They were puzzled by the suggestion that the two parolees break up; they saw no sense in it and they wondered quite bluntly how the parole officer "could be so goddam dumb."

Experiences like this give meaning to Gisela Konopka's view that "A helping relationship must be built on trust. The group worker therefore cannot 'manipulate' a group in the sense of working toward his or the agency's goal, even if well-meant, without letting the members know about this and working it through with them. Not every step of his method must be consciously shared with them or explained, but the intent must be made known." [8]

AUTHORITATIVE QUALITY OF THE GROUP PROCESS

Probation and parole officers who have tried working with groups have been accumulating experience that teaches us much about adapting the group work technique to the authoritative setting. To many officers it still seems preposterous to ask the advice or help of a group of parolees. The traditional approach would simply be for the officer to order Carlo to sell his car — right now; to order parolee B to stop seeing parolee A. Whether or not the blunt orders are appropriate, it is obvious that some matters do have to be handled directly by the officer himself and not entrusted to a group. There is just no substitute for good

[8] Gisela Konopka, *Social Group Work: A Helping Process* (Englewood Cliffs, N.J.: Prentice-Hall, 1963), p. 84.

judgment on the part of the officer in making intelligent selections of situations and techniques.

But just as a parole officer should avoid asking for group decisions in certain situations, there are many case problems that the group can solve more effectively than the officer can by himself. A good example of this occurred in a parole group where one parolee was helped to take a realistic view of his vocational plans. Fred had enough experience around machine shops to have convinced himself that he was a machinist, but he was being completely unsuccessful in getting and holding a job as such. Because he would not retreat from his own view of himself as a machinist this meant that he was remaining unemployed. The parolee who already feels some hostility toward his parole officer is not ready to accept from him any advice that might have an ego-deflating effect. So the officer encouraged the bringing up of the topic in the group sessions.

Over a period of several weeks the group dealt with Fred's vocational aspirations. They even watched for job openings and referred him to them. Eventually, they all saw what the real problem was. Fred simply wasn't qualified as a machinist but could not face that fact and was giving all sorts of excuses about why he couldn't get work. He blamed union shops, automated machines, unfair prejudice toward his prison record, etc., etc. Finally the group gave one full discussion period to the problem and beat down Fred's excuses one by one. There was endless discussion of minutiae about machine shops as the men argued over every tiny point. They pointed out the ads in the paper Fred had not answered; job tips that they had given him but he had not followed; discrepancies between his claimed qualifications and their knowledge of his background. Without the necessity of intervention by the parole officer they relentlessly made Fred see that he was deceiving himself and that it would be no disgrace to admit his limitations and take the sort of work that he really could do. The technique was effective and Fred, with this group support, accepted a revised view of himself and settled down to steady work operating a floor scrubber.

Generally the group process can be very effective for this broad type of problem solving. Given enough time to consider the problem thoroughly, the group will come up with dependably sound attitudes. But the group leader is on dangerous ground when he tries to get a highly specific kind of action and when he cannot fully share with the group all the premises upon which a decision must be based.

Just as honesty regarding the specific issue is important, we must also be honest about the general purpose of the group. A group discussion took place in a halfway house for parolees where the staff sincerely wanted the group to exercise a responsible decision-making function in regard to release plans for members of the group. The group on this occasion was speaking back hotly at the staff because group recommendations for a member's release had not been followed. In sharply profane language they were wondering what sense there was in their being asked for decisions when their decisions were ignored. Somehow the staff had managed to convey the idea that "It's up to the group to make the release decision." This was not a promise that the staff could actually carry through in the face of irresponsible decisions made by an immature group. The staff would have been all right if instead they had said the completely honest thing: "*We* make the decisions about release, but we do want the recommendations of the group and will follow those recommendations if they are not too much of a compromise with what we see as responsible action."

ICE BREAKING

Certain conditions of awkwardness are likely to be felt as a group first begins its meeting and the group members cautiously take each other's measure. The leader may feel the need of some artificial stimulant to get the discussion going and focused on a fruitful topic. Generally this will be less true with an adult group where the process will be relatively simple and straightforward. It should be sufficient for the leader to explain the general purpose of the group in very brief terms and then leave it to the group to start conversation in whatever direction they wish. If they really seem to need help the leader might begin with an impersonal discussion of a type of problem that belongs to no one individual in the group but is more or less common to all. After getting started on this relatively safe ground the group will ordinarily move along to the more personal discussion content that will meet their real needs.

A bolder opening move with a new group is to make no opening gesture at all. It takes a little more nerve for a leader to invite a group of

87

probationers or parolees to a group session and then sit down with them without saying anything. What will happen is that someone soon asks, "Well, what are we supposed to do?" Or, "What are we here for?" So the leader sets the pattern of the process immediately by turning their very first question back to them. "Well, why did you come?"

It's a method that at least surprises and arouses curiosity. It may cause annoyance. But it does get some talk going and immediately puts the group to work to find a purpose and areas of discussion content.

This technique has had a greater use in the general field of training in human relations. Juvenile court judges have experienced it in training institutes for judges where the "T-Groups" have been used. In these situations the leader surprises and disturbs the group by giving it no structure, no guidelines. "What makes the T-Group unique is that the trainer (instructor) does not prescribe what the trainees are to talk about or to do, lead the discussion, or even lay down procedural rules for the group — e.g., how one gets the floor. All these things are, instead, done by the group itself." [9]

It cannot be said that any one technique is the right one. It will depend largely on the leader himself. Unorthodox and even bizarre approaches will sometimes be acceptable and effective because of the particular talent or personality of the leader.

Generally with younger age groups there may be more need for discussion stimulants. Teen-age girls in a newly formed group are likely to be slow and reluctant in getting into meaningful discussion if they are just put together in a circle of chairs and told to talk, especially if the subject is to deal with highly personal family matters or sex information. In fact, this would be hard for most people. Despite the sex experience of most delinquent girls they lack the sophistication that would enable them to talk about it with comfort in a group, and so the attempted conversation is dissipated in embarrassed giggling. It has been found helpful for such groups to use an activity such as making fudge or popcorn. There can be a substantial reduction of discomfort if some busy and enjoyable manual activity is going on at the same time as discussion.

As a further development of this idea one probation officer and co-leader starting a new group of girls held a brief, get-acquainted meeting and set up their next meeting for dinner together. A settlement

[9] Howard R. Sacks, "Human Relations Training for Law Students and Lawyers," *Journal of Legal Education*, Vol. 11, No. 3 (1959), p. 328.

house had an unused apartment in its building and this was borrowed for the evening. The girls met there, bringing the food items as prearranged and the six girls and the male and female co-leaders got to work in a completely casual way, like a family, making hamburger patties, peeling onions, and brewing coffee. They all sat down to dinner together and later found themselves in the kitchen together washing dishes. They were still talking as they sat around the kitchen table some time later.

The leaders had not said a word about group discussion, but as an utterly natural outcome of the dinner table conversation the talk turned to the "problem" of parents, just the topic the leaders would have picked. It was only the second time that any of the girls had met each other, but in this easy situation they were quickly comfortable and before the evening was over they were, in fact, a discussion group without any formal word or gesture having been used to institute them as such.

With boys' groups the more likely stimulus, when such is needed, is an activity that has an element of adventure. Examples of this are discussed more fully in Chapter 4. With either boys' or girls' groups that are reluctant to move into discussions of intimate material there are ways to get the discussion going first on a nonthreatening, impersonal basis. It should not be done by selecting "topics" to discuss. The leader who just arbitrarily announces that "At the meeting next week we will talk about dating" is being too artificial and if his planned discussion next week turns out to be a good one it will be only for accidental reasons. For the best success the discussion should grow out of real, natural, and immediate situations. The chances are that if this group really does need to talk about dating there is something in the current experience of one or several of them that can be used as a natural springboard for the discussion. If not, a springboard can be supplied. One leader has found that it sometimes works just to take the youngsters to a movie, a movie that may have some content that is akin to a subject the group might discuss. At the next meeting it is no problem to begin a quite natural discussion of some social problem that was presented in the movie. After discussing how the characters in the story handled or mishandled their problem it will not be long before the group finds its way to discussion of similar problems that are closer to home. In a somewhat contrived sense, then, this is still a discussion that arises out of a natural situation.

Phonograph records have been used similarly. There are records available with talks on dating, personal hygiene, marriage, etc., and sometimes these can be useful to get a group started in areas which interest them at the same time that they find it difficult to relax and talk about them.

Another variation of these approaches is the idea of presenting a problem situation by acting out episodes with puppets, a device that is used at the Philadelphia Youth Study Center.[10]

With adult groups some leaders may find it useful to use a "transplant." After a group has met regularly for a long time and has come to its natural cessation it is likely that one or more persons in it are so enthusiastic about the process that they are willing to help get another group started. Such persons can sometimes be used to join a newly formed group and help to give its members reassurance at the same time that they supply stimulation for the discussions. This method has also been used with delinquent girls' groups.[11]

ROLE PLAYING

From time to time a group may be wrestling with the problem of understanding why people acted as they did in some provocative situation and it may be that a bit of role playing would clarify some of the questions more quickly than straight discussions. Acting out parts in the course of communicating with others opens up a wide range of possibilities. The most structured use of the technique would be the play or skit, written and acted almost formally to demonstrate and teach better attitudes or ways of problem solving. Or there is the more extemporaneous psychodrama that a psychiatrist will use with a group of patients as he has them impulsively assume certain roles and act out their feelings toward other people.

The least structured and least conscious role playing is the simple quoting of other people in everyday conversation. As we might see it in a group discussion, one person is describing an incident or perhaps a conversation with his mother. He quotes his mother's purported exact words and in doing so mimics her facial expression, bodily posture, and tone of voice, usually with exaggeration of those qualities that led him to feel as he does about her or the situation at the moment. This is a type

[10] A *Primer of Short-Term Group Counseling* (Pamphlet issued by Philadelphia Youth Study Center, September 1, 1962), p. 67.

[11] Norman Fenton and Kermit T. Wiltse, *Group Methods in the Public Welfare Program* (Palo Alto, Calif.: Pacific Books, 1963), p. 268.

of communication that in varying forms occurs in almost any conversation; and, at a simple level, it is role playing.

It is a fairly easy step for a group leader to carry the device a little further and have two or more persons work together to re-create conversation, complete with feelings and perhaps some action. It is constantly astonishing how easily and fully people can immerse themselves in the feelings of the parts they play and capture the essence of the other person's viewpoints and attitudes. This can be a highly useful device to lift people out of their own concerns and help them appreciate the forces that affect their protagonists.

In a group of girls on probation such a situation arose when they were apprehensively discussing an immediate problem concerning one of their number who was absent that evening because she had just run away from home with a boy who had escaped the day before from a state training school. The girls wondered what would, and what should, happen when the two were caught. The group had co-leaders, Corinne, their probation officer, and Will, her supervisor.

Will suggested that they act out the situation according to what they presumed to be happening. The girls immediately picked up the suggestion and cast Corinne and Will in the parts of the two runaways. Many times the role playing is done while the actors walk about and physically carry out the parts, but in this case they all kept their seats. The girls eagerly started the action by describing the characters. Their ideas popped out thick and fast as they constructed personalities for the two. Corinne, now "the girl," was seen as a sharp dresser, but unhappy and having problems at home. She loved the boy and hated her parents. Her father was always drinking and was never home at nights. Her mother hated the father and took it out on the daughter.

Will, now "the boy," was cool, reckless; said he loved the girl, though actually he did not.

Four of the girls quickly lined up in other parts, the probation officer (reflection of Corinne), the girl's mother, the policewoman, and the judge. As quickly as the girls cast the parts they poured out directions for the action. The girl was to receive a phone call. Obediently Corinne simulated the phone conversation.

The call is from boy — mother is present and listening — talk has to be careful. Girl tells mother it's a girl friend asking her to go to the drugstore with her. Mother argues but then reluctantly agrees — mother stirs the action by yelling at girl to get off the phone.

Corinne began to get caught up in the part as she yelled back at the girl who played her mother and told her to get off her back. She verbally left the house with her mother still yelling at her. The action continued, made up of constant, excited directions from the group and with responding dialogue between the two adults who were now well established in their parts as girl and boy.

Girl meets boy at the corner — they talk about going to a party — girl knows where to get some liquor. They go ("Now we're at the party"), and there is lots of drinking — girl gets sick — throws up. Boy has a borrowed car — they leave and he suggests they go to a motel in next county. Girl has misgivings — wants to go — yet doesn't want to go. Boy accuses her of dating other boys — she denies it — says she just spread that around to fool her mother — says she really loves him. Boy gets smart and demanding — says girl should show him that she loves him ("But he doesn't show any kindness or tenderness"). They go to the motel. The next morning they leave the motel — girl in tears — girl scared — wants to go home.

The policewoman now entered the act. The group decided to have her stop the car to question the pair.

Boy says girl is his sister — policewoman says brother and sister don't sit that close together in a car — she also notices that girl has been crying — she takes them to headquarters. Questioning gets intense — girl is questioned first. Who is she — where has she been? Girl lies. Where did she meet boy? She can't remember. Why did she run away? Because she loves boy. Have they been drinking? No. "Then what's that on your blouse?" Girl says she spilled mustard from a hot dog. Policewoman doesn't believe it. Where did they stay last night? In the car. Policewoman says she has talked with girl's mother and knows that she took money from home — is also sure that they stayed in a motel. She asks what they did at the motel. Girl says they just slept. Policewoman drops the subject. [The girls knew it was out of character for the policewoman not to pursue this question, but the girl playing the policewoman was herself in character in showing reluctance to demand actual talk of sexual activity.] She asks girl about home. Girl says she hates it and doesn't want to go back. Policewoman questions boy — he looks at the ceiling — is uncooperative — lies — won't answer questions.

At this point the girl who was trying to play the policewoman, with flushed, angry face, gave up in complete frustration and, dropping her character, glanced at Corinne and asked with exasperation, "Are all the kids this uncooperative with the police?" The girls reset the stage and instantly the boy and girl were delivered to the juvenile detention. Now the "probation officer" entered the action, visiting and questioning the girl in detention.

Probation officer asks girl why she ran away — girl says because she wanted to and she loves boy. Had they planned it? No, he just called and they went. Where did they meet? On a street corner. What corner? Didn't remember. Probation officer pursues the matter — must know all the details — which corner?

At this point Corinne became truly exasperated herself and snapped back angrily that she didn't mark the corner and didn't see what difference it made anyway. After more of the aimless, provocative questioning for such details by the probation officer, another instant scene shift was decreed and next they were in court.

Girl's mother is present and she and girl are hostile to each other. Girl accuses mother of not caring about her — mother denies it and insists she cares, but girl is skeptical and says she wants a foster home. The "judge" asks girl how a foster home would help her. Girl says people would care about her and be nicer to her. Judge says girl would have to make changes too and asks what changes she would make. Girl says she would mind people better if they cared about her. Mother cuts in to say she does care. Girl and mother break into loud argument. Judge asks probation officer for recommendation. Probation officer recommends foster home. Why? Says she thinks girl needs it and would stay out of trouble better. Judge asks mother for her opinion. Mother says she wants girl at home. Judge continues the case for a week and orders girl held in detention.

The illusion of action in this episode became very real even though there was no moving about. The feelings became so intense that anger did arise at appropriate times and the group went considerably overtime without realizing it. It could hardly be said that they answered the questions that prompted the role playing, but there were some very apparent values in the experience. For one thing, from the action of Corinne and Will the girls got a new realization that probation officers know a lot about what goes on among delinquents. This had been apparent from the natural way the boy and girl carried off conversation about getting liquor, deceiving parents, going to the motel, explaining the soiled blouse. The girls also saw clearly that Corinne, their probation officer, understood how they felt about their mothers' yelling at

93

them and how it felt to be questioned endlessly on petty details. The anger in Corinne's reaction to the questioning had been unmistakably genuine. In addition the girls got a taste of what it's like to be a policewoman, a probation officer, or a judge, and to have to deal with stubborn, deceptive delinquents and make decisions affecting families.

It is perhaps too easy to assume that all the value of this type of experience is for the clients, the members of the group. While the process is more than justified on the basis of gains made by the group members, a bonus often received is the value it has for the leader too. In this episode, for instance, the impact of the experience on Corinne was perhaps even more profound than it was for the girls. As her probationers in the parts of policewoman and probation officer questioned her she knew that they were playing the roles in exact imitation of the usual questioning process, and for the first time she had a taste of how it felt from the girls' viewpoint. Corinne came out of the experience with an amazed awareness of the stupidity of much of the grilling that goes on in such situations, and with a new and helpful perspective of herself in relation to her probationers.

Usually role-playing episodes like this should be followed by general group discussion about the experience. Just as group discussion will naturally lead to opportunities for role playing, the role playing will in turn lead to an enriched period of discussion as the group reviews and pursues the meanings of all the feelings evoked by the acted episode. While each group member may have received some value from the experience it is also possible that each member felt a different kind of impact from it, and there can be additional value for them in sharing these reactions.

It must also be assumed that any role-playing episode that cuts at all deeply into people's feelings has an element of risk. A young person who has been deeply affected in some sensitive area by the experience should not have to leave the meeting that evening with his emotional hurt untended, or even unnoticed. The doctor who administers a healing treatment watches for signs of unwanted or dangerous toxic reactions, and in the same way we must be aware of these possibilities in our work. A discussion of the episode just played, even though very brief, will give the perceptive leader a clue to how the experience has affected each group member and whether there is any reaction that needs special attention.

Of course, the mere fact that someone is upset and tearful is not in itself any cause for alarm. In a girls' group in which the members were discussing what makes a "good" meeting of their group, one girl commented, and the others agreed, that in one sense a good meeting is one in which everyone has a good time; but then she added that not so much is accomplished at that kind of meeting. She thought that in a truly good meeting she might be upset and unhappy, but it would be a good meeting because that would mean that they were really getting at her problems.

Generally, the role-playing technique should not be hastily tried with a new group. It needs participants who are sufficiently comfortable with each other to let themselves go in acting parts without being too self-conscious. Persons who are new to each other will not so readily enter into the acting in a productive way. By the same token, those persons who have become an experienced and well-knit group can assume parts and feel the appropriate emotional intensity with surprising ease.

The role-playing episode described above was useful in enlarging understanding of other people's viewpoints. At other times the issue may be a more practical, problem-solving one, but this, too, can lead to attitudinal improvement. In a group of adult parolees, for instance, one member has lost his job following an argument with his foreman. The problem now being considered is the way in which this man should have handled his dispute with the boss. So in the group he is invited to act out what happened while another member of the group performs as the foreman. It is ostensibly a simple issue of how a man should handle himself so as to keep his job; but as the group members study and participate by turn in the action, there can be much exploration of motivation', attitudes, and subconscious feelings.

Even such a simple episode can get all group members thoroughly involved. For one thing, the action need not be limited to just the main protagonist and one other. It may start out that way but then it can be done over and over again with different concepts of how the action should have been handled. In fact, the man who started the whole thing with his argument with the boss may get the greatest help by seeing several of his colleagues portray their impression of him. It is not uncommon in these experiences for the member to be amazed at how stupid he obviously was as he sees himself depicted.

One of the most common variations of role playing is the reversal of roles. After the parolee has acted himself in an argument with another group member in the role of foreman, the leader may ask that they trade roles and go through it again. This parolee who has been carrying a sharp resentment toward the foreman is thus beguiled into the task of acting that foreman's part. If the group is a strong one they will not let him get away with a less than honest representation of the foreman's approach to the issue, and so there is a good chance that the parolee will pick up from the experience a new awareness of the other man's position.

Sometimes it can be said that one good role-playing experience demands another. In this case, for instance, the affected parolee may have acquired some new bit of insight into the reasons why he reacted as he did to his foreman. He may be able to see that it was a reaction pattern he uses all too often in various kinds of situations. So the role playing which helped open his eyes to his basic problem should be followed by other role playing to give him some simulated practice in applying his new-found insight.

Role playing, like the group work method generally, is a highly fluid method which is subject to endless innovative variations. While there are certain important general principles, a skilled leader may use great freedom in adapting the technique to the group and to the situation at the moment.

One interesting variation is the use of an alter ego. This would be used in a fairly sophisticated group with members who are accustomed to recognizing underlying motivations as contrasted with ostensible ones. After some group members are assigned their parts to play in the episode, one or more others are assigned as alter egos. Or it may be that just one principal character has an alter ego assigned to him. As the action begins, the alter ego sits immediately behind his assigned character and whenever he reads his character's motives or feelings differently from their surface appearance he speaks up as if voicing the more secret thoughts and true motives of the other person.

Member: I don't think we would get very far with that suggestion.
Other self: What is Jones trying to do, promote himself into the chairmanship? I'll have to block that. If I do not I stand to lose status.[12]

[12] Alan F. Klien, *Role Playing in Leadership Training and Group Problem Solving* (New York: Association Press, 1956), p. 95.

Techniques like this require a fairly experienced group and also should be tried only by a leader who is trained and experienced enough to be quite sure of what he is doing.

SELECTION FOR GROUPS

There are two aspects to selection of persons for groups. There is the problem of choosing those among a large caseload of probationers or parolees who would be suitable for the group process, and there is the other problem of selecting from among these qualified ones the particular persons who would fit together as one group.

The first problem is less of an issue today than it was a few years ago, as more and more the casework and group work methods are being considered universally appropriate. It now seems apparent that nearly all our clients can benefit from group work and that usually they will profit most from a combination of the two methods. Exceptions remain, of course, but a probation or parole office will usually find that if it has any client who is not assignable to a group it will not be so much because of personality characteristics as because of mechanical problems such as his hours of work or his residence location or similar reasons that make it impracticable for him to get to group meetings.

The more important and interesting question is how to pick those several individuals who will successfully coalesce into a group with therapeutic potential. One basis for grouping may be the particular purpose of the group. In one situation it may be a grouping of persons from a neighborhood who will be discussing their problems or behavior in the context of that environment. Another group may be adult parolees who are facing a common problem of adjusting to the first weeks of community living after release on parole. A group might be formed of persons who had all been arrested for the same kind of offense, such as narcotics use or forgery of checks.

It is not essential that each group have such an expressly identified common denominator, but the leader should at least see in his own mind a common goal for them to reach by a common path, and be able to state the goal for the group if they are uncertain of it themselves. It needs to be stated in terms that are superbly simple and practical — no empty moralizing is suitable here.

If a group is formed to explore a problem that is external to them it is not so necessary to be concerned with selection of personality types among them. For instance, if it is a group from a certain neighborhood and the purpose is some aspect of neighborhood improvement the group can function even though there is a wide age range in it and some imbalance in personality types. However, in probation or parole work we are usually more concerned with a helping process aimed at the group members themselves in a very personal way, so in our selection of them we must be concerned with a combination of types that will function together productively in a process that depends upon highly personal interaction.

It would be fine if we could point to some exact rules for grouping, but this is an inexact skill and even if we do have definite principles in mind concerning personality types we will often have to compromise with certain practical exigencies that control the availability of individuals. In selecting adults, the group will sometimes almost select itself. It may, for instance, be as simple as taking into one group all the men on one officer's caseload who live in a certain housing project and who are not working on night shifts. And this may work out quite all right. Probably the worst that could happen would be that the officer has to ask some member to drop out if he presents too much of a hindrance to the group's effectiveness. Generally adult probation and parole groups will be selected less on the basis of individual personality characteristics and more on the basis of the caseload, the residence location, the work schedule, and the client's degree of motivation or interest in using the group experience.

Group therapy with children has produced a more refined body of experience regarding grouping, and some of the principles developed there may have applicability to some extent with adults also. In working with children's groups the most general principle is that a variety of personality types should be assembled, producing a balanced group. Of course, this is desirable with the adult group too since it brings to the group the stimulation of different viewpoints, a variety of social experiences, and the opportunity for group members to profit by comparisons between contrasting approaches to life situations.

Another general principle is that we should not introduce into a group a youngster who is a natural type for group rejection — by that group. A boy who has a distinctive physical appearance that makes him the instant subject of a belittling nickname will not have a helpful experience in a group that promptly sets him aside in this way. He must be accepted truly as a group member if the experience is going to help him mature; but if he is ridiculed, even subtly, he is outside the effective group dynamics and is forced to find some protective device for handling his rejection. He may, for instance, become the group's clown or mascot. This way he salvages an illusion of group acceptance and defends himself from the harsher kind of rejection; but he still is not, in this condition, able to use what a group has to offer.

A person who is a natural whipping boy can actually be helped greatly by a group experience if he is put in the right group. It needs to be a placement where, because of his age or some other superior quality, he can slightly more than hold his own with the others until he gains a more secure self-image. S. R. Slavson states that a group "must consist of children who potentially have therapeutic value to one another. Obviously, a beaten down and rejected child would only be more traumatized if he were to be assigned to a group where he would be beaten and persecuted. A frightened, withdrawn, and sensitive child becomes only more frightened and withdrawn in a tumultuous and aggressive environment . . . they must have an environment in which their particular difficulties are counteracted and their needs are met."[13]

In balancing the personality types there should be wide differences in degrees of aggressiveness. A juvenile group can contain at least one dominating, aggressive member, but too many of this type would destroy the group's potential, for the leadership effort would be dissipated in a constant problem of control. One aggressive member can be controlled by the group itself and in that case the process of control will itself be part of the therapy. The best group will have a balance of aggressive, withdrawn, seductive, passive, hostile, dependent, or other types that serve both to counteract and to stimulate each other.[14]

With adults, a grouping on the basis of age is not as important as most other factors will be. With juveniles it must be remembered that a difference of even a year in age can sometimes make for a substantial social gulf, so the range in a teen-agers' group should preferably be no more than two years.

Though use is being made, particularly in institutions, of large groups

[13] S. R. Slavson, in *Group Psychotherapy and Group Function*, edited by Max Rosenbaum and Milton Berger (New York: Basic Books, 1963), p. 235.
[14] S. R. Slavson, *An Introduction to Group Therapy* (New York: International Universities Press, 1952), Chapter 5.

of fifty or more, these have a purpose that is not identical with the purpose of the discussion groups that are intended to involve fully and affect strongly each group member. In the large group the dynamics are substantially different since there cannot be active involvement of every member. It is not possible for more than a few of the more verbal persons to talk. This means that the situation becomes, in effect, a small group discussion with a large number of observers.

To have a small group discussion that has maximum impact on each member it is necessary that lines of relationship connect each member of the group to each other member. As any member of the group talks, his feelings reach the other members along these lines of relationship and his words and feelings are given a particular character and impact according to the nature of that particular relationship. After all, we are seldom deeply affected by expressions from someone who means nothing to us. If the group is too large these lines of rapport are weak — it is not possible to maintain acquaintance with and a "caring" sort of feeling for everyone in a room full of people. If a group gets much larger than six or eight persons, consequently, its capacity for investment in the process and its ability to dig deeply are noticeably impaired.

GROUP WORK WITH PARENTS

For many years there have been attempts here and there to work with groups of parents of delinquents. The early efforts were often disappointing in their failure to achieve sustained interest or to develop any convincing impact. Probably the most common reason for a lack of success was the usual lecture format for the meetings. Even when group discussion was used it was often a prescribed and formal discussion of the material presented. More recently the technique of natural, free discussion, such as has already been described for use with client groups, has been extended to parents' groups, with distinctly greater success. The difference in basic philosophical approach can be seen in such a simple thing as seating people in a circle around a table instead of in rows, facing a speaker or chairman.

The increased use of group discussions for parents accompanies the increased awareness of the vital importance of working with the total family situation in each case. One author comments: "The hypothesis is now made that where there is a disturbed child there is a disturbed family." [15] Certainly one of the most significant developments in the social work field is that we have begun to see the futility of working only with a single patient when he is a symbol of a total family problem.

The use of parents' groups is a splendid device whether their children are in groups themselves or are being worked with individually on the probation caseload. But parents' groups tend to develop more often when the children are in groups too, for the involvement of a juvenile in a group tends to produce more parental involvement and leads more surely and naturally to the provision of a group for the parents. The group for the juveniles creates constant issues for the parents to face or chores for them to help with. The group occasionally wants to go somewhere, to do something. Parental permission must be gained, and parents may be importuned to help with transportation.

In one probation office the use of groups raised the problem of permission for smoking. Though the probation officers had always in their casework contacts discouraged smoking by the juveniles, it was apparent that it was a meaningless effort, for any youngster could abstain from smoking during the short period of a casework interview, and the probation officer seldom really had to confront the problem. But when group work came with its one and one-half hour meetings and its occasional outings the staff was brought face to face with the issue. It was decided to put the question to the parents, and since it needed to be answered by them in concert if possible, the value of their having their own group discussions is obvious.

The much more basic reason for a parental group is that we cannot work with a young person in isolation. The problems that have brought that juvenile to court are problems that have certainly made themselves felt in the home. We would like to think that if we are able to ameliorate the child's adjustment we will hear sounds of gratitude from the home as the improvement is felt there. This may happen, but not necessarily. We may even get complaints instead of thanks. A family finds ways to adjust to problem behavior of a member so that life can go on in tolerable ways. Sometimes the alleviation of a long-standing problem at home will upset the compensatory adjustment that other family members have made and they will react with pain and protest to improvement which they

[15] John Elderkin Bell, *Family Group Therapy* (Public Health Monograph No. 64, U.S. Public Health Service, U.S. Department of Health, Education, and Welfare, 1961).

101

do not recognize as such. Caseworkers and group workers are both aware of the need sometimes to give help to a parent or wife because the client is beginning to improve and in doing so has upset the adjustment mechanisms in the home.

A marital relationship may be considerably affected. Father and mother may have developed an unspoken and delicately balanced equilibrium in handling their adjustment to each other at the same time that they contend with a difficult child. If the child's conduct begins to change it can threaten the parental armistice and cause a sharp reaction from either spouse who might fear loss of the marital stability. When this happens, the threatened parent is likely to be on the phone to the group leader protesting the group process and attempting to withdraw the child from it.

If the parents are meeting regularly in their own group the resentments, anxieties, or other painful reactions to their children's changed behavior can be expressed and dealt with as they arise. The parents are not left with a sense of mystery about the experience their children are having. In their own group, under the same leader their children have, they have a feel of what it is that the children are doing. In the presence of other parents they feel less inclined to take unilateral action about withdrawing a child, for they see other parents also expressing anxieties, yet sticking with the process. And gradually there can come a great sense of relief in finding that other people, too, have problems and worries in the parental role, and that comfort can be found in talking about it.

The leader must be acutely aware of the parents' feeling of failure and the need to alleviate this rather than adding to it. It starts with the invitation to meet with a group. It is so very easy for the parent to feel that in being asked to join a group of parents he is being labeled as the cause of his child's delinquency. In formulating his invitation the probation officer must try to base it on practical, nonthreatening reasons, but without deviating from reasons that are entirely honest. He would not be honest if he asked them to get together because they need to arrange transportation and other services for the children's group; but he would be smart to use his contacts with them about transportation problems to suggest that there might be other interests in common that they could talk about in a group of their own once a week.

Actually, this can be accomplished in a more authoritative way too.

The juvenile court judge may need to set the process in motion in the courtroom at the time of the disposition hearing. Parents who would never be able to respond to an "invitation" to join a parents' group may need to be prodded into it by the judge at the time he has their anxious attention in court. There is still no need to do it callously or punitively. The judge can make it clear that he considers the parents' involvement in the treatment plan essential and that he must insist that they attend at least a specified number of the parents' group sessions. He need not suggest in any way that this is because they are at fault and must be corrected, but may assure them that while the probation officer can help the child he needs to have the parents' cooperation.

This procedure is usually effective in getting the parents involved, but the kind of handling they get when they arrive at the meeting will determine whether they stay with it and derive value from it. A coffee pot helps, especially if the women can help in the brewing instead of having everything already done for them. The probation officer's approach needs to be a disarming one. These are often people who have been blamed, or feel as though they are being blamed, for failure in raising their children. They are afraid that here again they will be blamed and lectured about how they should do better. So the approach must be a low-pressure one, essentially an invitation to talk about whatever is on their minds.

Parents will be puzzled about how they can get help from just undirected talking and may have a vague feeling of being cheated. This is the leader's chance to gain in his rapport with the group as he shows understanding of their feelings in freely admitting that it seems peculiar just to talk. But he can assure them that it does indeed help and if he says so with self-confidence he will have gained greatly with them when they begin later to see that he was right.

Parents will want specific answers. They will want to know how to handle a certain situation at home. A son or daughter may be showing some improvement and the parent will want to know what is being done with him in the other group; "Tell us so we can try it too." They may ask for diagnostic explanations. Again the best response is to bend the questions back toward the group, giving the members constant practice in discussion, in sharing each other's views. A therapist who works mainly with disturbed children and their parents comments, "On the whole it is better not to explain the child's psychodynamics to them, even in terms they would understand, for they often interpret it as criticism of themselves or infer that the therapist is more understanding of the child and takes his part. As a result they may become resistant to treatment or resentful toward the child and so defeat the purpose of therapy. For that reason the therapist does not answer this question but listens instead for the emotional undertone in their discussion and points it out in such a way that they will feel understood and accepted rather than criticized." [16]

Questions will inevitably arise in both the juvenile group and the parents' group about what is going on in the other. The leader needs to take the firm stand that each group is the privileged guardian of its own privacy. The members of either group must be serenely confident that the leader will reveal absolutely no content from one group to the other without permission from the members. A boy may go home and tell his parents what his group discussed, and the parents likewise are free to discuss their group with their children. Generally, however, there is not an appreciable amount of such information exchanged between the two groups, but one of the most noticeable results of the parallel groups is the improvement in the relationships between the parents and children. And after all this is probably the most basic factor there is in the prevention and control of delinquency.

Stressing this principle of keeping the content of parents' meetings and the children's meetings confidential from each other is not meant to suggest that a family problem should not be discussed with parents and child together. When there are separate groups it is only a matter of basic integrity to give each group its own privilege of sharing or keeping to itself its discussion content. But it is also very true that the various members of a family can be assembled as a group and under skilled leadership they can be led to discuss the problems of their relationships with candor. Sometimes it is as hard for the social worker to face this prospect as it is for the family members, so concerned is he with the right of the individual to privacy of his feelings.

But much is being learned about dealing with families openly as a unit, with no secrets retained. It is being recognized that family problems, which invariably involve impediments to communication, cannot be fully resolved by a helping process which reinforces the barriers to

[16] Helen E. Durkin, *Group Therapy for Mothers of Disturbed Children* (Springfield, Ill.: Charles C. Thomas, 1954), p. 27.

communication. As one psychiatrist comments, "What is the propriety of a therapist's dealing openly with intimate matters when more than one member of the family is involved? Can confidential material be so handled? Under what conditions must an individual's privacy be completely safeguarded? Under what conditions may his personal secrets be exposed to family scrutiny for legitimate therapeutic purposes? With great frequency I have found that these intimate matters, these so-called secrets, turn out not to be real secrets at all. Far more often they are common family knowledge, surrounded by a tacit conspiracy of silence. What is involved here is not so much a true secret but rather a barrier to emotional communication, a barrier to the free sharing of certain experiences. Some forms of privacy are needed and healthy. Others are pathogenic. When a therapist supports a sick need for privacy, he affirms guilt and fear; he reinforces the patient's isolation." [17]

Parents are not the only family members who should be offered this kind of service. In adult work there is no reason why wives of probationers or parolees could not also be worked with in groups. The staff that has the time and energy to do it would find great potential effectiveness in working with a discussion group of parolees while a parallel group of their wives also meets weekly, with the two groups having a joint meeting at periodic intervals.

In San Francisco the Federal Probation Office has made good use of the discussion process for relatives of prospective parolees. The staff was interested in preparing the homes of parolees to receive them constructively. To start the process the staff first talked to the future parolees instead of the families. Staff members visited the reformatory and met with the inmates (youthful offenders) who would be returning to the San Francisco area and told them of the plan. They encouraged the men to write to their families and ask them to participate. Then notices were sent to the families by the probation office. Responses came from nearly all the invited families and the group soon was started with wives, parents, and one fiancée.

One problem the situation presented was that the process started out, properly enough, as an informational one; movies were shown of the institution, and in other ways the two probation officer leaders tried to answer the families' questions. The group members, in turn, tried to use

[17] Nathan W. Ackerman, *The Psychodynamics of Family Life, Diagnosis and Treatment of Family Relationships* (New York: Basic Books, 1958), p. ix.

the leaders as question answerers instead of discussion leaders, and attempted to manipulate them according to their individual interests. The degree of anxiety in such a group runs high. The staff was surprised to find that the members actually feared that their participation in the group could work against them. They worried that if they made a bad impression on the group the probation officers would report this to the parole board and there would be less likelihood of a favorable parole decision. This is another convincing reason why the group leader must be nonthreatening in his approach; and it is also additional evidence of how much need there is for this kind of work to involve the total family.

As we see the many fascinating attempts to develop socially therapeutic programs using groups of clients it is apparent that here, as in so many areas of treatment philosophy, we have moved from one strongly held position to its opposite. And we shall see this phenomenon reflected in other chapters of this book. Parole officers who earlier in their own careers were enforcing the nearly universal rule that parolees could not associate with each other are now instead bringing them together for their mutual help — and with a sense of satisfaction that enforcing conformity under the more repressive rule in the past could never match.

4

Special Purpose Programs

In addition to the discussion groups that are becoming more and more familiar in probation and parole, activity-centered or task-centered programs that focus on specific kinds of needs are being developed, often with considerable inventiveness. These take a wide variety of forms and for convenience here they will be referred to as special purpose programs. Usually they are designed for juvenile offenders rather than adults, probably because the juvenile offender appeals more to the public conscience, and public support of these programs is essential. Because of the extra costs involved it is not usually possible for public agencies to finance them in the initial stages of development, if ever, through their regular budgets.

One is tempted to say that the special purpose programs reflect the American love of gadgetry, for in the whole perspective of rehabilitative efforts some of these programs do appear to have the characteristics of gadgets. But, if intelligently conceived and administered, social gadgetry can be sound and effective; it can serve research and experimental purposes and can lead to real progress in basic rehabilitation programs. It often has the virtue of catching public attention because of its imaginative character, and this is a fully legitimate asset to exploit as long as soundness of method and the welfare of the client are not sacrificed to publicity purposes.

The Citizenship Training Group, Inc., in Boston is perhaps the oldest and most firmly established of any special purpose program in this country. Actually, it is somewhat misleading to include it in this category, since it does not focus on one particular aspect of the delinquency problem any more than probation does. However, it does belong here as a highly structured social group program especially designed to serve a juvenile court. A brief look at it will introduce us to some of the strengths and problems of special purpose programs.

Started nearly thirty years ago by the Boston juvenile court, it is an after-school, club-like program, to which boys newly placed on probation are assigned by the court. It is like a club in its outward organization and operation, but its purpose is to help probation officers to gain a better understanding of the boys and to give the boys an actively constructive, socializing experience.

Like most special purpose programs, the C.T.G. uses group discussion as a major technique, combining this with activities which seduce the interest of the boy and keep him happily involved in the rehabilitative process. For a physical setting, the program has space in a venerable downtown building occupied by the Young Men's Christian Union. This organization, operating a program not unlike the typical Y.M.C.A., has, since the beginning, given the C.T.G. a home in its building, but otherwise has no administrative connection with it. For many years the space was donated to the C.T.G., but now a rental fee is charged at a rate about half the actual cost. The space includes a gym, a craft shop, library, interview and conference rooms, and office space. The gym is well frequented by the active, restless boys, but older visitors use up energy enough just in walking up to these fourth-floor facilities in the elevator-less, old building.

On a selective basis, about 15 percent of the boys placed on probation are assigned by the court to the C.T.G. as a condition of probation. Each boy so assigned must attend the program for two hours after school every weekday for twelve weeks. It is an open-ended group program, able to operate with boys entering it at any time instead of keeping intact groups. The two hours each day are filled with a mixture of educational, recreational, and creative activities interspersed with medical and psychological testing, casework interviews, and group discussions. The craft shop and gym provide a chance for the boys to gain some self-esteem through creative and physical accomplishments, as well as to work off excess energy. The library offers opportunity for some quiet intervals and is a good gathering place for the boys who arrive early or stay late. This kind of program presumably is organized for treatment purposes primarily, but it has been found equally useful as a diagnostic method. Nor is it just the medical and psychological examinations that provide data for diagnosis. The opportunity the staff has to observe each boy in a social situation two hours a day gives an advantage that can seldom be duplicated in a conventional probation case.

While a boy is in the C.T.G. program the staff there takes full responsibility for working with him. At the end of his three months he is returned to the court for action, which usually means he is put on the regular probation caseload. Ordinarily the boys assigned to the C.T.G. are those who need especially close supervision. About twenty-five boys can be accommodated at any one time. The boys are required to come directly after school in the afternoon and they go directly home afterward. The C.T.G. furnishes transportation for those who need such help by giving them bus tokens when they leave for home — one to go home on and one for the return trip the next day.

During the summer the regular program is discontinued and a day camp is operated on a voluntary basis for both the currently assigned boys and the former boys. Boys newly assigned during the summer are scheduled to start in the program when it resumes at the beginning of the school year. The staff has its vacation when the program closes entirely during August.

Although three professional workers and one clerical employee on the C.T.G. staff are paid from the regular Boston juvenile court budget, the remaining costs of the program must be met from various private sources. The C.T.G. is incorporated and has its own board composed of citizens who represent various interests and organizations in the community. The juvenile court judge is the president of the board.

The C.T.G. has worked splendidly in Boston where the juvenile court has been able to operate its program with the help of physical facilities made available by a private social agency. The program might not have been possible otherwise. The success of this arrangement, however, is due to some elements that are hard to duplicate elsewhere, and administrators who seek to copy the Boston court's relationship with a cooperating agency need to consider some of the problems carefully. Not only did the Young Men's Christian Union of Boston make space available to the court without cost during the program's first twenty-five years, but it did not ask for a controlling voice in the operation of the C.T.G. (The C.T.G. bylaws do provide that a representative from the Young Men's Christian Union shall be on its board.) This is unusual. Ordinarily a private agency will have neither the funds nor the inclination to give valuable space outright year after year to support another agency's program. The few private agencies that would be able to furnish rent-free space to another organization would usually be interested in having a voice in the conduct of the guest organization's program, and perhaps an active role in it. The agencies available to work cooperatively with a court are likely to be either church supported or community supported through the United Fund or Community Chest. If the latter, the Community Chest may discourage a no-cost arrangement since this would mean Community Chest support of a public program.

If the host agency is church supported, especially if that church has an evangelistic bent, it is likely to want to inject some religious elements, with a denominational bias, into the program, whatever the financial arrangements. This may seem acceptable at first, but the center can rarely survive under these terms, for this situation is not the same as that when the court sends a child to a denominational facility for care and treatment by that denomination. In such a case the court takes into account the family's church preference, and the placement is made only if everyone is aware of and accepting of the religious setting. If the court wants to establish a program like the C.T.G. that may be used for any or all probationers without regard to religious preference, then it must be as denominationally neutral as a public school. No church-related agency may use it to exert denominational influence. But if such influence is expressly prohibited, the denominational agency will often be unwilling to give its support.

If the difficult problem of housing is met, and even if free housing is somehow obtained, there remains the problem of financing the program. It is unlikely that the court itself can get the budget to carry the full cost, and the alternative is that someone has to be perpetually concerned with money raising. The Boston C.T.G. proves that the year-after-year financing can be accomplished, but it requires time, energy, and persistence on the part of the director.

A PARTIAL RESIDENTIAL PROGRAM

A variation on the after-school program as an adjunct to probation is a weekend program. In Minneapolis the juvenile court developed a Weekend Ranch Program which, like the Boston C.T.G., started with the help of a private social agency. The Volunteers of America owned a large ranch about thirty-five miles from the city, and while it was being fully used during the summer for children's camping, it had very little use the rest of the year. An arrangement was made for the court to send groups to the ranch from Friday afternoon to Sunday afternoon every week of the school year. The court furnished the director of the program and the Volunteers of America furnished food as well as lodging — in fact the Volunteers paid all the costs of the program except the salary of the program director. (Any contributions from private sources went to the Volunteers.)

The weekend program is still very active although in a different setting. After operating for three years at the ranch provided by the Volunteers of America, it was necessary to move because of other programs that developed on a full-time basis there. It now operates from a cabin on the grounds of a local boys' training school and has been otherwise modified in such minor ways as were necessary to adapt to the different kind of housing. Private financing carried most of the cost of the program for its first three years but now it is supported by regularly budgeted funds from the probation office. (The probation office is part of the Hennepin County Department of Court Services, as is also the local training school mentioned.) The description of the program here mainly relates to the first three years when it operated in the ranch setting, even though the basic principles involved have not materially changed.

The decision of the Minneapolis authorities to develop a weekend program instead of an after-school facility like the C.T.G. was not based on a conviction that the weekend schedule was necessarily better. Either method has its advantages. The major factor in the decision was simply that the physical quarters available had cooking and sleeping accommodations and the ranch was such a distance from the city that it could not be used after school. However, it was also apparent that the weekend offered the advantage of getting the boys away from home and into a twenty-four-hour program during the two days of the week when they were out of school and at loose ends, and when their parents in some instances were most likely to be drinking. Another advantage was that when the boys and their probation officers lived together around the clock there was even more opportunity for the officers to observe and understand the problems of their charges than there would have been in a program in which they were seen only during afternoons. At bedtime, for instance, feelings that may be haunting a child tend to come to the surface and if a probation officer is at hand then, he has an unusual opportunity to give help when it is needed.

At the same time, however, the weekend, with its residential feature, is more expensive than an after-school program. It introduces the extra costs of cooks and food preparation (the group was served seven meals per weekend), beds, bedding, and laundry. There is also a problem of staff scheduling. The program director, for instance, was a full-time member of the court's probation staff, but it became impossible to define for him a forty-hour week. One weekend of duty — twenty-four hours a day — would more than fill his quota. But it was still necessary for him to work on other days of the week too, because he had to formulate plans, make phone calls to parents, confer with court and probation officers about case referrals, and the like.

Obviously, then, it is impossible to state categorically which program arrangement is best. This can be decided only on the basis of the resources available in the particular community.

The Weekend Ranch Program was designed to serve boys from twelve through fourteen. This made it a homogeneous age group, and boys at this early teen level proved more responsive to the idea of a ranch setting than older boys. It was necessary that the twenty to thirty boys in the program not have severe physical or mental handicaps that would prevent them from participating in the program activities, but this does not mean that only nice boys were welcome. In fact, the intent was to refer only probationers who were quite delinquent, severely hostile, and likely to get into other trouble soon if they could not have more intensive help than the conventional probation process provided. They were boys who had weak or unstable homes and in most cases they were showing their hostility in disruptive behavior in school.

Unlike the C.T.G., which prescribes a three-month period for each boy, the Weekend Ranch Program was an assignment of indefinite length. Each boy was kept in it for the period of time that seemed to be of benefit to him. Of course a certain number lasted only a very few weekends and then were out of it either because they got into more trouble or because they turned out to be completely unsuitable. For those who stayed with it, their participation was likely to last anywhere from six months to over a year.

While the referrals were made by probation officers from their case-loads, it was found that there was more success in getting family support and participation if the assignment to the program occurred in the courtroom, instead of being handled directly between the probation officer and the Weekend Ranch staff. If the judge himself spoke directly to parents and boy in the courtroom and sternly emphasized his expectations, the families took the program more seriously and made more effort to cooperate.

Every Friday afternoon after school a school bus available to the Department of Court Services picked up the boys at prearranged spots and got them out to the ranch in time for supper. The program director and his associates were already there and after the meal they set up various recreational activities for the boys. The assistants were college seniors, usually sociology majors, and they received a flat amount of pay for the weekend, in addition to their food and lodging during the two days.

On Saturday the program was primarily work assignments. However, much of the work had a recreational quality for these boys. The ranch had a large dairy operation and these city boys found fun in the novelty of feeding the calves or even cleaning the barn. There was usually a chance, too, for some romping in the haymow afterward. Other boys worked in the kitchen and while dishwashing was no pleasure to them, there was the disposal of the garbage afterward to be looked forward to — this meant getting out a pony cart, hitching up two ponies, and driving about a mile through the woods to a dump. Then there was tractor driving. The boys had an opportunity to learn to drive one of the tractors and after a prescribed number of hours of instruction they were given a specially prepared "license" to drive under certain conditions.

After Saturday night supper came the discussion groups. With boys of this age a discussion session is substantially different from what it is with the older teen-ager. These younger boys are more hyperactive, have a shorter attention span, and have more attachment to their families. Discussions among older boys are normally concerned with how to get along with each other, but the younger boys still need to get along with adults, so the adult leader will be more involved in the discussion and will be actively developing and using his relationship with the boys.

The wonderful advantage of holding discussion sessions in the structure of a living situation like this is the wealth of discussion content provided by the group life. The boys in such a program all have problems in getting along with other people and these problems show themselves in the group living in ways that become painfully apparent to everyone. If the group on Saturday night is discussing control of one's temper, for instance, it is not just an academic discussion, but a real concern about what could have happened that very day if Jimmy had not ducked quickly enough and had been hit by that flowerpot thrown by Arnold in a fit of anger. And the leader helps them to wonder what would happen if the next time a temper explodes they are in the barn and the nearest thing is not a flowerpot but a pitchfork. One Friday night the boys were aware that a new boy was masturbating after they were all in bed. The next evening it was the topic of discussion, and because it arose naturally it evoked more real concern in the group than it would have if it had been artificially introduced.

Activities do not exist in this kind of program only to provide content for group discussion, but this is one of the kinds of usefulness the activities serve. Actually, a program rich in activities conducted with sensitivity and skill serves in many ways to encourage a maladjusted child's growth toward normalcy. This is a fact not understood by conservative critics who see group work programs as mere fun and games — a coddling of delinquents. Such critics miss the point that a lack of wholesome emotional stimulation is likely to have contributed to delinquency in a child. For him the social group work program must try to provide some of the deeply satisfying growth experiences that he needs if he is going to have the internal serenity that leads to a well-adjusted adult life. It is far more than just a matter of keeping him busy because "the devil finds work for idle hands." Probably more important than anything else is the opportunity for him to get to know adults who are warm, giving people, with an interest in him that does not falter at the first sign of misbehavior on his part. He meets and gets to know such adults as he works and plays under staff members who understand his needs and know how to use the relationship they develop with him. A craft class, for instance, offers a chance for the child to develop pride in himself as a person who, to his delighted surprise, can be creative, but it also lets him be companionable with an adult with whom he may come to feel a sense of acceptance and security.

The soap carving, the rope making, the leather working, all serve the immediate and direct purpose of enriching the lives of children whose experiences are otherwise "enriched" only with TV westerns and such deviltry as they can find in the street. But we are still not getting our money's worth out of these activities if they are not also conducted in such a way as to give the child a refreshing and deeply satisfying new relationship with adults who can foster a belief in the essential decency of the adult world and encourage in him a willingness to take his place in it as a responsible member.

Well-meaning people are always tempted to deal with delinquent children by direct teaching of behavior or by giving advice and admonition. Children who are what we like to call normal are able to use advice and instruction, but children who have learned to dislike, distrust, and fear adults are hardly prepared to use advice from adults. The help we give such children must first be in the form of actual experience — new experiences of having fun with strong adults who, astonishingly, never fail them.

Parents too have problems and need to have constructive experiences with persons in authoritative roles. The Weekend Ranch Program encouraged the parents to drive out to the ranch on Sunday afternoons to get their boys themselves, and to come early enough to have their own discussion session. In fact, it was made quite clear to them that they were expected to attend.

The parents sat around a table, with every effort being made by the staff to keep the atmosphere as relaxed as possible. A coffee pot and a plate of cookies helped much in this regard. Parents invariably approach a situation of this sort defensively and reluctantly. They are expecting to be lectured and perhaps blamed again for their son's delinquencies. They gradually thaw as they find that the leader is not pointing a finger of blame at them but is just helping them to talk as they wish about problems of raising children. All have worries in this area and once they find that their feelings are being dealt with respectfully they are more than willing to discuss them. The talk first is full of the other people and situations that are at fault. Teachers, schools,

115

bad companions are all worked over. But then some of them begin to notice improvement in the boys' behavior at home and they begin to comment on it in their meetings. They ask what is happening in the program that causes the progress; they want to apply the same techniques at home. Gradually some of them recognize that they themselves have to change.

In general it was found that neither boys nor parents entered the Weekend Ranch Program with any enthusiasm, or even any real willingness to stay and participate one bit more than the court required. However, it was also found that once they had got a good taste of it, the court's big stick could be put on the shelf, for both parents and boys in most cases continued to participate because of the satisfaction they were finding in the experience.

Though the Minneapolis weekend program operates the year around, the feature of it which has received the most notice has been the summer activity — a raft trip down the Mississippi River. This was an idea that was born in one of the discussion groups during December of the program's second year. The leader was beginning to encourage the boys to think about what they would do during the summer when the school vacation would mean that they were no longer limited to the weekend for any plans they might make. The leader's action here was a deliberate part of the treatment program. A nearly universal characteristic of these boys from lower socioeconomic homes is their lack of inclination to plan beyond the present. The middle-class family plans for the future and expects its teen-age sons to look years ahead — toward college and eventually a career; the family at the lower end of the social ladder, however, does little or no planning and a boy from this kind of home grows up thinking only of gratification in immediate terms. These boys also have little awareness of the world outside their own daily experience. Their families do not go on trips; do not talk of national or world events; do not stimulate the children's interest in any events not affecting them in a direct and tangible manner.

This environment nourishes the seeds of delinquency in the boys it envelops, for they grow up with low self-esteem, low aspirations, and no motivation to study in school because they see no application of the history, geography, English, or arithmetic to anything that is part of their life.

The planning and carrying out of a raft trip on the river was seen as a device that could combat some of these negative characteristics in the boys. First of all, the idea of building a raft and going down the river into a world never before heard of was a sufficiently exciting prospect to catch a boy's attention and hold it for six months of planning. In this, most of these boys were having their first experience in planning for anything more than a very few days away. Furthermore, in doing the planning it became necessary for them to learn many things that they had never known to be important. The problem of logistics that a trip of this sort involves are endless and the boys were caught up in all of them. For example, they had no experience in reading a map and little concept of distances and the relative locations of other parts of the country. Now their forthcoming adventure gave them a motivation to study the maps of the river areas that they did not feel in geography class.

A petroleum company contributed forty oil drums to be built into four long pontoons, and enough lumber was contributed from other sources to build a deck sixteen feet by twenty-five feet. Two outboard motors were supplied on loan from a manufacturer. The boys helped put the raft together every Saturday during the spring. A boy who had been failing in arithmetic was confronted by the problem of how to compute the number of square feet on the surface of an oil drum and from this to compute the number of gallons of paint that the forty drums would require. The buoyancy of an oil drum had to be determined and the weight of the raft itself figured so that the allowable weight of the payload would be known. Food consumption had to be estimated and a determination made of how many pounds of food could be carried, how long that much food would last, and so how frequently they would need to stop for new supplies. The same questions had to be answered regarding fuel consumption.

After maps of the river were consulted and locations spotted where the raft would have to stop for fuel and food, letters had to be written to the mayors of those towns, asking about the docking facilities and the availability of supplies. Boys who had been unimpressed with an English teacher's instructions about composing a letter suddenly found they needed and appreciated such advice, for they were writing to important people on an important subject. The replies to their letters brought gratification, for the mayors were cordial in their responses and their promises of welcome gave the boys a new sense of anticipation.

As the summer came nearer the group was visited by representatives

117

of the Red Cross, the Army Corps of.Engineers, and the Coast Guard, who talked about the river itself, the channels and how to stay in them, navigation fundamentals, safety and first-aid measures. The excitement of preparation was a motivation for the boys to absorb all this learning and also to stay out of trouble. This trip was going to be too good to miss by getting locked up because of any misbehavior now.

The first summer of the river trip the raft with fifteen boys and three staff members aboard left Minneapolis in mid-June and arrived in New Orleans twenty-eight days later. The rest of the boys were sent to New Orleans by bus to ride the raft on the return trip while the first group came back by the bus. The return trip could not be completed because the heavy raft moved too slowly against the current in a long, long river. But the difficulties were minor ones and the sense of success was great.

After the lessons learned the first summer, the full trip was not attempted in subsequent years. The trip became a regular summer feature of the program, but now, instead of going one way the full length of the river, the raft goes halfway and returns with St. Louis being the turn-around point.

The trip itself accomplishes therapy in many ways. While the endless panorama of new vistas with each bend of the river and the variety of river traffic going by are a constant source of diversion, the 300 square feet of deck is a very limited space for daily living for nearly twenty people. The close day-after-day proximity brings out every aspect of each person's way of relating to other people and provides an urgent kind of content for the nightly group discussions. A typical problem on an early trip was the behavior of one of the younger boys, small for his age, but always full of noise. His uninhibited hostility was constantly evident in conduct that everyone felt as belligerent and obnoxious. During the raft trip a substantial improvement occurred in his socializing ability. It was due simply to the fact that all day, every day, he had the experience of being checked in his irritating behavior by both adults and boys. But the process was made tolerable to him because the adults were strong and pleasant young men who liked him even though they controlled him, and who were just as ready to join him in some fishing, swimming, or other purely enjoyable activity as they were to correct him.

Sometimes there is an experience for the group as a whole that has

118

constructive effect. It might be arriving in a small river town on a Sunday morning to be met at the dock by the mayor, who arranges for police cars to give them transportation to church. Boys accustomed to being chased by the police thus have a chance to taste the experience of being honored and served by police and mayor. There were many experiences of this kind and each time that such boys get a chance to see themselves as respectable and important their desire to maintain this image is increased.

On one trip the raft docked at a town immediately after a severe storm that had swamped nearly all the boats at the riverfront. The boys rose to the challenge and spent the afternoon wading and swimming from boat to boat, bailing them out and floating them again. The boys found themselves to be minor heroes with the townspeople as a result, and here again was a new experience for them in discovering satisfaction in a constructive role.

Occasional delinquencies happen on these trips and even these serve a kind of usefulness. At one stop two of the boys were caught trying to break into a concession stand at the riverfront. For the other boys it was a rude shock. Though they all had been guilty of worse behavior in their own delinquent activities, this sort of thing was now beginning to seem out of place amid the good feeling they were developing with people in the river towns. This time it was no longer possible to feel unconcerned and hard-boiled when the sheriff came to the raft and questioned everyone. It didn't fit. It was a letdown, and the two culprits were made to feel the heavy disapproval of the others. Delinquency that had formerly been a regular and accepted part of living now was inappropriate; and this was a healthy discovery. In their group discussion the boys themselves decided what disciplinary restrictions would be imposed on the two for the rest of the trip.

In the course of the normal young person's development it is usual, and is considered important, for him to have wholesome and stimulating high points in his social living. An occasional exciting adventure with a group of peers is part of a child's socializing growth, and it has a continuing effect in the form of satisfying memories. An adventure such as this river trip fills a great need of this sort for boys who have had a severe dearth of good social experiences. There is far more to it than just riding down the river.

There are, for instance, countless interesting contacts on the river

119

itself. Families and individuals going by in private boats pull alongside to chat and exchange news of the river. Sometimes the same ones are encountered again on the return trip and there is the pleasure of recognizing them and talking about experiences in the interim. Fishing boats stop to see what kind of expedition the raft is and they enjoy introducing the boys to new tastes in fish. Occasional enormous barge tows are encountered; the boys have had visits to some exciting and impressive craft of this kind.

Experiences ashore are just as important. The town of Hannibal has always been particularly hospitable because of its love for the Huck Finn story, so the boys are always entertained royally there with tours of the Tom Sawyer points of interest. Other towns get interested too and show hospitality in their own ways. In one town the mayor met the boys at the dock and took them all to lunch at a good restaurant in town. The boys at that time had been on the trip long enough to need haircuts, and they were uncomfortably conscious of their rumpled clothes as they sat down in the very respectable restaurant. But the warmly enthusiastic hospitality of the restaurant owner and the mayor put them at ease and impressed them with the genuine likability of such people. At other towns, local people invited the boys to watermelon feeds, took them on tours, and made arrangements for them to get showers, haircuts, laundry, and so on.

Boys who have had no knowledge of the rest of the country and no interest in it come back with a new appreciation of things they have been ignoring in their school classes in history and geography. In general, it has been found that the boys who are the most severely disturbed are the ones who made the most progress. Some who entered the program months before in a nearly psychotic condition return from the river trip as remarkably normal youngsters. In such cases there is usually a later but only partial regression. A very satisfying net gain remains.

The romantic quality of the river trip is something that catches attention and serves certain agency purposes in addition to its primary aim of being a therapeutic framework. It dramatizes the efforts to treat delinquency and in doing so promotes community support of the program and the agency that operates it. There is a tendency, however, for the river trip to draw attention away from the fact that the program operates the year around and that a vast amount of the help that the boys gain from it comes from the regular, unspectacular weekly contacts and group experiences that go on throughout the school year. This program is no different from any other in respect to the fact that in order to help a maladjusted youngster it must provide a way to understand the problem fully and then must attack it with persistence and patience.

One of the Weekend Ranch cases illustrates clearly the heart of the treatment process and is well worth presenting here to show in specific detail the impact of such a program on one boy; at the same time this summary demonstrates the universal qualities of the treatment process, for this type of case could be found, with minor differences, in any of many other settings. The validity of the treatment process described here is not negated by the fact that this case would fall among the failure statistics if it had been evaluated at the conclusion of the boy's stay in this program.

Mike Sweeney was a thirteen-year-old boy who was in the Weekend Ranch Program for forty sessions. Three weeks after being released he was committed to a training school for involvement in three burglaries and an auto theft which apparently occurred just before and following his release.

Mike was the oldest of six children. The parents, both of whom had juvenile records, were married two months after Mike's birth. They were divorced, remarried a year later, separated, and were again talking reconciliation when the father committed suicide the year Mike was seven. Mr. Sweeney shot himself, then staggered into the house where most of the family saw him die.

Mike showed signs of difficulty in school as early as the first grade. He always had a poor attendance record, with frequent truancy. In second grade he did a lot of fighting because the kids teased him about his parents' bizarre sex life, which was conducted rather openly. When Mike was nine, Mrs. Sweeney began seeking outside help because Mike was truanting from school and was incorrigible at home. About the same time Mike was in court for stealing a bicycle. At thirteen he stole $75 worth of tools and a car, and drank liquor.

When Mike was referred to the Weekend Ranch Program as a result of this offense he showed signs of emotional disturbance. His mother indicated that he seemed to delight in abusing animals and she was sure that he had strangled their pet squirrel. One day Mike was found by his sister lying on the bed holding a BB gun to his stomach. The mother reported that Mike was absorbed with watching his sisters undress, and she had caught him peeking into the bathroom and the bedroom. The entire family felt that Mike was getting to be "just like his father."

After his first few weekends in the program the staff listed the following problems that Mike was showing. He (1) was insecure in the group; (2) boasted and bragged of his prowess at almost anything; (3) sucked his thumb; (4) was sure people thought he was nuts; (5) lacked social skills; (6) had difficulty accepting external controls and limits; (7) had little internal control; (8) was unable to accept his father's suicide, was ashamed of it, and fearful of people discovering it; (9) had borderline intelligence. To supplement these observations the staff had his mother's report that Mike abused animals, was obsessed with sex, and was "just like his father." On the positive side, Mike (1) was physically strong; (2) liked work; (3) was determined to succeed when given a task; (4) tried to please the group; (5) liked the ranch.

The staff tried to cope with Mike's identified problems in the following ways:

1. Insecurity in the group. Mike was not pushed too hard although he was required to participate in some activities. When it was apparent that he was feeling under too much pressure he was allowed to leave his small group. (The total group was divided into smaller units under specific staff members.) He was assigned to another group with three boys he knew from school, because they were more friendly and less threatening to him than the other boys. The worker was aware of Mike's need for support and made him more secure by always showing him especially clearly what was expected of him.

2. Boasting and bragging. These boasts were discussed in the group meetings and it was pointed out that nobody was best at everything. As Mike became aware of his reason for boasting, i.e., his desire to be a big shot in the group, the boys decided to remind him of what he was doing every time he resorted to boasting. He was soon able to accept the fact that he didn't have to act big any more to be accepted.

3. Thumb sucking. This was never discussed except when Mike brought it up himself. His thumb sucking gradually became less frequent although it remained unreduced while he was sleeping.

4. Illusion that everyone thought he was nuts. It was assumed that this was Mike's way of questioning the staff's attitudes toward him as a result of the psychological tests that had been given him. His counselor explained the need for psychological testing and pointed out that others

in the group had been tested, and everyone took tests in school. When Mike brought up his mother's comparison of him with his father, the counselor suggested that his mother was referring to physical likeness rather than mental unbalance. It was pointed out that if the staff really thought he was mentally ill they would send him to a hospital. He became able to accept this and seemed to be satisfied that the staff was not questioning his sanity.

5. Lack of social skills. Mike was taught new games, new work skills, and some craft skills. The group meetings discussed his group relationships and ways of improving them. The counselors encouraged acceptable methods of adjustment by praise and recognition, discouraged unacceptable ones by showing disapproval.

6. Difficulty with external controls and limits. This was related to two other problems in Mike's case: a lack of internal controls and a lack of native intelligence. The staff set few limits but enforced these firmly, fairly, and consistently. They tried to check him on every infraction, but also tried to convince him that he was able to accept controls. This was only partially successful; Mike will probably always have trouble with controls if for no other reason than that he is not able to see the consequences of his acts at the time he does them.

7. Little internal control. Mike had been able to get by with his uncontrolled behavior at home and in some ways had even been encouraged to act out. The staff used wood working, horseback riding, and tractor driving to set "limits" that he had to accept because no authority was able to do it for him; i.e., if you don't saw on the line the wood is cut wrong and doesn't fit. A worker could remind him of this and help him with the learning, but he had to follow the line himself.

8. Fear of father's suicide being known. Mike made up several stories about his father's death. He asked one of the counselors if he could tell him about it and proceeded to invent a story about how his father fell out of an airplane. The worker candidly asked him why he had lied, and made it clear that he knew the true story. From such incidents Mike learned that the counselors accepted him even though his dad had committed suicide. It was pointed out that his father had been sick and was not responsible for what he did. Mike was not responsible either and while he did not have to shout the story he did not have to be ashamed of it. The matter was discussed with Mike's mother

and she was asked not to try to hush it up at home or tell the children not to tell, nor encourage them to lie about it.

9. Borderline intelligence. Mike had to be worked with very patiently, with careful, simple explanations of everything.

The strengths listed for Mike were worked with in the following ways:

1. Physical strength. Mike was given jobs to do that the others could not do. This gave him some status in the group and helped his acceptance by the others.

2. Liking for work. Many potentially useful experiences existed for Mike on the ranch because of his liking for work. This was a major way that the farm setting itself was helpful to him, for he could derive status and acceptance in the group as a result of what he could accomplish.

3. Determination to succeed. Many times Mike learned things because he stuck at them when others would have given up. Since he had a harder time learning new things than most of the boys, his willingness to stick with something was very helpful and was encouraged by appropriate praise.

4. Desire to please the group. To exploit this the staff gave Mike suggestions about new ways of gaining the group's approval. The staff also helped him with his social skills as he tried to do what the others did.

5. Liking for the ranch. Mike's desire to stay at the ranch may have offset some of his other problems, such as lack of foresight, since, as he saw it, he would have to be good if he were to stay in the ranch program.

Then there were the problems reported by his mother. The staff saw no evidence of the abuse of animals. Mike cared well for ranch animals, especially the horses. His dog had pups and he built her a box and fed and watered her and the pups. Although he may previously have done some of the things reported by his mother, no more of this was seen. With regard to his supposed obsession with sex it was pointed out to his mother that he was probably curious and this was normal. The staff encouraged the mother to discuss with Mike the questions about sex which he seemed to have and to give him some sex education. The conclusion, finally, was that Mike had not really shown more than a normal interest. His mother's complaint that Mike was "just like his father" was a serious problem and difficult to solve. Though the staff tried to get

Mrs. Sweeney to reduce her allusions to this idea she still continued to compare Mike with his father too often.

As stated at the outset, Mike got into additional trouble despite the help he was given in the program and he was committed to a training school. A later staff report comments on this: "The additional trouble that Mike got into following his release from the Weekend Ranch Program was a matter of participating in thefts with some other boys and seems to have been again a part of his need for acceptance by the group in which he finds himself at the time. Since Mike has been at the training school the report is that he is adjusting well and he has shown some deep concern about having 'let down' the people at the ranch. Altogether, despite the recent setback, it appears that Mike did obtain some very real help from his ranch experience and that this will contribute substantially to the next steps in working with him."

This optimism in the final comment seems to have been justified, for four years have now gone by and a recent check shows that Mike is functioning adequately. After a period of restlessness in the institution Mike settled down and did well. He was later supervised on parole for a lengthy period and finally discharged as having made a fairly satisfactory adjustment. He continued to live at home with his mother and though she did not change materially, Mike became better adjusted to her. He got a job as a truck driver and with his determination to succeed he was handling the job successfully at the last report.

There was never a true research project built into the Weekend Ranch Program, but after its first three years a careful evaluation of the cases handled was undertaken. During that time 69 boys had been introduced to the program and had stayed for periods of time ranging from one session to ninety-eight sessions. At the time of the evaluation there were 13 boys still in the program and they were not evaluated then. Of the other 56 there were 9 who had been removed because of new delinquencies and 14 who had been removed because they were inappropriate selections and for various reasons could not use the program. This left 33 boys who had been admitted and discharged as having completed the program satisfactorily, plus the 13 still present and apparently doing all right.

A follow-up of these 33 boys a few months after their discharge showed that 11 had later been committed to institutions. For 4 of these there was no clear evidence that they had been helped by the program, but 7 others, including Mike, showed signs of having received help from the program that might yet bear fruit. Nine boys had made satisfactory adjustments to all appearances and 13 had made obvious and substantial improvement. This does not seem to be a high ratio of success except in relation to the fact that all the boys were originally referred to the program as almost certain to be in further trouble very soon.

A program like this presents a challenge to the leader's ability in perpetual inventiveness. There was for instance, an aspect of the raft trip that first time which could not be duplicated in later years. The first boys were the true adventurers. They envisioned the trip and saw the raft take shape with their help. It was "their" idea, "their" raft, "their" trip; and the fact of their investment in it gave them a commitment to make it succeed and a sense of pride in the success that was achieved.

The boys who go into the program now can never experience this same value — unless the leader is highly resourceful in developing new aspects to the program that can give each new group its own challenge and sense of uniqueness. It is difficult, but possible. A leader must avoid every temptation to follow the previous pattern in introducing a new group to any program of this sort. The new group must work its own way through the plans, the formulation of rules, and the like. It would be much easier for the leader to tell how, on the basis of experience, it should all be set up, but there will be much less growth for the participants if he does so. They should, if possible, formulate their own plan, and if they are using equipment, or a club room, or anything else that a previous group created, it would be desirable if it could be repaired, remodeled, renamed, and otherwise coaxed into a new identity as the creature of the new group.

A river trip is only one way that the high adventure idea can be developed. In the first year of the Weekend Ranch Program, for instance, the summer's adventure was quite different. It consisted of a canoe trip in northern wilderness lands during the early summer and then a long overland hike as a separate adventure. A hike of fifty miles or so to some terminal point such as a state park is very adequately productive, as is a canoe trip, of all the elements needed in the way of adventure. It too requires detailed planning that provides education and a challenge to the boys.

A privately operated program with a similar approach is found in the

Salesmanship Club Boys Camp, operated by the Salesmanship Club of Dallas, Texas. A number of years ago the camp changed from a summer program only to an all-year program for the treatment of maladjusted boys. Although it is not operated by a court or correctional agency it serves boys whose problems come from severe emotional disturbance that in most cases has led them into delinquent conduct.

The boys live in tents in a primitive camping setting, and while they do not have school in the usual form, they are required to do as much as possible of the planning and the work. It is a kind of continuing adventure that encourages them to gain proficiency in many new skills in order to meet the daily requirements of living. Satisfaction of many of their basic needs is subject to their own contrivance. The program includes periodic lengthy canoe trips which are exploited educationally like the trips described in the Weekend Ranch Program. The heart of the treatment is well described in the camp's descriptive literature:

A camper's status in the group depends on his contribution to its welfare. Here there can be no camouflage, no evasion. A boy is recognized for what he is and what he does. Daily living is at a relaxed tempo which reduces tensions and enables the group to solve most problems as they arise, and counselors have the opportunity to counsel with boys individually or in groups as the situation requires.

Educationally, the program is life-wide, encompassing the complete process of living. No formal classes are held, but all the learning tools and processes are used in solving the numerous problems that arise in day-to-day living. This helps surmount the problem of motivation so commonly encountered in the boys we serve. Books are used freely, but mostly as a resource and reference.

Such a camp represents a most elaborately structured example of the high adventure idea. At the other end of the scale is a very informal application of the idea by one man, a youth parole counselor for the Nevada Youth Training Center. Working from his home in Las Vegas, he takes small groups of boys, about five at a time, on brief trips and hikes into the surrounding desert country. These are done informally according to the interest and whim of the moment on the part of the boys. The parole counselor leads them in nature study and teaches them desert survival. There are always old mines, caves, and ghost towns to explore when they want to. An important element here is the fact that the adventuring is almost entirely something the boys themselves push for. There is no "program" to which they are assigned. On their own initiative they come around to the counselor's house and suggest a trip. This is a superb example of clients themselves asking for an experience that provides a perfect framework for the parole counselor in giving "treatment," for in this completely natural setting a helping relationship develops quickly and can be used with special effectiveness.

One of the more unusual and specialized adventure programs for juvenile probationers is a flying instruction course operated by the probation services under the juvenile court in Minneapolis. This type of program is aimed at the older teen-age delinquent who has low aspirations and low self-esteem, with consequent lack of interest in school. The intent of the program is not to route all these boys into aviation but rather to give them an experience that is exciting enough to capture their interest and that proves to them that they can learn a highly technical operation and become proficient in it. It is hoped that they may then be less inclined to drop out of school and settle for unskilled jobs.

Up to twelve probationers at a time are accepted into the program by referral from the probation officers. The group, once formed, is kept intact through the fifteen weeks that the course runs. At the end of the course there is a simple graduation ceremony and dinner for the participants and their parents. Then a new group is formed and the course is repeated. There are three courses per year (two for boys, one for girls). The program is under the direction of a social group worker in the probation office and is presently financed with a foundation grant. It depends to some extent upon voluntary interest and help from several people who are associated with the aviation business at one of the small local airports.

The instruction sessions are held on Saturday mornings at the airport, and they are conducted with serious academic emphasis. The subject matter includes such topics as theory of flight, structure of the airplane, airport layout and control, weather observation, and navigation. These topics have enough of the romance of flying about them to keep most of the boys — and girls — working at the arithmetic involved, but to make certain that their interest is stimulated further before the novelty wears off, the group has an actual flight about the fourth week. By then they have learned a few of the basics of flight theory and airport control, so the flight at this point gives them the chance to see how the principles work. Half of the group is taken up in one or two light planes to watch the pilot demonstrate the things that have been presented in class. The others go to the control tower to observe the operation there. When the first group returns to the ground they trade places and the plane goes up again.

At no time do the boys and girls get any instruction at the aircraft controls, but at the end of the fifteen-week course they have a final exam which consists of an all-day, cross-country flight which the participants themselves have to plan and conduct. Before leaving they must call for the weather information pertaining to all points on the proposed triangular course. They determine proper cruising altitude and speed; they plan the navigational process to be used, computing ground speed and wind drift; and they determine estimated time of arrival at each point. During the flight the pilots of the planes (three planes are required for a full class) fly just as directed by their passengers. If the plane gets off course it is up to them to find their position and correct it. Each is not only caught in the excitement of getting his own plane there as planned, but also feels the competition with his classmates in the other planes.

Somewhat surprisingly, this program does not initially have any great appeal to the boys and girls who are referred to it. Some difficulty is found in getting them to accept referrals or to stay with the program more than a week or two. This is not seen as any indication of program failure but rather as an indication of the real need for such a program and of the fact that the right probationers are being assigned. It is designed to help youngsters with poor self-concepts, and such boys and girls, of course, will shy away from something they presume to be too technical and difficult for them to handle. Not only are they afraid of failure in new situations, they also have been so inexperienced in normally stimulating activities that they have developed no inclination to respond to opportunities like this. But if they can be held past the first few sessions, they invariably begin to change. In fact, for those who remain in the program there has been a remarkably high percentage of what would ordinarily be called success cases.

The effect begins to show up first and mainly in improved socializing ability. Untidiness, sullenness, aloofness, indifference, all begin to melt away almost visibly. The boys and girls show increased interest and alertness as the study material proves to be exciting and something they can handle. Attitudes in general begin to improve markedly. A follow-up program provides the real test of this. The airport management do-

129

nated a room for the boys' use and most of the boys graduating from the courses have continued coming to the airport each week to meet in the club room and keep up their association with the program. This has not been affected in the least by the voluntary nature of the follow-up program, or even by the fact that many times a boy's probation may have been terminated by then.

As graduates of the course the boys can help around the airport, servicing transient planes, or they may have chances to tinker with old aircraft engines. If a boy has shown special interest and aptitude there are chances for him to develop a continuing relationship with a pilot and perhaps go with him on occasional trips. While the program is much too new at present to permit reliable evaluation of its effect, its first year demonstrated that it has great potential for helping certain selected youngsters.

A program such as this will ordinarily be dependent on private financing to get it started, but it is not expensive. In the Minneapolis program the instruction is given by a veteran pilot and flight instructor who has a natural rapport with boys and great interest in this kind of challenge. He is paid a token wage by the probation office. When flights are to be made he enlists the help of various associates as pilots of the other planes. The contributed funds pay for the teaching materials and the use of the planes twice during each course. This too is a program that has the sort of appeal that invites support, so the financing from private sources has not been found difficult.

WORK PROGRAMS

Perhaps the most common of the special purpose programs are those that provide work experience. The purposes are varied but simple, obvious, and valid. A program may be planned to give teen-agers a chance to earn some spending money on Saturdays so that they can more comfortably stay in school and compete with friends who get allowances. Or the purpose may be more concerned with teaching good work habits and a sense of responsibility. Still another approach may be to assign work as a measure of therapeutic punishment for an act of delinquency.

In Salt Lake City the juvenile court has developed a paid employment program for boys and girls on the probation caseload. Boys who are fifteen or over may be referred to a forestry job in which they are paid seventy-five cents per hour. The boys live at home and report each morning to the U.S. Forestry Service office, from which they are taken in trucks to the work sites. They work in groups under Forestry Service personnel, repairing bridges, clearing trails, cleaning camp grounds, etc. The money for the boys' wages is paid out of budgeted county funds, while the costs of supervision, transportation, and tools are handled by the Forestry Service.

Forestry work has a distinctly masculine character about it that appeals to the boys, and the tin hats they are issued seem to be much more useful as status symbols than they are as head protectors. This program operates most actively during the summer when school is closed, but during the spring and fall it offers work on a reduced basis for boys who are school dropouts. It is not dependable as year-around employment, being limited to seasons when the forest areas are open.

The work for girls is in a Veterans' Administration hospital in Salt Lake City. This is a newer development and at first the results were so discouraging that it was nearly discontinued. The girls referred to it are school dropouts who are available to work full time, also at seventy-five cents per hour. Supervision of the girls is shared by the hospital administration and Red Cross volunteers. The girls must pay their own bus fare in getting to work, as they would on any job, but the hospital then furnishes them lunch without cost. An initial difficulty in the girls' work program was related to the very reason why this kind of experience is so needed by girls such as these. They felt their difference from the other staff members so acutely that their discomfort and defensiveness caused them to drop out quickly. They did not have the poise to function with self-assurance among the professional people in the hospital and they knew that they did not look or act like the other employees. Their makeup and hairdos were designed for a different social setting and were in painful contrast to the more tasteful appearances of their co-workers.

This problem had to be met by a substantial revision of the training process and by better screening. There are many girls coming before the juvenile court who are just not ready for hospital work. It is necessary to pick girls who can tolerate authoritative supervision, since supervision in hospital work is necessarily close and stringent. They also have to be girls who will not attempt to act seductively toward patients. For girls who fit these requirements this job placement seems to be a very successful kind of training. No systematic evaluation of either the forestry work or the hospital work has been attempted, but after several years' experience the court is highly pleased with the apparent results of the program.

In the hospital work new girls enter only when a group of twelve can be started together. They are given two weeks of training, including careful instruction in personal grooming. They are called "Volunteens" and they wear a simple uniform which gives them a sense of status. Their work is sometimes in the central supply rooms and sometimes on the wards where they serve much as nurses' aides would, making beds, feeding patients, and running errands.

An interesting feature of this program is a typing course that is built into it. The girls work just seven hours a day and then in their final hour they have either a group discussion (two days per week) or typing instruction (three days per week). The girls seem to respond positively to both these supplementary activities, which also serve to keep them together as a group.

The juvenile court in Minneapolis has used a similar hospital work experience for girls but on a weekend schedule, limiting it to girls who are staying in school. In this program the girls work at a nearby state mental hospital where they help in the diet kitchen, in the laundry, and on the wards of senile patients. They seem to enjoy the work with patients best, even though these are severely regressed patients who are helpless and infantile in their senility. This is part of an experimental work program for juveniles being conducted by the Minneapolis court with the help of a foundation grant. Teen-age probationers — both boys and girls — are paid $5.00 per Saturday as an encouragement to stay in school. The boys and girls work in groups of eight each with a supervisor in charge. The foundation grant pays the salaries of the work supervisors as well as the wages to the boys and girls. The probation office coordinates the program and provides professional supervision for the work supervisors. The jobs are public service projects of various kinds. While the girls do hospital work, the boys are employed at a publicly owned children's camp, a settlement house, and a church. The camp or church furnishes tools and materials for any work done but has no other cost to bear. The boys do painting, cleaning, minor repairs, and simple landscape work.

Probably the earliest and the most thoroughly developed employment program is operated by the juvenile court for Hamilton County, in Cincinnati. It has been administered with imagination and vigor, exploiting in a variety of ways the value of work projects for boys and girls. Here again the work projects for girls are mostly in hospital settings, while the boys have done the sort of maintenance work already described, plus gardening and apartment cleaning in housing projects for the elderly. The latter has been a particularly useful kind of work, for it would otherwise be done only by the tenants, if at all. In this way the elderly tenants are treated to a thorough cleaning and repainting of their apartments periodically; and similar cleaning of any apartment is done when there is a change of tenant.

Cincinnati had felt the impact of the migration of many impoverished families from southern rural areas who moved north looking for work in industries. There was little interest on the part of these families in education for their children and when the children had no money for school fees, lunches, clothing items, or recreation, authorities had considerable difficulty in keeping them in school. The employment program consequently was designed to meet a severe need felt by the court as it saw delinquency fostered by the teen-ager's lack of job skills, his tendency to drop out of school, and his lack of any legitimately acquired bit of money for personal needs.

Cincinnati's work program during the school year has had both an after-school schedule during the week and a Saturday schedule. On weekdays a boy may report to a work group twice a week. The work supervisor will pick him up in the vicinity of the school right after classes are out and the group of boys will be at work by 3:30 P.M. They work until six and then are taken again in the work supervisor's car and dropped off at or near their homes. They are paid $2.50 for this two and a half hours of work. One group works just once a week and the other two work two afternoons each.

In the Saturday work schedule the boys receive $5.00 plus carfare and lunch. Always the wages the boy earns are paid to him in cash at the end of the day's work. In these programs much more than mere work is involved, for all the boys need counseling help. Often the money they receive is very poorly used; it may be spent for wine; it may be wasted in other profligate ways. In such cases either the work supervisor or the boy's probation officer gives persistent counseling to help the boy appreciate his money and spend it more usefully. Job attitudes and habits come in for attention too, as the work supervisors have occasional opportunities to talk with boys as a group during lunch or other work breaks. The same is true for girls.

Ordinarily the paid work is voluntary for each boy. He applies for it voluntarily and may discontinue it if he finds reason to. But some boys are assigned to work by specific direction of the court at the time their cases are disposed of. This, in a sense, is a sentence imposed by the court, to work for several Saturdays without pay. These boys work as a group doing such things as washing police cars or clearing brush along river banks. As they complete their assignments in unpaid work they are in many cases graduated into the paid work groups.

A similar practice is in effect in the Minneapolis program except that there the paid work program and the unpaid work are more definitely separate. The latter is known in Minneapolis as the Restitutional Work Program and boys and girls are specifically assigned to it by the juvenile court to work for a specified number of hours. The concept behind it is that a person does not really "pay his debt to society" by spending time in a correctional institution, or even by being on probation, and in some cases he should be given a chance to make restitution by performing an unpaid service for his community to offset the cost of his delinquency to the community. So in this program boys and girls work, sometimes in groups, sometimes in individual assignments arranged by a member of the probation staff who gives nearly full time to this program. The cooperation of many agencies and institutions in the area has been obtained, so a child can be sent, for instance, to the director of a settlement house with the understanding that its staff may use the boy or girl in any needed work on the premises for a specified number of hours; these may stretch over several Saturdays to complete. The settlement house director gives the probation office a brief report on the child's performance. The agencies cooperating with this program also include parks, police departments, hospitals, and various suburban village offices.

The operation of a comprehensive employment program such as that in Cincinnati requires the assignment of a full-time staff member in the probation office to supervise the program and the employment of a number of part-time work supervisors. In addition, other people will be involved in a variety of ways. Both the judge and the chief probation officer, for instance, spend a portion of their time, particularly lunch hours and evenings, in activities related to the support of the program in Cincinnati. The employment program there costs about $25,000 annually to operate and most of this money is raised in the community through the constant efforts of the judge, the chief probation officer, and a very active citizens' committee. Some organizations in the county help the program financially on a continuing basis. Much additional income comes in the form of irregular $25 to $50 contributions from a multitude of groups of all kinds.

Any court or probation office that proposes to operate a program like this with this kind of financing must be prepared to expend great energy in order to keep it going. The method in Salt Lake City is more reasonable in terms of administrative time, for there more use is made of volunteers, and the money for payments of the children's wages is appropriated from public funds and paid from the probation office budget. In Minneapolis the program is operated with one foundation grant that will carry it for three years; as yet there are no plans for the manner of continuing after that time.

A work program in Ely, Nevada, offers a significant contrast to the Cincinnati program and should be mentioned here as a demonstration that efforts of this kind need not be limited to the big city. Ely is a prairie town of 4,000 people, set in open country in a state where the entire population is a little less than that of the city of Cincinnati. In Ely there is one probation officer who doubles as the school attendance officer. Like Cincinnati, Ely has a juvenile court judge who has ideas and likes to get things done. As a result, there is an ambitious job-finding program for Ely's youngsters, scaled down to a size and character to fit the town.

The probation officer, with primary concern for his probationers, engages in a substantial, continuing campaign to find any jobs that could be taken by teen-agers. Use is made of newspaper ads, posters, and radio announcements, urging people to report to the probation office any need they have for someone to do relatively unskilled work. Job offers are welcomed whether they are permanent or just one day's work such as housecleaning or lawn mowing. The probation office functions as the clearinghouse for all offers received and, from a list of youngsters who have registered as wanting work, the officer selects those to send to the jobs. The program is advertised as Y.E.S. (Youth Employment Service), and even though it is a service of the juvenile court it is not limited to probationers. Any boy or girl in the community may make application through the probation office for work.

The experience in Ely seems to indicate that this kind of plan is useful, though difficult. Except for the probation officer's salary and office expenses, which would have to be met anyway, there is no cost for the program. It functions mainly in the summer when the officer has more time for it because his school duties do not occupy him. The major difficulty is that the recruitment of jobs, despite constant and energetic advertising, lags substantially behind the demand for them. There are always more boys and girls on the applicant list than can be provided with work. In this situation, however, every job recruited and filled is pure gain, and the court deserves much credit for a very fine and meaningful effort.

No systematic research has been attempted with employment programs, so there is no reliable indication of the degree of their effectiveness. Generally in all such programs there is the usual fraction of participants who do not make good use of the experience, but the administrators are honestly convinced that such programs are very much worthwhile. Subjective but careful observation suggests that two-thirds or more of the juvenile employees make some form and degree of progress in their work experience, and in many cases the progress is impressive. As in any helping process, however, where pronounced progress is made by any probationer it is not simply because of the work experience itself, but because this has also given him a chance to develop a relationship with some adult connected with the program and to use that relationship in a therapeutic way.

5

Controlled Culture as a Treatment Tool

One of the serious handicaps that has plagued the correctional process from its beginning is the highly selective communication that exists between client and staff, between the offender and the person in authority. The inmate talks to the guard, the warden, or the psychiatrist, but may tell him only what he wants to tell or only what he thinks his listener wants to hear. The probationer may seem almost verbose as he discusses his problems with the probation officer, but the more we succeed in learning about the mental habits of the clients in these settings, the more we realize the extent of their reserved feelings and of their ability to present a façade of free communication behind which they can still maintain their own way of thinking and acting.

This is seen in its bluntest form in the correctional institution, for even in the gentlest, kindliest training school for delinquent children there is an inevitable permanent game of staff-against-the-inmate-and-vice-versa. The imposition of rules from above and the circumventing of rules from below is a process that makes for a gulf between the people who would correct and the people who need correcting but who cling to their patterns of rebellion to the fullest extent possible, with subterfuge if not with clear defiance.[1] The delinquent or criminal who is a part of a delinquent street culture feels loyalty only to that culture, which requires that he hold out against the blandishments of authoritative people from the world of squares. Actually and truly to cooperate with the squares in authority, even just engaging in unrestricted and non-dissembling conversation, would be an act traitorous to the only cultural values he knows.

Where significant gains are being made in overcoming this fearful handicap to the correctional process they have resulted from a promising technique of group work: the delinquent is given a new cultural context which then carries him into a more constructive living pattern, just as his street culture had carried him easily into a delinquent pattern. This seems so simple and obvious that one wonders why it was not thought of long ago.

It has taken us a considerable time to realize that in the institution or in probation or parole work we have often enforced rules of behavior that not only have failed to produce the changes we sought but have sometimes even guaranteed the continuance of the basic problem. If we are successful in enforcing a rule of no fighting, to take one example, what we have actually done is to mask the real problem — of insecurity or whatever — and to delude ourselves into believing that by controlling one manifestation we have solved the problem.

It requires courage to decide instead to work with delinquents in a setting which permits a substantial part of the problem behavior to show itself so that it can be understood, evaluated, and worked on, a setting that permits free communication between staff and client as they explore the problem behavior with a common purpose in mind.

The most specific current use of this technique was developed at New Jersey's Highfields. When the Lindbergh family gave their estate,[2] Highfields, to the state of New Jersey it eventually became the locale of an experiment in group therapy with seriously delinquent older boys, most of whom would otherwise have been candidates for reformatory commitment. Though it may at first glance appear to be an "institution," it actually is much closer to probation than to traditional custodial institu-

---

[1] LaMar T. Empey and Jerome Rabow, "The Provo Experiment in Delinquency Rehabilitation," *American Sociological Review*, Vol. 26, No. 5 (October 1961), p. 679.

[2] See George Waller, *Kidnap: The Story of the Lindbergh Case* (New York: Dial Press, 1961), p. 194.

tionalization. It demonstrates an idea that should be very tempting to the administrator of any probation service that serves a substantial urban area.

The original Highfields is still in active operation, but a number of facsimiles have been created in recent years. The discussion here will encompass the essentially similar programs now in use in four other such residential treatment centers in New Jersey, plus several in New York and Kentucky, as well as the original installation.

THE TECHNIQUE

There is no pretense that this kind of program can reach every type of delinquent. As with any other specialized program, the selection of cases for it requires skill, and the success of the program will be considerably affected by the court's aptitude in choosing appropriate cases. The most likely candidate is the adaptive delinquent whose antisocial behavior has been a part of his loyalty to the mores of his delinquent group on the street. To oversimplify the concept, the boy who accepts and follows the culture of the group on the street may be similarly able to accept and follow the synthetic culture which surrounds and absorbs him in this unique treatment setting. On the street he needed no adult to tell him the rules to follow. He took his cue from the peer group and was satisfied with the values and code of the gang. So when he comes to a Highfields type of residential treatment center he is presented with little or no instruction from adults. He is referred instead to the gang. But this gang — the twenty boys in the treatment program — has a different sort of cultural pattern and code of values to present. It is no less viable and provocative than the street culture, so it has the ability to attract, ensnare, and hold the new boy while it presents him with a new and more constructive pattern of interacting with people.

This is the refreshing and constantly surprising aspect of this type of program, which is so much in contrast to the conventional training school for delinquents. For here the usual plethora of institutional rules is virtually abandoned. Here the academic school, the athletics, the craft work, the clinical services, the casework, and likewise the shakedowns, the line-ups, and the head counts all are virtually nonexistent. Television, an inevitable fixture in most institutions, is usually not found here. The waking hours are crowded with activities that are a part of the treatment process, so no time is left for sitting at the television screen where a boy could lose himself in withdrawal from the all-important interaction with others. The pleasures and comforts that we attempt to provide in a conventional institution are out of place in this unusual setting, because the boys are present for a short period of time, usually four months, and in that period they must concentrate all their attention on correction of their problems. Anything that draws their attention away from that goal does them a disservice.

Then, too, the boys have constant responsibility for the treatment process, for they are to a large extent their own therapists and their synthetic culture is the instrument of change.

To build this special culture it is necessary to get across to the boys a simple sequence of ideas — though the task of getting this across is not a simple one. They must grasp this concept: "You want to get out of here and the only way to get out is to lick your problems. The way to lick your problems is to talk about them." Obviously this is a difficult concept for a boy to accept because it is so contrary to the code that he followed on the street, where it was axiomatic that you do not admit your problems (i.e., squeal on yourself) in the presence of anyone from the dominant or authoritative culture. Moreover, there is a companion concept in this synthetic culture that is almost harder for the boy to accept. It may be expressed thus: "You also want to help your pals get out of this place and the only way to do this is to help them lick their problems. The only way for them to lick their problems is to talk about them, whether they want to or not; so to help them you must bring up their problems and help them talk about them." Here is a truly jarring reversal of the street code where the most severely proscribed action would be the squealing on a pal. But in the treatment center a reversal takes place and, unbelievable as it seems, the boys actually do learn to talk about their own faults freely and then go on to bring up all the specific misbehavior of their friends in the group and subject it to absolutely exhaustive examination.

The over-all program that accomplishes this vital self-help process has a daily schedule based on the barest essentials. No attempt is made to provide classroom study. During the day the boys do hard manual labor at nearby institutions, and in the evening they talk. The talking is done in the "meeting" which is the heart of the treatment process. Promptly at 7:00 P.M. one group of ten boys sits down for its meeting, and just as promptly adjourns at 8:30. From then until 10:00 P.M. the second group has its meeting. Usually the director of the center conducts one meeting and the assistant director handles the other. However, this staff leader plays a very quiet role, saying little and usually sitting outside the circle of boys. The descriptive name which has been given to this process is *guided group interaction*. The idea of the meeting is so firmly established in the Highfields programs that there is none of the waste motion usually to be expected in getting a group of ten boys to come to order and then to stick to the business at hand. With no prompting from the leader they launch into the discussion. It is in tiny but surprising signs like this that the strength of the special culture becomes evident.

THE MEETING

A meeting is only rarely a generalized or free-ranging discussion. Almost always it is a discussion focused on one boy; or it may be split, with the first forty-five minutes devoted to one boy and the second forty-five minutes to another. The boys make their own decision about this in the first minutes of the meeting when one or two, or maybe several, of the boys in turn ask for the meeting and give their reasons for wanting it. It becomes quickly apparent which boy has the most support in his request this time and so he proceeds. If he is relatively new it is likely to be a matter of "telling his story." He simply recounts chronologically the history of his own delinquent career. As he tells it the others interrupt freely, probing endlessly for more details and exposing the rationalizations and all the usual tricks of self-delusion. If he is very new to the program it does not come easy for him to tell of all his misconduct with honesty and completeness. It is likely that he will be selective of details and make the usual efforts to salvage the best self-image he can. For this reason some leaders do not let a boy talk about himself in the first days of his stay in the program. They reason that he should not be put in a position that, in effect, makes him lie about himself; so it is sometimes the practice to have a boy wait until he has been at the center for several weeks before he is given a meeting. This avoids the waste of time that would be entailed if he were to talk at a time when he really is not ready to talk truthfully.

The ability of the boys to talk with complete, self-searching truthfulness about themselves and each other is the sine qua non of the technique. Furthermore, they must do this talking largely on their own initiative with a minimum of prodding by the staff.

To the person steeped only in experience with the usual training school or probation setting it seems such an unlikely proceeding as to be nearly incredible. But it truly does work, and an essential reason for its success is that the staff's approach to the boys is even more unlikely as viewed from the conventional correctional setting. Obviously no experienced delinquent is going to give a matter-of-fact account, for instance, of stealing money from another boy the day before if the listening staff member is ready to administer an indignant scolding followed by disciplinary measures. But in this setting there is no such reaction. To overdraw the picture only slightly, the staff member is as matter-of-fact about it as the boys are. His reaction is a purely clinical one. He is genuinely interested in the behavior problem that has shown itself, but he discusses it with the same kind of uncensorious concern with which he would discuss the boy's earache or sprained wrist.

Every ordinary instinct causes the average person to rebel at this kind of handling of delinquents. We have always assumed that they must be corrected — punished — controlled — shown who's boss. This permissiveness, this apparent coddling of hoodlums who are thus allowed to run wild and laugh at authority, is the despair of people who, after all, are citizens of good will and intelligence.

But a closer look at the workings of this kind of program reveals that it has an authority and a measure of control that is intrinsically greater than the control imposed by rules and administrative discipline in a conventional institution. Let us look in on a couple of the group meetings and see if the control is not clearly evident. For instance:

Exactly at seven o'clock the ping-pong paddles are dropped and ten boys go into the front room where they promptly put chairs in a circle and sit down. The director of the program (who is the leader for this group) may be talking to someone else at the moment but this makes no difference. The boys do not have to be marshaled. They sit in their circle and without waiting for any staff direction they start their meeting. This first group tonight is fairly quiet, but not either slow or dull. One boy asks for the meeting this time in order to tell "his story." Another boy, though, wants the meeting too because he is anxious to be released soon and wants to get the group's support for his readiness to leave. They agree on making it a split meeting and the first boy, with forty-five minutes to use, tells his story, a rambling account of stolen cars, irresponsible drifting, and defiance of home. The other boys listen and on no face is there any suggestion that the process is being taken other than seriously. From time to time boys interrupt to ask questions. These may just be for clarification, but more often they are probes that point to defects in the story, that attempt to hold the mirror up to empty rationalizations.

When the second boy has his chance he argues for his release. He has made progress with his problems, he insists, and he should be permitted to go. But the others are unconvinced. They remind him of episodes that he is neglecting to tell. They reinterpret the rationale he is presenting and relentlessly show him the holes in his arguments. He defends himself, and the others needle him the harder, giving him no sympathy. At the end of the meeting he is obviously seeing a somewhat revised picture of himself and even though he is not altogether convinced that the others are right he is bowing to the group opinion and seems glumly accepting of the situation. The leader closes the meeting with tacit acceptance of the group's opinion that the boy is not yet ready to leave.

During the meeting the leader sits at a desk just outside the circle, observes closely, and occasionally asks a question or makes a remark. Never is there any tone of rebuke in his voice, only a completely interested, clinical searching for meanings in the things being said. Even when the language in the group is profane, obscene, abusive, the leader shows no hint of disapproval. But there is no mistaking the control inherent in the group, for the boys attend instantly to the leader when he chooses to ask any question or make any remarks; and they talk with him on his level of concern and with utter frankness.

The degree of control built into the culture becomes still more evident in the second meeting. Hardly more than a minute elapses while the first group leaves the room and the second group comes in and gets its meeting started. Immediately it appears that this will be a truly frenetic session, for a struggle for leadership is going on and we can see here in one meeting the stages of progress from new boy to old boy. Certain boys stand out in relation to the problems they show, or in respect to their "age" in the group. One boy, Pete, is surprisingly dressed in a white shirt and tie. He has lately been affecting this more formal dress and this goes with his older status in the group. He has matured considerably, though not as much as he likes to believe. He had been the dominant boy, but this position of informal leader has been usurped in recent weeks by another boy, O'Day, who is far more verbally agile than Pete.

O'Day has now gained a leadership position largely because he thinks rapidly rather than soundly and can be louder and more profane in his rapid-fire talk than any others. But now O'Day is being challenged too and he and his protagonist, Angus, are the principal "discussants" in to-night's meeting.

It would be impossible to report the dialogue from such a meeting be-cause much of it would make no logical sense on paper. Its meaning can be deduced only by the observer who is physically present and knows the boys, their special relationships, and the background of the feelings that are striking sparks between them.

Through much of the meeting O'Day and Angus are engaged in argu-ment that is so heated that it brings them to their feet, standing nose to nose in the circle, shouting obscenities at each other with great violence of feeling. At the same time other boys in the circle attempt to inter-rupt and often try to get the two to sit down. It is a general scene of ap-parently uncontrolled behavior that would suggest to the observer that fists and knives will be flying at any instant. However, the fists do not begin to fly and it is clearly apparent that the situation is not so uncon-trolled at all. What makes it appear wild is the complete freedom the boys have to dispute with each other as long as they do not fight physical-ly. And further observation of such a meeting brings the realization that here in fact is tremendous control, for in the hour and a half of vio-lent verbal exchanges no boy lays a finger on another. This despite the fact that they are calling each other names that would have provoked in-stant fighting in the street culture. Experience shows, too, that the boys generally respect the principle that feelings expressed in the meeting will not be carried outside the meeting room.

During the meeting while the two principal protagonists are holding center stage other types of interaction are going on in the group in a less boisterous fashion. One red-headed boy has very little to say to the group as a whole, but he frequently gets up and goes about the circle to talk privately with various boys. His activity has all the earmarks of an earnest bit of politicking. Still another boy is unique for his complete lack of activity. While all the others are excitedly involved in the dis-cussion he stays aloof and quiet.

Another evidence of the tremendous controls inherent in the culture is the fact that on those occasions when the staff member chooses to inter-ject a question or a comment he has no need to shout to make himself heard. No matter how high the decibels at the moment he speaks in an ordinary tone of voice and the boys, aware that the leader is saying something, immediately become quiet and talk with him on his voice level. During the last ten minutes of this session the leader takes charge of the discussion and focuses attention on O'Day, who supposedly is the object of this meeting. First he asks O'Day to tell what he thinks the other boys think of him at that point. So O'Day, who for the previous hour has been acting like a wildly belligerent rooster, now sits quietly and calmly describes himself as the other boys undoubtedly see him. And with only nominal prodding from the leader he admits just how obnoxious he really has been.

Then when the combined needling of the leader and other boys is making O'Day feel the pressure quite severely, the leader suddenly switches the attention away from O'Day to the quiet one who had stayed remote during the whole meeting. The redhead is bypassed in this instance; his turn will come later. He happens to have an urge to be seen as the intelligent, logical force in the group and with it he has a need to enjoy the favor of the staff. At this point, however, he does not have the maturity and skill to play the role effectively and so he is not yet ready to be used. A few weeks later he will have a more senior status in the group and then the leader will be ready to use him to help convey the approved cultural code.

In switching the attack from O'Day to the quiet boy during the last minutes of the meeting the leader is acting on his awareness of the problems of both. O'Day has a low tolerance for frustration and on occasions in the past he has resorted to heroin when under emotional pressure. It is necessary to let the group keep pressure on him to recognize and modify his irritating qualities, but there is a point beyond which he cannot be pushed without danger. The leader has sensed the point at which he must draw the group's fire away from O'Day. It is slightly surprising that the boy then attacked is the one who has been the quietest. The leader asks the latter why he is almost the only one who has not got angry in the meeting. The boy can give no satisfactory answer. In the ordinary life situation this would have been the boy most subject to praise, for he alone has been sitting quietly through it all, doing no interrupting, shouting no obscenities, offering no provocation. But here this can only be seen as withdrawal and failure to make any effort to help himself or his friends with their problems. The leader's attempt to

145

needle the boy to learn to get angry shows its reasonable basis in the final exchange of the meeting.

"So why can't you get angry about anything?"

"Don't know."

"Well, you've got to get more worried about yourself. You haven't ever asked for a meeting yet — you're not that concerned about yourself. How will you ever get help with your problems that way?"

"Guess I won't."

"So what if you're out on the street and some of your buddies come by in a stolen car — and you know it's stolen — and they holler for you to come and go with them."

"I'd tell them I don't want to."

"And then what if one of them gets out and comes up and says to you, 'You get in that car, you damn bastard you!'"

"I guess I'd get in."

"Yeah. That's just it. You've got to learn to get angry enough to have some backbone, don't you?"

"I guess so."

A meeting like the foregoing is not quite typical in its level of noise and hostile interchanges, but this kind of session does happen occasionally and even though it appears on the surface to be a useless exercise in verbal pyrotechnics it actually serves a healthy purpose. It is one more experience for each boy in discovering that problems *can* be worked on with words and that provocative words do not have to be followed by fists. It is also an experience in finding that adults can be helpful people, and not phony.

This quality of non-phoniness is of the greatest importance in working with these boys who have seen so much of naively unrealistic, if not outright phony, attempts at helpfulness. The staff never tries to curb the flow of profane and obscene language that characterizes the natural speech of these boys — the staff recognizes that profanity is a part of their culture and it is futile to think that they will give it up. Any rules against it or even any attempts to discourage it would have no effect and, what is worse, would serve to drive a wedge between the therapist and the boys. It would point up for the boys the gulf between boys and staff, when instead it is vital to close that gap so that there is a truly felt oneness of purpose between boys and staff. The staff has more important problems to help the boys with than the niceties of speech, and any campaign against these lesser problems would be a distraction defeating to the major purpose of the program.

CONTROLLED CULTURE AS A TREATMENT TOOL

The most titillating question — and perhaps the hardest to answer — is this: How does the staff go about building this culture? Even persons who have done it find it hard to describe the process. It is a matter of long-suffering patience and consistent, firm, day-after-day working with a small group of boys until they begin to get the idea and then can go still further and actually believe and trust the staff in the strange new relationship that is offered them.

In several instances the new culture has been started in a newly opened treatment center by "culture carriers" or "transplants" — boys who are already well indoctrinated in it at another center. As a starter, seven or eight such boys may be transferred to the new center and then new boys are brought in one at a time until the transplanted group, like a yeast, has given the culture to a whole new group.

When the culture has to be built without such transplants it is a long and slow process, taking anywhere from six months to a year. Basically it is a matter of the leader telling the boys time after time, in simple, direct language, how they are expected to talk about themselves and each other. To be convincing he must be superbly consistent in handling himself so that in every detail his conduct supports the ideas he has been expressing.

The following is a verbatim excerpt from a meeting which occurred during the culture-building process in one center. Although words can be quoted exactly here, one essential ingredient cannot be reproduced. That is the quality of voice and mood of the speaker. It can only be reported that the skilled leader who is quoted here spoke without rancor and with warm, genuine concern at the same time that he was deeply serious.

Leader: Each of you guys has a history of not facing things at the time they happen.

Bob: What do you mean by that?

Leader: You don't know what I mean? What do I mean, Jim?

Jim: Well, you mean — like when you do something and get caught you try to bluff out of it and say it was something else.

Leader: Yeah. And denying that problems exist; that things are really problems to you. And you're treating the group the same way. Instead of nailing down the important things that will help you get started, you're just really not getting started. You don't face this. You go to talking about something else. Or if a guy is getting in trouble around here

147

you don't talk about it; you talk about something else. Maybe you don't see them. I do. Maybe it's just because I've been here so long. But you all have a way of denying that something exists; something that is a real problem. I don't know what you're going to do as a group because right now you're in pretty bad shape. Your meetings have never gotten off the ground, and most of you have been here nearly two months. You got to learn to do what you think is best as a group, because not one of you can get out without the help of the others. How much Danny helps his problems is dependent on how much Charley helps his problems. You can't do things singly, you've got to do them together as a group, and until there is some feeling among you as to your group you're never going to get off the ground.

But where the leader has sometimes to scold he also can praise as a part of the culture-building process. The same leader found occasion to comment this way at the end of a later meeting.

Leader: I think you guys are about the best meeting I've seen. You've demonstrated how well you can see what a boy's problems are and to be in a position later on to discuss it. You listened to the story and you're aware of what people do around here and you put these two things together quite well. People don't get away from you easily, so when you really want to help a guy I think you're going to be able to do it. You've demonstrated this real well. I think later on you'll feel the effects of this. Guys will be getting out sooner if you keep on the way you're going, 'cause you're always acting as a group. You're pretty sharp kids — you picked up on a lot of things that people do and you know what's going on. Larry, with a lot of other groups you could have gotten away a lot easier, because you do have a good way of getting away from people.
Larry: Yeah. Working all the angles.
Leader: They may make you feel very uncomfortable like they're hurting you, but I think you'll be able to use it. It's not always easy to take the way other people see you and if you can get over the feeling they're hurting you —
Larry: I thought they were being helpful.
Leader: Yeah, I think so. I don't think anyone was trying to carry any feelings for you from outside. I don't think anyone here really dislikes you.
Larry: No, I don't think so.
Leader: The way they put it to you tonight they just did a very good job of showing you how they see you.

The standard population size in all programs of this kind is twenty, and this figure is soundly based on experience. Twenty is too large a group for a good discussion of the kind developed here, but, on the other hand, the ideal discussion group of ten would be too small for holding the culture. So the happy solution is to have two groups of ten each live in one treatment residence and this provides a total of twenty boys to hold the culture once it is built. Ideally, new boys enter and old boys leave just one or two at a time. In this way the one new boy coming in and bringing with him the contamination of the street culture is met and out-influenced by nineteen boys who absorb him into the synthetic culture. It is only in this way that the culture is perpetuated and kept constantly functioning as the effective treatment device. A program of this kind is in trouble if, as sometimes happens, boys must be released when new boys are not available to take their places. When the number drops to a dozen or fewer and then several new boys are sent by the court all at once, the old boys in their reduced number have real trouble holding the synthetic culture, and the leader may find himself having to start the culture-building process again.

The meetings are held just five evenings per week, but because of the overriding importance of maintaining the culture the two evenings off are not consecutive. It is much harder on the staff to have Thursday and Saturday evenings free instead of, say, Saturday and Sunday evenings, but it is the meetings that sustain the culture and the staff does not incur the risk of weakening that culture by allowing more than forty-eight hours to go by without meetings.

The work program during the day is also an integral part of the process of building and holding the culture, rather than just a practical way of using the boys' time. In the first place, the culture must incorporate some new attitudes toward work, for in the delinquent culture no encouragement is given to the development of work skills. "To many of these boys, who have begun to internalize a delinquent style of life, work has a low social value. It is regarded with contempt or it is viewed as inimical to their best interests. Since 'only suckers work' these boys come to Highfields with little or no desire for steady, full time work and without substantial training and experience in work situations."[3] But what is perhaps of more immediate importance is the need for meaningful social interaction every day. The work becomes a vital source of content for the group discussions. The problems a boy has show up on the job while all the boys are working together. Irritating qualities in

[3] Lloyd W. McCorkle, Albert Elias, and F. Lovell Bixby, The Highfields Story (New York: Henry Holt and Company, 1958), p. 25.

personalities make themselves felt; provocative behavior of many kinds appear; petty stealing, fighting, lying, or just plain laziness and irresponsibility will certainly be evident for all to see. The work not only furnishes an inexhaustible supply of grist for the discussion mill every evening, but has the peculiar value of providing an altogether natural setting for problems to arise. If a boy is an agitator or a thief this problem is not being talked about in abstract terms. Instead, the boys in their meeting are talking about something that was seen and felt that same day and in a way that involved them personally. This underscores the problem for them and gives its solution a quality of urgency.

The way in which work projects are conducted supplements in another way too the special nature of the treatment process. While the boys are removed from the influence of the street culture during their stay in the program, they are at the same time exposed to a more conventional culture. They have some daily contact with adults who serve as work supervisors and with other adults on the staffs of the institutions where they work. Their noon meals, for instance, are eaten at these institutions with the staff. This exposure is augmented at least once a week when the group is given a chance to go to town on Saturday, to spend money as they wish in the stores or to go to the movies. On Sundays there are opportunities to go to church. The money available to them for these excursions to town comes from earnings on the daily job. The different centers pay the boys at rates varying from fifty cents to a dollar a day. Since this is an open setting for probationers instead of the conventional training school, the usual practice of withholding cash is not followed. The boys can carry their money as they wish. It is much simpler this way and some of the feeling of institutionalization is avoided by letting them have their own money to use in supplying their personal needs.

An important extension of this community contact is the occasional weekend furlough, when a boy goes home. It is far more than just a brief holiday for him. It is a chance to test his ability to get along with members of the family when previously there was perhaps severe friction among them. It is a chance to meet his buddies on the street and see if he can resist the invitations to return to drinking and stealing. Sometimes the furlough is a significant turning point in a boy's treatment process, for it may bring him realization for the first time of the true enormity of his problems at home or of the influence of his gang on the street.

Discussion of relationships in the home is a crucial part of the process of uncovering problems in many cases and it is often a sign of progress when a boy finally shows a willingness to look honestly at the feelings between himself and his parents. In the following discussion, for instance, Henry is being questioned by the group about the reasons why he and his father get along so poorly. The lesson that the other boy points up from the discussion is a good example of the sort of counsel that Henry can accept fairly well from one of his peers, whereas it would be essentially ignored when coming uninvited from an adult.

Henry: Dad thought that because Mom took up for me and she fussed at my little sister, well, he thought she loved me more than she did my little sister, so he would jump on me all the time, and he would start fights and things, and beat on Mom, and I'd throw something at him and hit him to keep him from hitting Mom.

Leader: Why don't you tell us how you used to use your father's getting drunk and all the other troubles that went on to your own advantage; like skipping school and all that.

Henry: Well, first of all, I stole a lot, and Dad would catch me at it and whip me for stealing, so I hated him and all that stuff, and I'd run outa the house, and I kept on for a long time saying "Mom's the only one who treated me right." And even when he was sober and did something that I didn't like I'd say, "You ain't nothing but a drunk anyway — the only time you work is when you ain't drunk and you're drunk more than you're sober." I did that a lot. That's one reason I didn't get along with him. When he gets drunk he's — well, I don't know — he's just crazy.

Leader: What things did you use to get back at your father? What other things did you do to make it less punishment for you?

Henry: Well, a lot of times he asked me to do stuff around the house; some work, you know, and I never would do it, but I'd do it if Mom asked me to.

Another Boy: Did you ever try to help your dad out?

Henry: No.

Boy: Why not? [No answer.] You favored your mom a lot more than you did your dad, didn't you?

Henry: Yeah.

Boy: Any special reason why?

Henry: Well, she works and brings in all the money and everything. Well, there's another reason — every time I'd get some money or something, I'd tell my mom about it and he'd hear about it, he'd take it away for himself. And everything I'd get he'd take out and sell it. When I got that last money and I bought me some clothes he went out and got drunk and didn't have no money so he sold the clothes, then he sold the television, he sold the radio, he sold my record player — I got that back though — he'd start selling food out of the icebox in order to get money to drink on.

Boy: When your dad was sore did you get by with more with your mom than with your dad?

Henry: Yeah.

Boy: Is that another reason why you favored your mom more, because you could get by with more stuff on her than with your dad?

Henry: Yeah; and another thing — he was married before and had two other children and every time he gets sore about something he'd start bringing it up about how good the other children always were.

Boy: Did you ever get along with your dad?

Henry: Once for about three months we got along real good. He was away from home for a long time — about six months, and then he come home. I'd missed him; Mom had missed him; so we got along good for about six months. He didn't drink for some reason. Then suddenly he sold his car and got drunk and stayed drunk for about three weeks.

Leader: Did your dad ever come in and your mom accuse him of something and he would say "I didn't do it," and she would say he did and they would go on like that in a big argument?

Henry: Yeah.

Leader: Did it happen quite a few times?

Henry: Yeah, and I'd always join in on my mother's side of the argument.

Boy: Did you ever stop to think that maybe one of the reasons that your dad did all this drinking was that he seen that you were off on the wrong shoes? That every time he tried to help, to work hard and get help it done more harm than it did help? So that led him to go on to further drinking too?

Henry: Well — maybe.

Boy: Like you said, you never did try to help your dad and was always on your mom's side. Couldn't you see that it really hurts your dad to find that you was against him, right or wrong, drunk or sober; and yet you just kept on going at him?

Henry: I guess so, but I wasn't thinking about that so much as just getting by with things without getting caught.

Boy: Did you ever stop to think while you were doing all this that if you had been telling the truth maybe your dad would have had more reason to get along with you? Can you imagine how it'd feel if you had a boy and he was doing wrong and you tried to correct him, yet the boy lied to his mom and his mom took up for him — well, you know how you'd feel and you'd always be called a liar and told that you don't know nothing.

Actually, this dialogue is a fairly gentle probing. When a boy asks for a meeting in which to argue his readiness for a furlough or for release it is expected that the others will examine him ruthlessly. And they do. In a well-developed group the process may be relentless enough to strip the boy psychologically naked. The boys sometimes show surprising maturity in their determination to judge their fellows seriously and honestly. A group in its early stages will function superficially, making platitudinous comments that are presumed to be what the staff wants to hear. But an experienced group not only will be honest but will show surprising skill in getting under the rationalizations to expose to a boy his weaknesses and his self-delusions.

At the same time the process may not appear to be an efficient one in terms of economy of time and words. An observer at these meetings can easily get an impression of much time being wasted with endless wordy debate on picayune issues. The boys' talk will range back and forth over minuscule points of argument which the professional person would quickly settle or bypass if he had his preference. However, it is inevitable that the boys will use their meeting time this way and it serves a useful purpose. This is the way that they squeeze an issue dry and guarantee that no single aspect of it is overlooked. The boy who is being examined is more convinced by the conclusions that are presented to him because he knows that the examination was exhaustive and he had every opportunity to present argument and rebuttal.

When the issue in these meetings is whether a boy is ready for a furlough or release, the decision is left to the boys to a large extent. They know that the leader will make the final decision but that their opinion counts heavily. And they do not hesitate to vote against a boy's furlough or release if they are not satisfied with his progress.

An excellent example of this was Orville, who was received by one of the residential group centers following a number of delinquencies and probation violations. Among the delinquent acts was one the police and court did not know about. He and another boy had stolen $500 from a local merchant. It was unknown because the merchant himself was unsure how much had been taken, was uncertain, in fact, whether it had been stolen or whether he had just lost it. The boys in the treatment center knew about the $500 but they were a new group at the time and without the skill to handle the matter as yet.

Four months later, however, the time came for Orville to talk about being released and when he asked for his meeting he was surprised to find that the other boys had not forgotten about the $500 and were bringing this up as unfinished business. They insisted that it had to be cleared up before they would vote for his release. Orville protested loudly and insisted in turn that it was past history and not to be held against him now. The other boys were equally adamant that he could not be considered sufficiently improved until he settled the matter.

Orville worked desperately hard to clear it up, but not in a way that satisfied the group. He checked with the police and was able to report back to the boys that there was no complaint filed in the case. The boys were unmoved. They pointed out that he had to learn to look at the essentials. The real question was whether a storekeeper was still the unrepaid victim of a robbery. Orville was desperate and told how his codefendant in the theft had threatened to kill him if he ever told about it. He was advised to talk it over with the codefendant anyway. Finally Orville gave it a try and went to see the other boy to talk about some way to square the old offense. His prediction of his fellow offender's temper was right, and he returned to the center with generous bruises and black eyes as a result.

Again he pleaded to have the matter overlooked and again the group turned him down. They were adamant in insisting that he had to decide just who his friends were. He could decide to stick with hoodlums like the one who just beat him up or he could convince the group of his readiness for release by lining up with the right guys despite his fear of his former pal. The pressure and the counsel were finally effective, and once more Orville went back to the codefendant; this time he was able to convince him that they had to square themselves with the storekeeper. Ironically, they had to convince the merchant that they had indeed stolen as much as $500 from him, as well as convince him that they were the culprits. But once that was done the rest was fairly easy. The merchant was a reasonable sort and he worked out a satisfactory arrangement for the boys to pay him back with weekend work.

When Orville reported back to the next meeting on his accomplishment he was informed finally that he was now ready to leave. The evidence this incident gives of the potency of the technique is underscored by the fact that it succeeded despite the resistance of the boy's parents. This is a fairly usual problem, for the group treatment center, in giving the boy a new way of dealing with people, tends to alter the usual pattern of interaction within his family. This can make new tensions, and, in fact, the leader must expect that sometimes family members will become hostile toward the center as a result of their subjective misinterpretation of what is happening to their boy. We have seen this earlier as a problem in other kinds of work with delinquents.

Parents can obstruct the treatment process also because it is something so different from what they are ordinarily acquainted with that they are suspicious and distrustful of it. This becomes a specially difficult problem if the treatment center is close to the homes of the boys. As will be discussed later, two of the Highfields programs have operated with the boys actually sleeping in their own homes at night, and in such a situation the staff has found it necessary to spend many of their daytime hours in interviews with parents, especially at the time when the boy is first assigned to the center.[4] If the center is more remote from the boys' homes there will still be problems but these will arise primarily at the time of special occasions such as the furlough. This can occasionally produce a crisis and in any event can provide a testing of the boy's progress.

At one of the centers a badly deteriorated family situation was the dominant problem for Ted S——, and it was not until he went home on furlough that he began to face it and make a real effort to improve. The slow and painful struggle is reflected in these excerpts from the monthly summaries of Ted's case written by his leader.

First Month. This conforming boy made a surface adjustment in his first month in residence. He needs the approval of his friends and the staff a great deal. He seems unwilling to do things on his own. He is well accepted by the other boys in the house because he is very careful not to make enemies. Some of the boys are confused about his role since he doesn't act the way the others do all the time.

He always seems to feel as though he must put up a front to the staff and to the boys as he is never sure how to act. He is a good group member but is neither a leader who is willing to put his neck out, nor is he a follower. He prefers to talk about other boys rather than to draw much attention to himself. At times he is more honest than other boys in his group, which causes him some difficulty with the other boys. . . . So far he is too controlling to try any new roles or ways of acting and is careful not to identify himself with boys who are looking for trouble.

Second Month. Ted has made a good adjustment to the routine here during his second month in residence. [This is a comment which would be meant as fully complimentary if it were found in a case record at a conventional training school. Here, however, its import is negative in a setting where conformity is only evidence of failure to expose one's

---

[4] Unpublished Annual Report, Essexfields Group Rehabilitation Center, June 30, 1963, p. 14.

problems to the helping process.] He has not helped his problems any more than he did during his first month. He would like to stay out of trouble in the future but is not clear how to go about solving his problems.

During his third month Ted had a weekend furlough that was marked by a severely upsetting emotional episode with his mother and other family members. At the peak of his emotional turmoil during the incident his thought was to call up the director at the treatment center and ask him to come get him. Though he did not actually make the call, this was apparently a turning point for him.

Third Month. After spending a disastrous furlough, Ted has begun to settle down, making real attempts at helping himself. Previous to this time he relied only on his very capable ability to adjust easily in order to get by. Ted has a great deal of responsibility in the house, assuming the role of a helped boy. Other boys are dependent on Ted doing the right thing and usually go to him for advice and support. Lately he can see where his choice of friends has become important to him. . . . Ted has always acted as though he can take care of himself and only recently has he admitted that this is not always the case.

But with the counselor's report at the fourth month we see the real significance of the progress Ted has made, and also the dismaying prospect he has yet to face.

Fourth Month. This mature, sophisticated 17-year-old boy has made a good adjustment during his four and a half months here. He enjoys an old-boy status among the others. He has been able to keep himself out of difficulty here and is not affected by the immature activities of other boys in the house.

Ted comes from a deprived and extremely inadequate family background. His mother is an alcoholic prostitute who is presently cohabiting with a married man. Ted will have to go back to this type of environment. He will be living in close association with three brothers-in-law who introduced him to the art of stealing, drinking, and other illegal activities.

I feel the prognosis for this boy in any other environment but this might be fair. However, because of his limited sixth-grade education, his inadequate picture of himself, he cannot be expected to survive for more than several months. Any longer than this would be against terrific odds.

His one advantage is that he has a strong desire to get out of this environment. His desire is greater than any other boy's in the group and has enabled him to be a leader in the group. His chances for survival are enhanced by his introspection and his knowledge of the way other family members operate. However, this doesn't seem to be enough to give him a good chance for survival.

This appraisal of Ted by the leader is in agreement with Ted's own view of himself. All the boys in this treatment center are asked to write a statement, at the time of their release, telling about their experience at the center. Here is Ted's impression of the place, and its effect on him, just as he wrote it, occasional misspelling and all:

When I came here just the looks of the place made me feel like I didn't belong. Mr. M—— was on when I came and when I met him I thought he was an old fat square. And when the boys came in from work I was ready to fight any of them because I thought that was what I had to do to get along with out. But I found out different, then here. My attidude changed. I thought of them as a bunch of phonies. I didn't think anyone could be serious when they said this place could change them.

When I went to a few of the meetings I found out what was really on peoples mind and the way they felt inside. And then I told my story and got my problems. I didn't know I had problems that the meeting gave me. I started finding out where these problems came from and what made me do the things I did. I found out how ignorent I was to let some things get to me.

The meeting showed me how to get away from the things on the outside that get me in trouble. They taught me that you have to have respect for yourself and other people in order to get somewhere in life and stay out of prison. And I found out what being bad is going to get me, and I don't want any part of that any more.

THE CONCEPT OF "PROBLEMS"

Any observer of the Highfields technique is struck with the special kind of meaning that the concept of personal problems has for these boys. It has about it a great sense of urgency and it has too a certain vaguely naive quality. The latter derives from the overly simplified categories into which problems are divided. The professional person will see a delinquent's problems as being composed of a number of varied factors which are intricately intertwined. The boys, however, are inclined to see neatly separated problems which can be handily labeled and pigeonholed. Furthermore, as they see it, these problems can be worked on singly and are capable of being independently conquered one by one.

It is not important that this is at odds with the best professional approach. What is important is that it fits in with the young person's need to see things in black and white terms, and it gives him an approach to a problem that he can utilize because it comes naturally to him.

Early in the process of guided group interaction for any boy is his opportunity to "tell his story," at which time the others "give him his problems." It is simply a matter of the boys sizing up his shortcomings and listing for him the problems which they think are evident and which they think he will have to work on. There is something very official and wonderfully clear-cut about the way the group gives a new boy the problem of "easily led," for example. They have seen signs that he yields too easily to suggestions from others and they will thereafter bombard him with further evidence of this in meetings whenever they see other examples of the problem. They may at the same time give him other problems perceived in his story and in their daily dealings with him.

The names of the problems are more imaginative than any listing from a textbook, and tend to support the view that culturally deprived children are not so nonverbal as we tend to think. According to Riessman these children are actually richly verbal though we give them little credit for this since their vocabulary happens to be very different and consequently a handicap to them in responding to our professional evaluative processes.[5] Among the "problems" frequently recognized in the treatment centers are those with such prosaically self-explanatory titles as stealing, gambling, easily led, slick, sneaky, cheating. Some of the more colorfully named ones have particular significance in this type of treatment program. "Clowning," for instance, is mildly surprising as a problem since it does not denote problem behavior in the usual sense. It refers to the ordinary practical joking or playing around no worse than the normal and innocuous byplay that is always an enjoyable part of social living. But in this setting there is great and constant emphasis on the seriousness of each boy's task in working on his problems with no distractions. Each boy must pursue that task constantly if he is going to make enough improvement to be released in the four-month period that is fairly standard. If he is "clowning" he is not attending to business, not thinking about his problems, but wasting precious time. Another problem is "ball-busting," a habit of hurting people with verbal remarks that cut deeply. It is a term that comes naturally to the vocabulary of boys who know what it is to endure a sharp blow to the testicles. The prob-

[5] Frank Riessman, *The Culturally Deprived Child* (New York: Harper and Row, 1962), Chapter 8.

lem of the "flunky" has special meaning among these boys because of their need for being clearly masculine. It is a label given to a boy who doesn't stand up for himself, but lets others walk over him and use him. "Putting people down" is a problem label for a boy who always tries to get the upper hand by making another boy look bad to the group, especially in order to divert the group's critical scrutiny away from himself.

The list of problems is long, highly explicit, and subject to constant modification. Boys are expected to work on their problems and show evidence of this in their activities outside the meetings. In fact, one of the problems a boy might show would be his failure to talk about and work on his problems on his daily job.

Even with the rich variety of problem titles which are catalogued by the boys in any of these treatment centers there are some that are missing if we take a more conventional approach to the process of rehabilitation. If these boys were sent, for instance, to a training school or perhaps to a private military school, they would get disciplinary attention for swearing, something that is ignored in the treatment center. A problem of poor reading ability would be met with remedial reading instruction. There would be training in proper dress and personal habits of grooming, coaching in athletics, instruction in crafts, music, dramatics, and just plain good social manners. There might be rules to deal with the problem of smoking. But all these are completely missing in the Highfields program, for in it the single goal is very simply stated: to bring each boy to make enough improvement in his adjustment so that he can avoid further arrests.

It is a precise and narrow focus for a helping process that makes no pretense of trying to do more than that in the brief exposure each boy has to the program. If he needs also to learn to read better, to talk more politely and dress more presentably, there are other community resources to help him with this after his release, and he will be better able to use them if he first learns how to solve his problems without resorting to delinquent behavior. These centers are not intended to be the typical catch-all training school. They serve a fairly narrow spectrum of the delinquent population. Admission is mainly limited to delinquents who are sixteen or seventeen years old and who have been probation failures to the extent that a state reformatory is usually the next step if the residential group treatment center is not effective. They are boys who have parted company already with the public schools and for whom further attempt at academic education is useless unless they change their attitude toward it after the treatment experience.

THE MEETING AS DISCIPLINE

It is typical for visitors to a training school for delinquents to ask about the disciplinary measures that are used. The same question asked in a treatment center of the Highfields type may bring the curious response that misbehavior is not so much a subject of disciplinary action as it is a subject of discussion in the meeting. Where a more conventional institution uses rules and disciplinary measures to control and prevent misbehavior, the treatment center finds instead that misbehavior can serve a useful purpose in the treatment process. While mischief is not encouraged, it is expected; and the philosophy is that a boy cannot truly be helped unless he "shows himself." The problems that show are the problems that get help.

Some of the centers go further than others in leaving discipline to the meeting, but all of them depend heavily on the meeting as by far the most effective control in the program. Most of the centers recognize that some disciplinary punishment must be available, but in general practice a boy is not administered punishment for misdeeds if he will talk about any such behavior freely and *honestly* in the meeting. In fact, this is the stuff of which the helping process is made. The energetic probing of the misbehavior by the other boys is the most vital treatment process that can occur.

Disciplinary action in the conventional sense is not so likely to be applied for misbehavior as for refusal to face the quality of the misbehavior honestly. This might be something as clear-cut as trying to lie about an act, as when a boy steals something and then flatly denies it. But it might just as easily be much more subtle, as when a boy persists in various ways to "con" his way out of taking responsibility.

For such a boy it is presumed that a disciplinary measure should give him time to think, and this is part of the reason for a device known as "the pit" which is common to many of the centers. It is simply a nearby small patch of land where a boy can spend the day digging a hole. The digging is for no purpose except to use time and energy in activity which is boring and which allows time to think. Any staff member can give a boy hours or days in the pit, and the boys themselves in their meeting can give pit time. While working in the pit the boy is not with the group in their regular work and he is not earning his daily allowance.

The final control of such disciplinary measures is never turned over to the meeting, although recommendations on the amount of pit time a boy should spend are often invited; the director, however, always retains the right of veto. But, in addition to disciplinary action, decisions regarding releases, furloughs, or release dates are all made a part of the boys' responsibility, so we come right back to the fact that the meeting, after all, is the real source of discipline. This despite the program's apparent permissive character — in most centers boys are not even required to come to meetings. It would seem that something so vital to the whole program would have to be strictly required, but here again the nondirective philosophy is seen. There are occasions when a boy is feeling so much pressure from the meetings that he needs to stay away for a time or two. If, however, he is just deliberately flouting the expected practice the other boys will see to it that he gets involved. If necessary, they may take the meeting to him. They may follow him around and hold a rump session in his room, leaving him feeling the intense pressure of the group to return. Sooner or later he will yield to the expectations of his peers. The boys attend the meetings because this is the dominant activity available and the whole mood of the place calls for attendance. Sometimes a boy will indicate he wants to talk to a staff member about personal problems, but he is likely to be told to take it up in the meeting instead. He is truly surrounded by intangible forces that push him to the meeting and compel his involvement in it.

This is far more effective than a rule would be. The sanctions of peers will be a form of pressure that means more to the boy than a rule laid down by an authoritative adult.

Even orientation for a new boy is largely a function of the group. In a conventional institution the staff is likely to greet a new boy with printed lists of rules and perhaps much verbal instruction on how to adapt to his new setting. In a residential treatment center, however, the director may do little or nothing that resembles the usual orientation process. When a new boy is brought into the program he is almost immediately taken out to the job and left with the other boys. In this kind of program the boys are competent to explain the culture to the new boy and their explanations will be more quickly accepted than any from the staff. Also, since the group feeling and interaction is so essential in the treatment process it is considered important to get the new boy immediately involved in it. Accordingly, the reception the boy gets from the staff on his arrival is not a hearty, arm-around-the shoulder greeting. Instead he is turned over to the group with almost a casual, take-it-or-leave-it attitude. Often the staff member does not even mention that meetings are held, but leaves the new boy to learn this from the others.

In one of the centers it is the regular practice to send a new boy off to work by himself without supervision the first day. Even though it may be evident that the boy has been promising himself he will run the first time any staff member turns his head, he is received without fuss and after the secretary gets his name and other information for the file the director gives him a rake or shovel and sends him off to do some work on a remote corner of the property. It is considered essential that the spot where he works is out of sight of the building and that no one is observing him. No one goes out to get him or check on him at all until the end of the day when the other boys get back from work. Then the boys themselves go to get him.

This kind of introduction to the program is remarkably casual in appearance, but it is a carefully calculated technique. It tells the boy in a way that no amount of words ever could that this place is unique. It arouses his curiosity immediately and his curiosity keeps him there on that remote assignment the first day because he cannot understand this kind of approach. This kind of boy prefers to make such drastic moves as running away only when he has the system rather well figured out.

The center that uses this technique has not yet had any new boy run off from that first-day assignment, nor has there been any appreciable problem in sustaining attendance at the meetings. The boy finds many things here that are contrary to expectations and so is likely to be puzzled. The fact that he does not have to fight anyone; the fact that the boys talk to the staff with a startling lack of inhibition; the staff's calm attitude toward misbehavior — all these things are more certain than any rule would be to induce the boy to come to the meetings to find out what goes on around here. And by the time he has it figured out he is finding that the meetings are important to him.

THE ADMINISTRATIVE CONTEXT

The Highfields Residential Group Center near Hopewell, New Jersey, was originally made possible by the gift of the property itself and by gifts of funds from a foundation and from private contributors. These gifts were sufficient to finance the new program for two years, after which its support and administration were fully assumed by the state of New Jersey under its Department of Institutions and Agencies.[6] After a decade of operation it had sold itself so well to the New Jersey courts that inevitably there was demand for more such facilities. So in recent years the department obtained the necessary appropriations to open additional residence centers for boys at Oxford and Forked River. And while the residents of the treatment centers have been referred to only by the masculine gender, it must be pointed out that this was more for convenience than for accuracy. At Farmingdale, N.J., there is now a center for girls, known as Turrell Residential Group Center.

A minor variation on the original pattern is represented in still another center. Located in Newark, it was made possible by a Ford Foundation grant and is known as Essexfields. While Essexfields has always served only the juvenile court in Newark, and has now been accepted as a financial responsibility of Essex County, it receives its administrative control and direction from the State Department of Institutions and Agencies, just as do the other residential group treatment centers in New Jersey.

One aspect of the Essexfields operation that is distinctly different from other existing programs of this kind has already been mentioned — the fact that the boys do not live in. This gives it special significance for other localities that may want to try this type of treatment program, for the main attractiveness of this feature is the reduced expense. Since the boys sleep at their own homes, the program is saved the expense of maintaining sleeping space, beds, bedding, laundry, shower facilities, kitchen and dining facilities, food, salaries for cooks. Of course this is feasible only in a city with a dependable supply of appropriate cases within easy travel distance.

The Essexfields program is operated in an old row house in a high delinquency area of Newark. One of the professional staff members lives there, but otherwise the run-down, old residence has to provide very little comfort. There is a ping-pong table in the dining room, while the living room is the office by day and the group discussion room by night.

Many of the Essexfields boys live within walking distance of the building. Others have a short bus ride each day, but all are due at the building

[6] McCorkle, Elias, and Bixby, *The Highfields Story*, Chapter 1.

at 7:30 each morning with their breakfast eaten at home. Promptly at 7:30 their work supervisor drives the twenty boys in Essexfields' own bus to the mental hospital where a 400-acre campus easily offers enough maintenance work to keep them busy. The hospital furnishes the noon and evening meal to the boys and their work supervisor at no charge to Essexfields. After eating supper they return to the Essexfields building and at 7 P.M. the first discussion session begins. When the second session concludes at 10 P.M. all the boys go home. On Saturdays they report as usual at 7:30 but spend their morning in cleaning around the building and are free to go home from Saturday noon to Monday morning.

The boys' nightly absence from the tightly controlled program has not been a major problem, for when they have been doing hard manual work all day they are usually going to spend the remaining night hours in sleeping. At best, their available time for sleeping would be only from about 10:30 P.M. to 6:30 A.M. The Saturday noon through Sunday break is more of a threat to the synthetic culture of the program, for this can permit a substantial contamination each weekend by the street culture. However, it can also be a useful testing of a boy's growing strengths.

Except for Essexfields, which is a local service, the New Jersey centers receive referrals from any New Jersey court; on their release the boys and girls go back to the courts for continued probation supervision.

In New York the State Division for Youth has adapted the residential group treatment idea in its START centers (Short Term Adolescent Resident Treatment). The START centers serving boys are located at Middletown, where work is done for the Middletown State Hospital; at Auburn, where the work is a variety of nonprofit community projects; and at Brentwood, where the center is built on a remote corner of the grounds of Pilgrim State Hospital. For girls, New York has two new centers: one at Amenia, where the girls work at Wassaic State Hospital; and one on Staten Island, where work is provided by the Willowbrook State School.

In New York boys or girls in the START centers are probationers under local courts. In effect the State Division for Youth is providing a service which does not involve commitment to the state, but to which the courts may refer boys or girls as a condition of their probation.

The only residential group center of the Highfields type outside of New Jersey and New York is in Jefferson County (Louisville), Kentucky. Named Southfields, it was started in 1961 with Jefferson County furnishing the cost of the physical facility and the Ford Foundation financing a research project and assisting with the operating costs for the first three years. Southfields is a county service, drawing boys only from the one juvenile court in Louisville. For its source of work it uses the Central State Hospital, eleven miles away.

An experimental departure from the standard pattern was tried in Provo, Utah, where the Pinehills project started in 1959 with a grant from the Ford Foundation, and closed in 1964 when the grant was used up. Pinehills was to follow the same basic approach as Highfields, with twenty boys and the same development of a synthetic culture. There were certain differences, however, that made it a very brave attempt to adapt the idea to a rural area, but that also worked heavily against its success. The Pinehills program was not a residence program and did not even provide a regular work program except on Saturdays. Most of the boys were in school. Every day after school part-time transportation workers picked up the boys from their widely scattered locations and brought them to the house in Provo where the program was based. After their two discussion periods they were delivered to their homes in time for a late supper about 7:30 P.M. On Saturdays they were transported to the center again and supervised at work all day on various public service jobs. They were paid fifty cents per hour for the work. The Provo program was rare in its lack of a daily work program and in its consequent independence of any other state facility.

Beginning with Highfields itself, the treatment centers have almost invariably established themselves near a facility that will furnish a dependable source of public-service work. The New York practice in this respect has already been mentioned. At Highfields the boys work each day on maintenance jobs at the New Jersey Neuro-Psychiatric Institute. At Turrell the girls work at nearby Marlboro State Hospital. At Oxford the employment is mainly at a state fish hatchery, and at Forked River the boys are employed on a state game farm. The association of the residential treatment program with an existing state facility is a happy one due to the chronic staff shortages that seem to be an almost definitive aspect of state institutions. Whether it is a game farm or a mental hospital, the administrators of such facilities have found that the boys or girls are able to do many jobs that would never get done otherwise, and their services are performed at negligible cost to the institution. At a hospital, for instance, it is typical for the boys and their work supervisor to

165

be furnished their noon meal and sometimes a certain amount of their work supervision, but these would be the only cost to the hospital except for the supplies and materials necessary to the maintenance work. The work supervisor is a member of the residential group center staff and the money to pay the boys or girls their fifty cents or more per day also comes from the center's own budget.

In most instances the boys are working with property instead of people. The jobs are mainly concerned with grounds maintenance. At Turrell, however, there has been direct contact with the mental hospital patients. The girls were assigned to work in a ward that housed severely regressed and senile women; the patients were withdrawn and incontinent. With insufficient staff, the ward had seldom had adequate housekeeping, and the resultant stench made the assignment there a rather forbidding one for the girls from Turrell. The staff was prepared for rebellion from the girls, and would have been quite understanding of rebellion under the circumstances. But the girls went at the job of cleaning up the ward and when they had the soap and water work all done they began to give their attention to the patients. The experience has been a highly satisfying one, for the girls give the patients exactly the kind of attention they need and had not been getting. The girls become fond of the patients and seem to be challenged to do what they can to bring them out of their regression. They escort patients to the doctor or on other errands, they fix their hair, help them apply makeup, help them eat, and sometimes just play games with them. It becomes a source of pride for the girls who help patients to show progress and this supplement to its staff is a great assistance to the hospital.

THE STAFF

The basic staff needed for the operation of a residential group center is a director, assistant director, secretary, work supervisor, and cook. An additional position or two may be used according to the particular needs of any center. The positions of director and assistant director are professional and in most cases are filled by persons who have graduate training in social work. Whether the training is in social work or some closely allied field, these positions are more demanding of skill and dedication than almost any other work to be found in corrections. It is work that is confining and exhausting for both the worker and his family.

There is fascination in observing this small but greatly important trend which runs counter to social work's new-found comfort and pleasure in having "banker's hours." Social work in the generation previous to ours was often accepted by its practitioners as a career of dedication accompanied by some sacrifice of personal time and pleasure. It was assumed by them that the hours would be long, the personal involvement total, and the pay little more than reasonable subsistance. (An interesting historical note that reflects this is the fact that the early probation officers in England were called "Court Missionaries.") In the past three decades social workers have made great progress toward more comfortable living, have joined unions, and have taken for granted the forty-hour week and good competitive salaries. As social workers gained in the good things of life, social work as a profession lost something of its luster as a career of dedication. But here in the Highfields type of program there is a rediscovery of the indispensable quality of self-giving. Here the social worker must give himself, his time, his energy, even his family, to a degree that equals the investment of the most dedicated of early social workers. The reassuring difference is that this modern-day version of the missionary job provides a higher social status and a much more satisfactory level of income than was accorded the early practitioners.

What really makes the job attractive is the deep satisfaction in it for the professionally trained worker who is eager to use his skill to the fullest. It offers him the stimulating experience of being in intimate daily touch with the basic processes of change in people who are in crucial need of changing.

Typically, the director of any Highfields type of program lives with his family in an apartment furnished to him in the same building which houses the boys. It is usual for the family to eat in the same dining room with the boys. There may also be housing furnished for the other staff members, depending on the remoteness of the location and the effect of this on the availability of other housing. The staff quarters need to be comfortable and designed to give as much privacy as possible, a point which should be abundantly self-evident.

The two professional staff members in each center are involved in group discussions five evenings per week and the two free evenings, as already indicated, are not successive. Usually it is Thursday and Saturday evenings that are skipped. Here again is a significant difference from the conventional institution where too often administrative practices give priority to staff convenience. In these residential treatment centers the professional staff members never have a two-day block of time in which to be off. But, as we have seen, the inexorable maintenance of the special culture is so paramount that it is considered essential never to allow more than a one-day break in the group therapy pattern.

Obviously, the problem of having no weekends off is a burden to the staff, and this is compounded by the fact that evenings too are occupied. The last group discussion each evening adjourns at 10 P.M. and even then the staff is not free to relax until the boys are in bed and quiet. The only compensating factor is that during the day the professional staff members have the freedom to use their time as flexibly as the situation will allow. Actually, even during the day when the boys are all out on the job with their work supervisor the professional staff will still have many demands upon them. There are parents to talk to, records to read and keep current, court sessions to attend, probation officers to meet with, new referrals to study, emergencies to handle. The only comfort for the director's wife who wishes her husband would not have to work both night and day is that he is at least close to his home most of his working time and he is free to spend his time on personal and family matters whenever his attention to all these program duties is not demanded.

The obvious question of how to find professional persons willing to immerse themselves in their work to this extent gives rise to an interesting possibility: that a future source of such personnel may be the occasional boy among today's delinquents who has the potential ability to adjust, to grow, and to use his intelligence for developing skill in this profession. Some experience in this was gained almost accidentally in the Provo program, when one of the boys was used as a work supervisor. Since the work projects were done only on Saturdays the work supervisors were part-time employees who were not otherwise involved in the program. This proved to be a problem, for without thorough and continuing orientation to the program these supervisors were handicapped in knowing how to handle such boys and were too easily "conned" by them. As an alternative, the staff selected one of the older, more mature boys and paid him double his usual rate to take charge of the work group. The boy proved to be appreciably more effective than the regular work supervisor had been in keeping control and getting the boys to work.

It will be noted later that there is a slowly awakening realization that we can tolerate hiring a person with a "record," and should in fact actually recruit and train persons from among our former clientele. In the present residential group centers can be seen a beginning of this trend and it appears to have much promise of effectiveness. Obviously the work requires stability and skill, attributes which tend to be in short supply in the clientele, but the occasional delinquent who can become mature and skilled has additional qualities that are not so easily found in the conventionally reared middle-class person. He seems to have a more natural rapport with the delinquents under his care, and he and his family are more willing to give themselves fully to the all-out personal investment in the job.

THE PHYSICAL PLANT

The residential group treatment centers are located in a variety of building types, but where new buildings have been erected in recent years for this special purpose there is an interesting standard design that is common to most of them.

The original such program still operates in the fine, big, stone house at Highfields, and its paneled library is the main office and scene of the nightly meetings. Its location is rural, and by being back from a county road, hidden in a wooded area, it seems remote even though it is but a short drive from Hopewell or Trenton. It has been a satisfactory location and the centers that have been subsequently built have used similar locales.

The Essexfields building in Newark is of minimal quality, but this is no problem when the building does not need to provide sleeping, cooking, or eating facilities. Similarly, the Provo program was operated in an ordinary house which required almost no modification for the purpose.

The other centers are operating in buildings built for the purpose, and what might be a composite of the several of them can be described. The building is usually one story and brick. It contains a kitchen and an all-purpose room which is the dining room at mealtimes and is used as a day room, perhaps for ping-pong, at other times. To one side of this main portion of the building will be a wing with the sleeping rooms, and on the opposite side will be office space and a wing housing an apartment for the director and his family. A garage is sometimes included, and it seems a good idea to have the garage between the director's apartment and the rest of the building.

In the sleeping area for the boys there are no private rooms, since these would reduce the amount of interaction and allow a boy to withdraw too much from the group. In this program the meetings must feed constantly on the rich content supplied by the daily group activity. So the rooms are designed for four boys each, ensuring in this way the important constant interaction. The rooms have two double bunks and four lockers, little else. The whole building has a somewhat bare look about it, as though there was not quite enough money left to furnish it completely. But the effect is intended, and except for the ping-pong table there is seldom any equipment for the sort of recreation that would provide mental escape.

Nor is there any effort to beautify the building or make it comfortable. Drabness is avoided, but that is all. Though boys are treated with unfailing consideration, friendliness, and humaneness, they are not provided with creature comforts that would encourage them to want to stay. The building must work with the program so that every waking moment will produce interaction between the boys rather than allow opportunities for individual comfort and private reverie that would thwart or delay the intensive social therapeutic process.

There are no custodial provisions in the construction. Doors, windows, and locks are ordinary ones and even though no staff member remains awake on duty at night there is no provision for locking the boys in.

Buildings like this have mostly been built in the last five years and tend to cost a little over $200,000 each.

THE TREATMENT CENTER AND THE PROBATION OFFICE

Group treatment in these centers is a technique that is refreshingly promising, but it should be evident from the foregoing discussion that it is likely to be a waste of time unless it is supplemented by strong probation services. The treatment center makes no attempt to meet all a boy's needs. It gives him no academic education, no vocational training, no specialized counseling. But these omissions need not be the subject of apology. The boys and girls who go to the treatment centers have been social misfits because of some basic defects in their attitudes toward

170

authority and in their patterns of relating to others. These are the problems that are worked on in the treatment centers in the short four months of stay.

When a boy leaves the center it is not because it is assumed he is rehabilitated, but because it is hoped that he is now ready to make use of the rehabilitative service that a probation officer can offer him. At the time he was sentenced he was not a suitable subject for probation; he could only have been committed to a reformatory except for the availability of the group treatment center. And so the center's job is to give him a new attitude and a new way of dealing with authority so that he can then accept and profit by probation status.

The various treatment centers have had experiences both good and poor in dealing with courts and probation offices. It was fortunate the new technique got started in New Jersey, for in addition to having urban areas that could furnish a dependable supply of cases, New Jersey is a small and compact state geographically, making it easier for courts to become acquainted with the peculiar nature of this treatment device and easier for probation officers to visit the centers without excessive travel.

For maximum success, experience has shown it to be essential that the judge of the committing court be well acquainted with the treatment center's philosophy and method if he is to commit boys or girls appropriately and if he is afterward to give effective support to the program. Essential too is the probation officer's understanding and support.

These conditions are more difficult to accomplish than might be expected, for the probation officer's experience is likely to be with institutional programs that are substantially different from this one, and he is likely to distrust this new program almost instinctively because of its apparent permissive character. The director of a residential treatment center finds himself having to provide interpretation constantly as judges and probation officers come and go. If the judge has a sympathetic understanding of the program he will contribute greatly to its success, not only by his wise selection of cases, but also by the way he handles the occasional boy who runs away from the center or who for other reasons must be returned to court.

Boys are quick to manipulate any restrictive situation including the court itself if possible. In the Provo program, for instance, one boy, frustrated by his inability to manipulate the staff, decided that he could possibly do more with the judge. He demanded to be taken back to court. His wish was amiably granted and in court he was promptly committed to the state reformatory. In that instance the treatment center and the court were working together with mutual understanding and purpose. It was a lesson that carried a clear and immediate message to the other boys and contributed substantially to the strength of the treatment program.[7]

But if the judge misunderstands the program and commits boys or handles violators according to his own private notion of the punishment he wants to impose, he will often select the wrong kind of case, with the wrong interpretation to the boy and his family, and so will negate the value of the center's program for that boy, and the others too.

Hardly less crucial is the full understanding and support of the chief probation officer of any court that is using a residential treatment center. The administrator does not commit boys as does the judge, and he does not supervise cases as do his probation officers, but he sets the philosophy for the officers to follow. If he is cool to the idea of any particular treatment resource his staff is likely to use that resource ineptly and seldom. This will be particularly true in regard to the unorthodox program that the staff will not understand unless they have much encouragement from their administrative chief. A probation officer is accustomed to the idea of a state training school which takes his probation failures on long-term commitments, leaving the officer free to terminate such cases at the time of commitment. It is very easy for a probation officer to act the same way toward a probationer who has been committed to a residential treatment center. It becomes essential, then, for the chief probation officer to make it clear to his staff that boys who have gone to the center are still on the active probation caseload; that they will shift back to the community again in about four months; and that they must be visited and worked with at the center no less regularly than boys living at home.

All this carries obvious implications for the type of population setting needed for a successful Highfields program. It will work best where it can serve just one or perhaps a very few urban courts. The more courts there are to draw from the more difficulty the director will have in in-

---

[7] Empey and Rabow, "The Provo Experiment in Delinquency Rehabilitation," p. 690.

terpreting the program to a variety of judges and probation staffs. And if cases are to come from a wide geographical area with small town and rural populations, the types of boys available will be less appropriate than those whose delinquency springs from the peer group pressures in the congested cities. Like all devices for the control of delinquency, this one must be used only in the context to which its peculiar characteristics are appropriate.

6

Narcotics Addicts on Probation or Parole

In any discussion of the narcotics problem it is easy to be drawn into the controversy over whether the control of narcotics should be primarily vested in the medical profession, perhaps with doctors being permitted to furnish legal dosages to known addicts. While there are aspects to such a proposal which are appealing to many, the fact remains that in the United States, the effective majority supports the present prohibition of addictive drugs and probably will continue to do so during the foreseeable future. So we will be concerned in this account only with the reality that probation and parole agencies are likely to have an increasing amount of experience with the drug user and must seek more effective techniques for helping him.

A part of the reason for the ever greater incidence of crime by addicts is the way that enforcement of the drug laws affects supply and demand. The diligence of law-enforcement agencies in preventing distribution of narcotics tends to drive the retail price upward. The higher price levels put a greater burden on the user so that his burglaries and thefts, or her shoplifting or prostitution, must be stepped up in order to buy the required dosage. "In New York City alone, it has been estimated, addicts must raise between $500,000 and $700,000 every day — most of it through shoplifting, burglary, forgery, prostitution, and other illegal activities."[1]

A publication of significance is the *Final Report of the President's Advisory Commission on Narcotic and Drug Abuse*.[2] In considering the question of legal dosages to addicts under medical direction, the commission requested studies and reports from the American Medical Association and the National Research Council of the National Academy of Sciences. Those two bodies submitted a joint statement which declares that the administration of maintenance doses to addicts is medically unsound. The President's commission agreed and commented: "There is no certainty that an addict can be maintained at a stable level. A confirmed addict builds up a tolerance to his drug, and to offset the effects of withdrawal the dosage must be continually increased. Moreover, it would be an unwarranted admission of failure to resort to maintenance doses when research is just beginning to indicate more promising developments in the treatment and rehabilitation of addicts and habitual users."[3] The commission also was convinced that more discretion in the use of probation and parole is in order. It expressed disagreement with laws that provide rigid penalties with mandatory minimums and no eligibility for probation or parole. It urged that the availability of parole be seen as motivation for a man to make more effort toward his own rehabilitation. It flatly rejected the alleged deterrent value of rigid harshness: "The Bureau of Narcotics maintains that the present severe penalties act as a powerful deterrent. The Commission does not agree."[4]

The National Advisory Council of Judges takes a similar view, commenting that "In recent years the penalties for narcotics crimes have become more and more severe, the theory of the legislation evidently being that the greater the penalty, the greater the deterrence. The result in practice is to glut the penal institutions with small-fry pushers and addicts serving long terms, without any deterrent effect on the racket but with deteriorating effect on the prisoners and the correctional institu-

[1] *Narcotic Drug Addiction*, Mental Health Monograph No. 2, U.S. Department of Health, Education, and Welfare (Washington, D.C.: Government Printing Office, 1963), p. 2.
[2] Washington, D.C.: Government Printing Office, November 1963.
[3] *Ibid.*, p. 58.
[4] *Ibid.*, p. 40.

tions. We oppose mandatory terms in narcotics cases and the exclusion of narcotics offenders from eligibility for probation or parole." [5]

So the natural laws of supply and demand, as affected by the activity of law-enforcement agencies, will act to maintain, and probably increase, the number of drug users who are brought to court. And the signs are that probation and parole as well as other community-based techniques will be increasingly relied upon as control and treatment measures. We can hope that researchers, medical experts, and legislators will eventually find for us better ways of coping with the whole narcotics problem, but until they do the victims will continue to appear in our caseloads where they desperately need our help, whether or not they recognize this themselves.

HOSPITALS AND COMMUNITY TREATMENT PROGRAMS

The institution that has the longest and most intensive experience with the addiction problem in this country, and is our best known resource for the treatment of addicts, is the U.S. Public Health Service Hospital in Lexington, Kentucky, opened in 1935. It is operated as a hospital, although it was built with custodial features so that it can serve federal prisoners as well as those patients who are admitted voluntarily from anywhere east of the Mississippi. A similar facility is now being operated, also by the U.S. Public Health Service, in Fort Worth, Texas. It serves male patients from areas west of the Mississippi. (Female patients from any state in the country are accepted at Lexington.)

Among addicts and persons who work with them it is common to find a depreciatory attitude toward Lexington, largely on the basis of a popular belief that its treatment program is almost completely ineffective. Often people will dismiss the Lexington facility casually with the observation that all but 1 or 2 percent of the released patients promptly return to drug use. Even professionals in the field will err in judging a program of this kind by its failures, forgetting that its successes would rarely be seen.

The impression is inescapable, furthermore, that this pessimism extends to treatment of drug addiction generally and that such pessimism substantially hinders efforts to reach and help the addict. Since the typical addict has little enough motivation anyway for saving himself,

[5] *Narcotics Law Violations, a Policy Statement*, Advisory Council of Judges, National Council on Crime and Delinquency, 1964, p. 15.

his inertia and feeling of futility are reinforced by the frequently expressed and generally believed assertion that Lexington is essentially powerless to help. But this hospital should not be underrated on the basis of subjective impressions or incomplete research. Follow-up studies are hampered and distorted by the difficulty of locating many of the former patients after a few years have elapsed. It is common for 20 to 40 percent of the cases to be listed in the "unknown" column in the statistics. O'Donnell has pointed out that a substantial number of such unlocated ex-patients would probably be successes.[6] He also observes: "The circumstances in which retrospective studies are done make it certain that they will find only histories of relapse."[7]

A feature that depresses the figure for successes in much research is the tendency to list a case as relapsed without regard to the conditions or duration of the relapse. In a follow-up study covering several years a person may be listed as relapsed even if he used drugs for just a week or two at any time during the entire period. Though it might be a technically proper classification it masks the more dynamic information that such a case represents a most satisfying net gain. In all fairness too, we should discriminate between two kinds of failures in narcotics cases: those so labeled because of reuse of drugs and those who have engaged in other forms of proscribed behavior. It is too easy for researchers to list as failures ex-patients who have been incarcerated at some time during the follow-up period, whether or not drug use was involved. O'Donnell comments, "Two patients are treated, both abstain from drug use, one returns to his previous occupation as a physician, the second to his previous occupation as a shoplifter. The first is clearly a success; it is not equally clear that the second is a failure."[8]

Correctional workers, whatever the type of case, must be able to recognize that the goal in the usual instance is not to bring a client to the healthy, happy, normal condition of the average, law-abiding middle-class citizen. Even though a client's basic adjustment problem is not fully eliminated, success can still be claimed if he has achieved enough reduction of the problem so that it is no longer socially crippling to him. A probation or parole officer, in his approach to an addiction case, should not allow erroneous impressions of research results to foster in

[6] Dr. John A. O'Donnell, "The Relapse Rate in Narcotic Addiction," unpublished paper read before the U.C.L.A. Narcotics Conference, April 27, 1963, pp. 28, 29.
[7] Ibid., p. 2.
[8] Ibid., p. 17.

him a sense of futility which will surely reduce his effectiveness with that person.

A general finding of particular significance is that the best record is made by the patient who is released to probation or parole supervision, for he goes to a pre-arranged home and job situation in addition to having the continuing casework help. This is a finding that supports Lowry's comment that "Hospital treatment can initiate rehabilitation but it must be completed after the patient returns to the community." [9]

Probation and parole workers have tended to rely too heavily on a hospital or institution to do the whole job with this kind of client. The most important new realization in the correctional field today may be that hospital or institutional care, for clients with or without special problems such as addiction, will be far more successful if it is seen as an intensive and controlled means of getting those clients ready to use field services, rather than as the complete or final treatment service in itself. We have been unjustly judging a hospital such as Lexington when we evaluate its program by the rate of relapse of its former patients whether or not they had any post-hospital help. Any such research may be assessing the availability or quality of post-hospital resources rather than evaluating the hospital itself.

The treatment process at Lexington includes the usual withdrawal to terminate the patient's physiological dependence on drugs, and then casework, group work, psychiatric techniques, and vocational training. Withdrawal is aided by the use of a synthetic drug, Methadone, which eases the discomfort of the withdrawal symptoms. It is given by mouth, thus avoiding the use of a needle, and is gradually discontinued as the patient's body adjusts to a drug-free condition.

A large number of patients at Lexington are there as voluntary commitments, and this tends to heighten the pessimism in regard to addiction treatment, for a voluntary patient cannot be held against his will and a discouragingly large number of them leave the hospital before completing treatment. By leaving against medical advice and without follow-up care they are, of course, heading for almost certain relapse. The President's Advisory Commission, recognizing the hospital's ineffectiveness with the voluntary patient, but also the need for more re-

[9] James V. Lowry, "Hospital Treatment of the Narcotics Addict," *Federal Probation*, Vol. 20, No. 4 (December 1956), p. 51.

search, has recommended that "the Public Health Service hospitals in Lexington, Kentucky, and Forth Worth, Texas, accept voluntary patients only for purposes of research study in the future." [10]

Though some excellent hospital treatment services for addicts have been developed, the much more difficult job of developing community treatment resources and techniques has lagged seriously. It may be that the federal government's leadership in establishing installations at Lexington and Fort Worth has tended to delay the kind of progress that is now needed. "Unfortunately, the two Federal hospitals were rather large, and with their admitting of patients from the forty-eight states, there was no great rush for the states to develop their own facilities. Consequently, addicts have been treated too far from home, and the post-hospital treatment and supervision have, to say the least, been meager." [11] Other reasons for the lag are inherent in the baffling nature of the addict himself and, again, the general hopelessness that characterizes consideration of this social problem. For most social agencies, an effort to come to grips with an addiction case is like an effort to pick up quicksilver. The ordinary social worker finds that his usual techniques for introducing and carrying out the helping process will be ineffective when the client is an addict. The therapist has to do some relearning to function well in this area of social service, but experience is showing that techniques can be learned which have a satisfying degree of effectiveness.

The most energetic programs for community-based work with addicts have been in the states of California and New York where probation and parole agencies as well as more general types of resources have developed specialized approaches to the problem. In New York, for instance, a grant from the National Institute of Mental Health financed a five-year experiment, beginning in 1957. It took the form of an agency, known as the New York Demonstration Center, which worked directly with patients being discharged from Lexington in an effort to integrate them into community life. This program is still in existence, and now, under the name Washington Heights Rehabilitation Center, it is working almost entirely with addicts released to probation or parole supervision.

[10] *Final Report of the President's Advisory Commission on Narcotic and Drug Abuse*, p. 65.

[11] Dr. Warren P. Jurgensen, "Inpatient Treatment of the Narcotic Addict," speech delivered at the Chatham (Mass.) Conference on Perspectives on Narcotic Addiction, September 9–11, 1963.

The lessons learned by its casework staff have considerable significance for probation and parole officers generally.

An initial problem was the reluctance of social service agencies to accept referrals of addicts. Since the center was at first mainly a coordinating and referral service, its first job was to persuade employment agencies and others to accept as clients a few of the more promising addicts. This reluctant cooperation of other agencies was gained only by giving assurances that the Demonstration Center would carefully screen the cases before referral and would continue its supportive activity in the cases afterward.[12]

However, this problem was more easily solved than the problem of the addicts' poor record in accepting referrals. Casework experience showed that addicts were very poorly motivated for self-help, even to the extent of being notoriously unreliable about keeping appointments for casework or job interviews. It became apparent that the usual process of establishing rapport with the client was far less appropriate in these cases than the practical expedient of giving concrete help at whatever unscheduled moment the client needed it. Addicts were found to be wary of forming close relationships. They were manipulative, passive, and dependent. They could often be reached only in the immediacy of a crisis situation. A reaching-out technique became essential; the workers found that they had to make frequent visits to the home, write follow-up letters, and stand ready to respond to a client's needs whenever they arose. A tidy arrangement of office appointments does not suffice in this kind of effort, for the addict is likely to come to the office impulsively, ignoring schedules and responding instead to the pressure of the moment. The effective worker must be willing to make himself available promptly as the unscheduled need arises. For this same reason it was found important for the Demonstration Center office to be located as conveniently as possible in the client's neighborhood.

The social worker's basic treatment tool of relationship may be useless in the early stages of any of these cases, for the addict may be unable to tolerate the sort of rapport the worker wants to develop. Typically, the kind of close family relationships the addict experienced as a child had damaging effects because of the demanding, destructive, or seductive kind of love he received. The result is that now the worker who would

---

[12] Leon Brill, "Preliminary Experiences of a Pilot Project in Drug Addiction," *Social Casework*, Vol. 42, No. 1 (January 1961), pp. 28–32.

effectively help must let his client have a generous amount of time before he is expected to form any close relationship, and meanwhile the worker will provide simple, practical help at any time and in any situation in which it is needed.[13] When a close relationship can be developed it is likely to come from exploitation of problem situations, which may occur frequently in the addict's life.

The workers at the Rehabilitation Center do not see complete abstinence from drugs as the only criterion of success. They are philosophical in recognizing that complete and continuing abstinence is beyond the capability of many of the clients, and that if a client is doing no worse than occasionally "chipping" this may represent for him great progress, especially if his drug intake is so light or so infrequent that it does not interfere with his job or cause him to return to criminal activity. "In working with the addict, limited goals seem the only feasible ones. It is important to view addiction as a chronic illness in which periodic abstinence, even for a few weeks or months, is considered a boon to patient, family and community. Total abstinence over extended periods of time may be a goal beyond realization for most of these patients. Even if abstinence from drugs is established as a primary goal, it can rarely be achieved in a straight line. If it happens at all, it will occur through a series of stops and starts with allowance made for an indefinite number of relapses, slips and other acting-out behavior. Addicts continually fall back on drugs in an effort to achieve some balance in their lives, to bolster their strength in meeting people and social situations." [14]

Though this is a more accommodating approach than the law-enforcement professions usually find acceptable, it is possible for the police themselves to recognize that success in working toward abstinence "can rarely be achieved in a straight line." The head of the Vice and Narcotic Control Division, Oakland (California) Police Department, in writing about the use there of a Nalline testing program, comments, "The treatmental aspect of this program is accepted by the probationer who has learned that a positive reaction does not necessarily result in the filing of a new charge, but generally is processed by modification of the probation order. . . . Parole and probation departments must maintain a firm stand in enforcing the terms of probation without forfeiting their discretionary powers, and realize that the objective (rehabilitation)

---

[13] U.S. Department of Health, Education, and Welfare, Public Health Service, *Rehabilitation in Drug Addiction*, Mental Health Monograph 3, May 1963, p. 10.
[14] *Ibid.*, p. 9.

cannot be reached in addiction cases in the same manner as with the nonaddicted delinquent." [15]

Getting the addict to develop control over his habit is to a large extent a matter of setting limits directively and giving constant reminders of the inexorable process of cause and effect; this should be coupled with efforts to fill the client's time as constructively as possible by occupational and recreational activities. "In their attempts to help patients understand why they used drugs and to encourage abstinence, caseworkers used a variety of techniques: the setting of limits, giving of information and even of direct advice, pointed recognition of positive achievements, however infinitesimal, increasing attempts to enlist the family's cooperation and the accompanying of patients to certain community resources." [16]

There is a growing body of experience, too, with the use of specialized probation and parole officers to work exclusively with the narcotics cases. The Narcotic Drug Study Commission of the New Jersey Legislature recognized that hospital and institution treatment of the addict is ineffectual unless there are probation and parole services with especially skilled workers carrying caseloads of perhaps no more than twelve. "We recommend that the larger cities and places where narcotic addiction is prevalent establish a separate probation department of trained personnel. Each probation officer should have a small case load to make it possible for more intensive casework supervision." [17]

An agency that has had solid experience with this kind of specialization is the New York State Division of Parole. Its New York City office has for several years had a Special Narcotic Project, a unit of six parole officers who work exclusively with addict parolees. They are nearly successful in their intent of keeping caseloads to no more than twenty-five per officer, and they prefer (as does the Washington Heights Rehabilitation Center) the master's degree in social work as the educational qualification for the staff. In this unit too there is an emphasis upon the worker's readiness to give immediate practical, problem-solving service as difficulties arise, case by case. Employment is of great importance. The parolee must have a job immediately on his release and if he loses a

[15] Thorvald T. Brown, "Narcotics and Nalline: Six Years of Testing," *Federal Probation*, Vol. 27, No. 2 (June 1963), p. 31.
[16] *Rehabilitation in Drug Addiction*, p. 25.
[17] Narcotic Drug Study Commission of the New Jersey Legislature, *Interim Report for 1963*, p. 115.

job for any reason the worker makes every possible effort to help him find another without delay. Any period of idleness is an invitation to re-addiction. An important supporting factor is an office fund which can be used to meet the parolee's financial needs during these emergency periods, for he must have the necessary rent and food money between jobs or while waiting for the first paycheck. The parole officer also finds it essential to get his client involved in constructive leisure activities. With the addict this is not a simple matter of referring him to a community social center of some kind. If the client were a person who had a natural ability to walk into a social program and make friends he probably would not have been attracted to narcotics. Most addicts are non-competitive and shy of new social situations; they lack motivation for making new social contacts and they have little skill or self-confidence in handling themselves among "squares." Accordingly, the parole officer must become directly involved, taking the parolee to the suggested program and perhaps staying through it with him the first time or two. He must also directly and specifically enlist the help of the staff of the community center that is being utilized.

Since the attitudes of family members are crucial to success in helping the addict, the parole officer will spend much of his time in supporting improvement in the total family. It has been seen generally by case-workers that often the problem member of a family is serving a patho-logical need of some other member. Whether it is addiction, alcoholism or any of many other forms of personality weakness, the wife or mother may actually become dependent upon the continuance of this family problem which feeds some neurotic need of her own. In such a case pro-nounced improvement in the problem member of the family provokes a severe reaction from the neurotic wife or mother whose emotional crutch is thus threatened. To save his client then the caseworker must turn his attention to the family as a whole. Experience suggests that this is more than usually true with addicts, for the root of their drug habit is in the damaging family relationships that still persist and tend to preserve the client's need for drugs.[18]

In supervising the addict on probation or parole the question arises of how much authoritative surveillance will be exercised, and to what ex-

[18] Robert L. Wolk and Meyer H. Diskind, "Personality Dynamics of Mothers and Wives of Drug Addicts," *Crime and Delinquency*, Vol. 7, No. 2 (April 1961), pp. 148–152.

tent revocation will be resorted to for any relapse. The detection of recent drug usage is a knack that is developed by the specialized parole officer, who learns to suspect it from subtle signs that become meaningful to him. The parole officer in New York's special unit feels free to check arms for needle marks if it seems desirable. He also has available a urine test that gives dependable, though not perfect, indication of recent drug usage. This is the thin-layer chromotography test, which requires that a urine specimen be sent to a laboratory for analysis. The test takes about twenty-four hours to complete and it will detect the presence of heroin sometimes as much as seventy-two hours previously. It cannot be relied upon, however, for detection of drugs taken more than twenty-four hours before and even then the results can be doubtful if the client has been taking medicines or large amounts of water. But, in general, its reliability is easily sufficient to make the test a very effective kind of control.

The use of the test and the examination of arms are done selectively by the parole officer. Parole Board policy allows the parole staff reasonable latitude in deciding when to revoke parole. The parolee himself knows that the reuse of narcotics will not in itself automatically result in revocation. Under these conditions the officer has less difficulty in getting a parolee to admit his reuse so that they can then talk about the reasons and the ways to prevent still more lapses. If the parolee persists in denying use in the face of outward signs, the officer's next move may be to ask for a urine specimen and this often prompts the client to drop the pretense, making the test unnecessary.

The experience of the Hamilton County (Cincinnati) Adult Probation Department also supports this approach. "To emphasize to an addict that use of drugs and association with known addicts will be an automatic violation of his probation or parole, is to tell him that he cannot confide in you and immediately eliminates any possibility that might have existed for rapport and insight. On the other hand the probation officer must be careful not to allow himself to be utilized as an ally in the addict's illegal pursuits." [19]

The Hamilton County office has found the group work approach more satisfying than individual casework in working with addicts. After discovering that a nonaddicted probation officer was just not reaching an addict probationer they tried the use of group discussions

[19] Robert A. Roland, "Narcotics Addiction, a Symptom of Social Disorganization," paper presented to Annual Convention, Ohio Probation and Parole Association, June 1963.

for addicts and their experience is that there is a much freer flow of uninhibited communication. "In an atmosphere dominated by other high junkies [the addict-client] will relate feelings with a reasonable degree of truth, especially if he is called down by a fellow addict who is not high at that time. Being present in this atmosphere placed us in a position to learn a great deal about narcotics and the addicts. Although the tangible progress that has been made through this group with addicts thus far has been quite limited, we have gained insights that have been invaluable, and these insights are broadened and deepened with each meeting. . . . The members have come to realize that the group is a setting where they can come and freely discuss their multitude of conflicts in life and with society. A discovery made early by most of the addicts in their experience with the group is that their particular and specific conflicts and problems are not nearly as unique to them alone or even as a group as they believed them to be." [20]

Another office that uses a special narcotics unit is the Alameda County (California) Probation Department. Its experience and the type of casework approach it has found necessary are nearly identical with those in New York. In Alameda County, too, testing is used, but here it is the Nalline test instead of the thin-layer chromotography. Nalline, a trade name for N-allylnormorphine, is a narcotic which acts on the central nervous system, counteracting the effects of any opium derivatives present. The most useful effect of this is that an injection of Nalline will cause the pupil of the eye to reduce in diameter if no narcotics are present in the system — or to increase if narcotics have been recently used. This testing procedure, which must be handled by a doctor, requires the client to be seated in a small room under conditions of controlled light. A single light source shines into the client's face from several feet away and slightly to one side. The doctor controls the light brightness with a calibrated rheostat dial. He records the light setting and then measures the client's pupil diameter with a pupilometer. After recording this he gives the client a subcutaneous injection of Nalline in the upper arm. About twenty to thirty minutes later the client returns to the room and the doctor sets the light intensity just as it was before, so that the measuring of the pupil is done again under conditions that are identical except for the factor of the Nalline injection. If the pupil has reduced in size it is evidence that no narcotics have been used in the last two or

[20] *Ibid.*

three days. Once the testing equipment is set up and the procedure organized a large number of persons can be tested in a short period of time.

The Alameda County probation office is enthusiastic about this testing procedure as are the police.[21] They both feel that its availability allows probation to be used safely with known narcotics addicts and that it provides a control which keeps them drug-free while rehabilitative processes have a chance to take hold. They also see the psychological effect of the test as mainly positive — the clients who have any motivation to abstain from drugs are appreciative of a device that so directly discourages them from reusing and at the same time objectively proves to the authorities the fact of their abstinence.

In New York the Nalline test is rarely used. The Kings County probation office, for instance, considered and rejected it in the belief that it is not as reliable as the urine test, that it can cause harmful side effects, and that the use of the needle in the testing can whet the appetite for more drug use. In California, on the other hand, the urine test is a rarity and there is strong loyalty to the Nalline test, which Californians seem fully satisfied with on all counts.

The Alameda probation office, just as the New York Division of Parole, avoids using the test for a categorical revocation of probation or parole in case of evidence of relapse. It is regular practice to consider each new relapse in the light of a number of factors and to use degrees of disciplinary action. The parolee who has been showing some signs of wanting to succeed, the parolee whose violation is essentially minor and whose family would be hurt by his incarceration, might be dealt with by means of a "misconduct report" in his record.[22] This is a humane and sensible way of doing the parole job, even though it complicates research which is already complicated enough.

The New York Special Narcotics Parole Unit has tried to evaluate the success of its efforts and in doing so raises the old question of just when do we cut off the case and put it in either the success or failure column: on the day the case is officially closed? after the client has been off parole for one year? three years? As would be expected, the longer the evaluation waits, the lower will be the percentage of success if we con-

[21] Brown, "Narcotics and Nalline."
[22] Meyer H. Diskind and George Klonsky, *Recent Developments in the Treatment of Paroled Offenders Addicted to Narcotic Drugs* (Albany: New York State Division of Parole, 1964), p. 73.

sider failure as any case in which some return to drug usage occurs at some time during the study period. For this reason "The 14 month report revealed 51% abstinence, the 26 month report 42%, while the full three year final report showed just 35% 'success.'"[23]

But again, what is success? The New York City parole staff points out that a parole violation that does not involve narcotics in any way may be a parole failure, but at the same time should not necessarily be called a failure for the narcotic treatment program. When they studied 695 parolees assigned to the narcotics unit they found that 510, or 73 percent, had committed new delinquencies. However, 62 of these delinquencies involved no drugs, so instead of a 73 percent failure rate this would make a 64 percent failure rate in respect to reversion to the drug problem. In view of popular pessimism about arresting drug addiction, a 36 percent rate of success in holding these clients drug free is a most encouraging record. It is still more hopeful when considered in relation to the locale, for New York City, with the example and influence of fellow addicts all around, and the many, close-at-hand sources of drugs, is among the most inimical environments anywhere for the successful abstinence of the habituated person. "Addiction, as in large city minority groups, is pathological behavior which can be viewed as infectious. . . . Indeed we may regard the addict as a vector by whom the susceptible person is infected. The presence or absence of this vector is of immense etiologic or epidemiologic importance."[24]

To sound a further modest note of optimism, even those clients who land in the failure statistics after two or three years still represent a sizable gain because of the time they remained drug-free in the community. An addict in prison is costly to the community and an addict at large and on drugs can be even more costly because of the depredations he must make against the community in order to support his habit. To keep him drug-free for a year or two saves us considerably for that period of time and may, it is to be hoped, hasten the day when we can expect him to be permanently abstinent.

Though our concern in this volume is with the services provided by *public* agencies in probation and parole, there are important developments in voluntary programs for addicts, too, and because these are

[23] *Ibid.*, p. 75.
[24] Jurgensen, "Inpatient Treatment of the Narcotic Addict."

having their effect on the methods used by authoritative agencies we need to look at them next.

THE USE OF SELF-HELP TECHNIQUES

The most provocative movement toward self-help for addicts is found in the Synanon Foundation and though it is controversial, it is not to be ignored by anyone working with addicts. It is as yet mainly limited to the West Coast, but it is gradually extending its service more widely.

In its present form Synanon has been in operation since 1959 when it moved into a former armory on the beach at Santa Monica, California. It is an almost familial group of people of both sexes and all races, ages, and conditions, but having in common a problem in drug addiction to overcome and control. It has no "staff" in the usual sense, but is effectively operated by addicts who have kicked the habit and progressed to a condition of responsibility. This is the kind of movement that develops under the intense personal leadership of one unique personality. In this case it is a former alcoholic who discovered that he had something to offer to drug addicts, and with his intuitive but sound brand of psychiatry he devised a self-help approach that is the most refreshing new aid to the addict that is apparent at this time. The leader, "Chuck" Dederich, has a keen understanding of the psychology of the addict and he applies it in the most hardheaded, take-it-or-leave-it way. His compassion for the drug addict is immense but it is not expressed in a conventional manner. He can appear to be callous, indifferent, and even brutal in his verbal exchanges with addicts who ostensibly are asking for help. But his is a calculated and realistic approach and is remarkably perceptive of what each man's individual needs are at the moment. The effectiveness of it is seen in the reverence toward him on the part of Synanon residents and the obviously potent cohesive force that his personality provides for them.

The effective ingredient in the Synanon idea is hard to define since it is highly intangible and is made up of a number of elements. Synanon is a communal living experience in which the newly arrived addict finds himself, for the first time ever, in the midst of other "dope fiends" who are like him, yet different from anything he has ever expected to see. They are living together in complete freedom from drugs, without authoritative controls to enforce their abstinence, and they are more alert, social, and happy than would ever be true of addicts elsewhere. The new arrival is puzzled, to say the least, and his curiosity is part of the reason he stays.

Almost never does a confirmed addict come into Synanon motivated by a sincere desire to be permanently cured of his addiction. Even though he enters voluntarily, the newcomer has somewhat cynical reasons for knocking on Synanon's door. It may be that he is stranded and looking for temporary shelter. It may be that he has become so heavily addicted that he cannot support his habit and is mainly looking for a chance to kick the habit briefly before going back to it at a more manageable level. And sometimes an addict will enter, not to avoid drugs, but to find them. On the basis of all his previous experience he assumes that where there are addicts, there he will find drugs.

While the Synanon members know that they must take in persons who come with less than pure motives, they are also very skilled in screening out those who are not ready to use the program. The person who is accepted is required to begin his withdrawal immediately and does so "cold turkey." It seems, however, that this abrupt withdrawal is not so excruciating in the Synanon setting as is normally true. During the withdrawal the newcomer is right in the living room among all the hustle of people coming and going with housekeeping activities. He may lie on the sofa and be feeling miserable, but during this time he is given the complete, loving attention of anyone who comes near. Other residents leave him alone if he prefers, or sit with him to give him sympathy and to pamper him with whatever physical comforts might help. Again, this is a very new and surprising experience to him.

Surprise follows surprise as the newly withdrawn resident finds that he actually cannot get drugs here, and that there is an atmosphere of hope and pride throughout the house. The man or woman has entered Synanon for cynical reasons but his surprise and curiosity make him decide to stay for a few days to figure this thing out. If all goes well, by the time he has it figured out he will not, as he intended, leave and go back to his addiction. By this time he is addicted to Synanon instead.

Though he is pampered through his withdrawal like the emotional infant that he is, he finds that as soon as he is over the crisis he is put to work. And to make sure that he is made aware of his lowly state his first jobs are housekeeping assignments that bring him into close association with pots and pans, scrub buckets, and sinks and toilets. Later he will need tangible signs of progress if he does well and his promotion to more prestigeous jobs will bring this recognition. But whatever the job, his contribution to the household through a work assignment is the first unique and most inexorable fact of life that he will face in Synanon.

As in Alcoholics Anonymous, the Synanon program includes meetings in which self-examination is pursued. But in Synanon the meetings are three or more nights per week, and they are an intense emotional experience. In the meeting no holds are barred. Members are expected to be ruthlessly candid with each other. A member who may have been showing irritating qualities will find himself being exposed to every kind of analytical comment. The words that fly are blunt, caustic, profane — whatever is prompted by the uninhibited emotional feelings of the members sitting in that circle. No one is immune from attack and no one is expected to pull punches. The criticisms are expected to be sincerely expressed and constructively intended, but otherwise there are no rules of politeness that hamper the members in the free use of emotionally charged expressions. At all other times in the program reasonable decorum is expected. The house rules of no fighting, no drugs, no alcohol, are inviolate and the member who flaunts such rules is expelled. It is the nightly meeting that provides both a sanctioned release of feelings and the constant polishing process wherein members are made to see themselves and to work toward self-improvement.

Here is a treatment method that is absent from most probation and parole situations. Drug addicts are here sitting in a meeting, getting advice about themselves, but the communication involved bears little resemblance to the advice that a parole officer might give to his addict parolee. One central fact that runs through all experience with addicts is the addict's instinctive avoidance of rapport with "squares." But here it is one addict talking bluntly to another, and if advice about kicking the habit is being given it is coming from someone who has had the habit himself, who has served time for it himself, but who has nevertheless found a way to stay off drugs and grow up. The discussion, as Synanon residents describe it, is at "gut level," for no one is allowed to get away with superficiality or rationalizations, and when the words are from one addict to another they carry real "clout."

These meetings are called synanons. The word when spelled with the capital S refers to the over-all organization; with the small s it refers to the meeting, which began as a kind of seminar. The story is that the word "synanon" was inadvertently coined by an early member who was trying to pronounce the unfamiliar word "seminar."

In addition to the nightly synanon there are other daily meetings of much importance. These are seminars of philosophical discussion and public speaking practice. They serve a particular need of the addict, who usually has been devoting his whole energy to acquiring drugs, sometimes for many years. One effect of this kind of life is that he is intellectually barren to a surprising degree, even though his native I.Q. may be normal or better. He has not kept up with civic events and has not read books or newspapers. He has been unconcerned and unthinking about any of the affairs of other people or anything that was not connected with his own self-interests. This leaves him with gross feelings of inferiority and insecurity when he comes into social contact with normal people. He cannot participate in normal conversation; he cannot respond to the simplest observations about events of the day. This becomes a big factor in the early return of many addicts to drugs, which briefly give them the sense of serenity and security that they cannot achieve with their own inner resources.

Synanon recognizes that if a member is going to be kept drug-free over the long haul this intellectual impoverishment must be corrected. The daytime seminar is a simple nonthreatening device for this purpose. A small group meets in one of the rooms equipped with a blackboard. One of the members has already written on the board that day a brief statement that is quoted from some philosopher, or it may be some provocative line from a Shakespearean play or from any other such source. The statement is then discussed informally. It is always a sentence that is capable of different interpretations. One by one the group members rise to tell their own reaction to the thought expressed in the sentence. The process is as simple as that, but the effect is to stimulate members to think in abstract terms about philosophical truths. They are encouraged to become interested in reading some of the writings of the persons quoted. They also learn how to get on their feet and speak. They make the pleasant discovery that it actually is possible for them to talk on worthwhile matters in front of others. No visitor to Synanon can escape the feeling that the system must work remarkably well, for the Synonon residents are unfailingly poised, outgoing, and cordial as they greet visitors to their house. To augment this cultural development there is opportunity for little theater acting and participation in music.

191

Like the Highfields programs (see Chapter 5) Synanon creates a new culture which in many respects reverses some of the values of the culture which the addict has been accustomed to. It has succeeded in giving status value to constructive accomplishments, and the addict is highly responsive to the sort of recognition that gives him status among his associates. Where he had been getting his status by negative accomplishments such as the high level of his drug intake, he finds in Synanon that status there is achieved for positive accomplishments. The ones who are looked up to are the ones who can talk well in seminars, the ones who earn the better jobs, the ones who learn to deal perceptively and truthfully with themselves and others in the synanons.

Synanon has been the object of some criticism because members are not expected to be cured of their addiction and then leave the fold, releasing a bed for new admission. The Synanon attitude, in fact, implies that a severely addicted person may never be so fully safe from temptation by drugs that he should risk community living. Members are free to leave when they wish but they are not encouraged to leave. If a person leaves against advice while he is still unwell he is said to have "split." He may be allowed to return and many of the very successfully helped persons in Synanon have split once or more in their slow fight against the addiction.

The eventual separation of a stabilized, mature person who decides to leave and establish himself independently is a different matter. Even this is not encouraged, but there are times when it is mutually agreed that such a person can probably survive on his own and that he should go, with Synanon's blessing.

Actually, Synanon itself has great need for the services of anyone who has made this much progress, for all administrative personnel in Synanon are members who have overcome their addiction and have developed the degree of maturity that is necessary for dependable leadership. This is the main limiting factor in the spread of the Synanon locations. There is no such thing as hired staff. The program cannot extend itself to a new location until it has produced the necessary leadership through the slow growth of individuals, sometimes with setbacks and painful recoveries. But expansion is occurring, and in more ways than one. New Synanon houses are being established in other cities and more activities are being developed that reach out into the community. Ordinary citizens are being involved in the Synanon programs, and ways are being discovered to diversify and extend the base of financial support.

From the original single building at Santa Monica the residents there have spread out to occupy a complex of buildings up and down the beach, not only additional housing but also income-producing facilities. Synanon now owns filling stations in Santa Monica and San Francisco, fully operated and staffed by Synanon residents. Subcontract work for manufacturing companies is being done in a large warehouse. These activities provide constant work for Synanon members and broaden the financial base of the whole program.

There is now a Synanon house at San Diego, one at Reno, Nevada, and another in San Francisco where Dederich himself is living. Until recently there was also a house at Westport, Connecticut, and this was used as an assembly point for east coast addicts who were entering Synanon. Newly received members stayed there only briefly before being transferred to the California locations. One reason why the Westport residence had not developed into a permanent residence was that it was too small. Though it was a roomy and comfortable old mansion, it still could not serve as the headquarters for the large, energetic program that this organization likes to operate. Synanon directors believe that any Synanon house needs to have 150 or more residents. Santa Monica has at least 160. They like to have varied activities and jobs for everyone and a full range of possibilities cannot be realized unless there are this many people to carry all the assignments that would be involved. The Westport house has now had to close because of a court ruling on zoning, so a replacement location is being developed in New York City.

The Synanon house in Reno is an outpost that is aimed specifically at the Nevada prison population, and it results from a newer trend in Synanon interests. After establishing its treatment character securely and gaining a wealth of experience in helping addicts, the Synanon program began to extend itself to nonaddicts who needed to be helped with problems that have a basis similar to drug addiction. To oversimplify the dynamics: The addict is seen as a person who is grossly immature, and his immaturity, which led to his dependence on drugs, is in turn made still more pronounced by the deteriorating effect of the addiction. So drug addiction is a symptom of immaturity. For other people there are other kinds of symptomatic behavior that accompany their gross immaturity, and this may often be some form of criminal behavior. The feeling in Synanon now is that this program that has worked so well for addicts would work as well for other kinds of social misfits who may never have seen one bit of heroin, but who have pursued other kinds of destructive behavior. This has led to an exciting and highly significant new direction of service for the Synanon Foundation. Since it does have a somewhat different focus, the Reno program will be described in Chapter 7.

Synanon as a resource for the probation and parole services has more to offer than has so far been utilized. This slowness of the correctional field to welcome its help is partly due to the unorthodox nature of the program, partly to legal difficulties that have plagued the Synanon Foundation, and partly to the bureaucracy of the established correctional programs. The legal difficulties are related to the inevitable fears of the community when a Synanon house is established and it becomes known to the neighbors that "dope fiends" are living among them. In Santa Monica there was intensive, organized resistance from the community, and although the community reputedly has not suffered by a single untoward act on the part of any Synanon resident, the organization has undergone several years of court fights on a variety of actions brought against the organization for the single purpose of ousting them. The California correctional system has felt it necessary to avoid involvement with Synanon as long as it is under fire in the courts, and so has not used it as a resource. It appears, however, that the relationship between Synanon and the California parole system is relaxing and warming a bit, as inevitably it must. The people of Synanon tend to view parole officers with irritating disdain, though they are fully accepting of any probationers or parolees who come their way. They have modified their earlier stand and now are willing to accept such persons who may be sent to them on a non-voluntary basis.

Actually, the Synanon personnel sometimes make it easy for correctional personnel to dislike them. Synanon members tend to have an evangelistic quality in their view of themselves, and at times can talk with arrogant intensity about the virtues of Synanon and the uselessness of any other approach to the drug problem. The correctional worker dealing with Synanon can be aided in maintaining his balanced perspective of it by reminding himself that this very quality which he finds galling is part of the reason for the program's effectiveness. The fierce belief in the rightness of their mission is perhaps an essential factor in its success.

The Synanon members make no pretense of having a religious interest or a religious content in the program in the conventional sense. However, the values that are expressed as basic to the Synanon concept are solidly and aggressively Christian, despite the unchurch-like language of the synanons.

The financial support of Synanon is entirely voluntary. The members become expert at soliciting goods and services, and certain members are assigned to visit local merchants to seek gifts of all kinds of needed commodities. They manage to obtain dependable supplies of bakery goods, meats, and staple groceries. They also manage to win a number of friends who can make cash gifts. Since most of their physical facilities are rented they have high monthly bills to meet, but they have been able to remain solvent. Gradually Synanon is working toward a greater degree of self-sufficiency as revenue-producing activities are developed within the organization.

No Synanon member is paid any salary. Everyone, including the directors themselves, receives a small allowance of pocket money. All major needs are supplied through the communal sharing of food, clothing, and living facilities that Synanon offers. It is a tribute to the magnetic grip of the Synanon idea that these addicts, who have formerly been notoriously discontented with simple pleasures, are proud, happy, and satisfied with two dollars in the pocket and a life that is almost entirely limited to Synanon activities.

A RESIDENTIAL PROGRAM IN PROBATION

A truly pioneering effort to provide residential treatment for addicts on probation is Daytop Lodge, operated by the Kings County probation department at Brooklyn, New York. Financed by a grant of $390,000 from the National Institute of Mental Health, the program was begun in October 1963. A five-year lease was taken on an old mansion with spacious grounds on the southernmost end of Staten Island, and a staff of two persons was hired.

The residence has a population of up to thirty men sent there as a condition of probation when narcotic addiction is the basic problem and when it is not complicated by psychosis, assaultive behavior, or sexual degeneracy. Unlike Synanon, it does not accept women. Initially the court defers sentence for two weeks to allow the defendant to have that much time to try out the residence and see if he and the probation officer think that it should be continued. He then returns to court at which time he is given a suspended sentence to a penal institution and is placed on probation on condition that he remain at Daytop Lodge until the probation office recommends his release.

The program in general has many of the same elements found in Synanon. There is the same emphasis on work and on group discussions. There are differences, however, which are inevitable in view of the compulsory nature of admissions as contrasted with the highly voluntary character of most admissions to Synanon.

The new Daytop Lodge resident is permitted no contact with family or friends until he has begun to show improvement. This ordinarily means that his first three months there are without visitors or even phone calls. This is intended as a means of helping the man concentrate exclusively on his own problem without being distracted and worried by the problems of his family.

Each morning the residents assemble before work to recite the lodge's statement of philosophy. During the day they all work on housekeeping or maintenance jobs around the premises. Certain residents who have been present for a fairly long period and have achieved a good degree of maturity have status as "coordinators" and as such they control the comings and goings of the others. They receive visitors who come on business to the residence, take phone messages, sign resident members in or out, and assist the limited staff in a number of other ways. As in Synanon, this position becomes a status condition and a prize to be worked toward by every resident. It is also a very concrete, and sometimes painful, experience in maturing. Addicts do not assume responsibility easily, and they have a tendency to stick together. It becomes doubly tough for an addict to assume a role in which he must be truly responsible and responsible for supervisory control over some of his fellow addicts. When such an assignment is given a resident he ordinarily finds it a very difficult one at first, and the great sense of status it carries is important in keeping him at it and eager to be successful in it. The use of coordinators is both an economy measure in the operation of the program and also a substantial part of the treatment process.

At noon, following lunch, the group meets for a discussion of philosophical concepts essentially similar to that conducted in the Synanon houses. At least three evenings a week there are group discussions with groups of seven or eight each and with the group membership changing from meeting to meeting. In these meetings, which are considered the most important active ingredient in the helping process, the discussions are conducted with great freedom on topics mainly dealing with highly personal matter. Irritations that have arisen during the day can be exhaustively examined during the discussion session, and the personal problems of each man are subject to detailed discussion that at times can be heated and bitter. A man can be scathingly attacked and stripped of his defenses by his fellow residents, but, as they say, they always put him back together again at the end of the meeting. That is, by commenting finally on some of his better points they enable him to leave the meeting with sufficient restoration of his ego to be able to make use of the critical comments he received.

Here, too, there are absolute rules of no drugs, no alcohol, and no physical violence. It would seem in practice that there must also be a tacitly understood rule of no personal animosity carried away from the meetings. At least it consistently appears to an observer that there is a healthy fraternal feeling in the group.

As a new resident passes his ninety-day period of no contact with persons outside and as he shows evidence of reliability, he has occasional opportunities to leave the premises on errands with one of the coordinators. In fact, the program has moved more toward the use of outside work assignments for residents than was originally expected. The staff is now gaining experience in having men take jobs off the premises, working regularly every day, and coming back to the lodge immediately after work each day. This is a status level that is worked toward and achieved only after evidence of considerable maturity has been shown. Men who have such paid jobs are expected to pay toward their food and lodging costs.

There is nothing about the Daytop situation that provides any physical barrier to the acquisition of narcotics. With the most elementary tactics any resident could arrange to have drugs come into his possession. With some residents going off the premises to work it becomes still more easy for drugs to be brought in. Considering this, the record has been remarkably good, though not perfect. An important controlling factor is a highly intangible condition inherent in the dynamics of the group situation. The pattern of interaction built into this group calls for avoidance of any discussion of former activities as an addict, and instead produces much conversation directed at nonaddiction as a goal that is accepted by the whole group and as a basis of status in the group. Furthermore, there is the carefully cultivated and constantly demonstrated basis for hope that the drug habit can be conquered. Addicts are notoriously convinced that there is no cure for their addiction, and while this may be discounted as simply a convenient rationalization, it must be assumed that the appearance of a basis for hope of cure can be a potent factor in accomplishing that cure. Everything at Daytop is calculated to demonstrate to the resident that cure can be accomplished and that the proof of it is in the other residents all around him who have remained drug-free for longer than he would have thought possible.

There is another controlling factor, however, which is of a more mechanical nature. This is the use of the thin-layer chromotography test. The test is used largely on an unscheduled basis so that the residents never know when to expect it. The Kings County probation office now has its own laboratory to process the test results. This technique provides a type of surveillance which does not alienate the clients, since it is impersonal, and even the client himself can see and accept the practical sense it makes if he is going to be helped to leave drugs alone. The test is also so objective that no one can have any basis for resentment against it if it reveals his relapse. The probation office philosophy is that any kind of delinquent behavior, including drug reuse, will be evaluated carefully before any action is decided upon. There is ordinarily no misbehavior in the residence that would automatically result in revocation of probation.

Unlike Synanon where there are no staff members in the conventional sense, Daytop Lodge has a paid director who has an apartment in the residence. This is the only staff person, other than clinical, research, and probation personnel who visit the residence periodically. A probation officer is expected to visit his men at the lodge once a week and also see their families frequently.

Finding the right resident director for this type of program is all-important and is likely to be exceedingly difficult. Daytop Lodge had a succession of directors who worked hard and sincerely to make the program work, but after a year's operation its leadership was still undistinguished until the fourth director was hired, this time a Synanon product. He was the first Daytop Lodge director who had himself been an addict and his leadership seems to be demonstrating the advantage inherent in that background. Shortly after his arrival he sensed a condition that his predecessors had been unaware of — that most of the residents had been surreptitiously taking occasional drinks or doing a bit of chipping, while the façade of progress they had so convincingly presented was only evidence of their ability to discern just what the probation officers wanted to see, and then to maintain that appearance. When the new director faced the group with his blunt accusations of their "corruptness" there was reluctant but general confession which deeply shook the establishment, but which enabled it apparently to make a new and much better start.

It is encouraging to see that there is a gradually developing community support of the residence and its program, but the experience of Daytop Lodge, like that of Synanon shows that this support is given grudgingly and only after the residence has earned it by strenuous effort. When after the first addicts were moved into the old mansion and the neighbors learned from their newspapers that "dope fiends and felons" were living among them, the protest was explosive. For months afterward hot letters were written to editors, pickets paced the road in front of the house, and court actions were sought. The antagonism is still not eliminated but gradually it is being replaced by acceptance and support. One helpful technique in accomplishing this is the Saturday night open house. The general public is invited to come in on this weekly occasion and the response is so good that sometimes the number of visitors must be limited. The residents take much pride in showing their house and program on these occasions and undoubtedly many people have been won over by finding that the well-dressed, cordial, and likable young men who meet them at the door are actually the supposedly fearsome addicts. During the evening visitors are shown about the building, served refreshments, and given demonstrations of the kinds of group discussions that are held every day. But perhaps the most effective selling device is just the visitors' chance to stand and chat with residents and to discover that they are ordinary people with nothing sinister about them and with much that is appealing.

Another public relations device that serves at the same time as an important program element is a schedule of speaking engagements for the more advanced residents. As one of the most coveted symbols of status in the house, a resident may be assigned to go out to public meetings to talk about Daytop Lodge or addiction generally.

An objective and thorough evaluation of the success of residence programs like Synanon and Daytop Lodge is not yet available. Synanon has been reluctant to release any figures about this aspect of its operation. Daytop Lodge is conducting research through the use of control groups matching the group at the residence, but it is too soon to know what the results will be, even though it is already apparent that while there have been recurrences of addiction among the men on the regular caseload there have been almost none among the men at Daytop. Until the research reports are in we can gain considerable encouragement from the unscientific but persuasive evidence of seeing men and women in these programs living for months and years without drugs when previously they had been among the most confirmed of addicts.

7

The Client as Staff

Using the client as staff is not at all new, but the respectability with which the practice is now clothed is very new indeed. In an older form there was the familiar, vicious practice of using convict guards, with the purpose being only to save money. In its newer form it is a recognition that the prisoner, the probationer, or the parolee may have a skill to offer that can be used to great advantage in helping others, and that by calling on him for his unique contribution to the helping process we contribute substantially at the same time to his own rehabilitation. The skill that he has to offer is an extra capacity for rapport with his fellow offenders, an ability to talk their language with special effect because he has been a part of their same culture. Consequently, he is not easily conned, and he can cut through defenses that would be baffling to the conventional corrections worker. He meets his assigned client with the immense advantage of little or no cultural distance between them, while the professional is handicapped by having to bridge the cultural gap before he can be effective with the client.

As one writer has expressed it, "The nonprofessional has no need to validate his presence in the community, which gives him a considerable advantage over the professional from the outset. Communication can be short-cut and friction eliminated because much is taken for granted as a result of the common background. The nonprofessional has a sense of life's meaning to the client out of their shared experience." [1]

Such reasons are in themselves sufficient to make the use of indigenous workers more and more attractive in recent years, but there is the additional advantage that the helper himself is helped. The client who is tapped for work in helping others may sense that the assignment to guide others to improvement suggests that he himself is improved. More important is the inference that he is seen as having a skill, a competence, a basis for social status; and any device that enhances his self-esteem like this is a material contribution to his improved adjustment. Inherent also is the principle that a person is never more effectively converted to a belief than by the process of having to convert someone else.

Our clients tend to be people who have had little reason to feel that their lives are purposeful, for they are usually on the receiving end of help and so are seldom able to enjoy the ego-building effect of being important to someone else. Alcoholics Anonymous and Synanon have exploited this need with great effectiveness, for in either organization the member finds that one of the most basic expectations is that he will be ready at any time to help another person with his drinking or addiction problem.

Although the client who is being invited to be a helper to other clients is not given responsibility for counseling in depth, it is nevertheless desirable that human contact, and personal rapport on some sustained basis, be involved. This suggests the defect in the idea of the juvenile juries that have recurring popularity with some juvenile courts. Service on such a jury puts the young middle-class person in a pseudo-authoritative role in which he must recommend corrective action for another young person who may or may not be his cultural peer. He only sits in judgment, making decisions on the basis of superficial knowledge of the problem, and does not have a chance to give of himself personally to the other young people who come before him.

A plan with more promise of being helpful to both the helper and the helped is a program that was experimented with in Champaign, Illinois.[2] In that program the same sort of young people who might else-

---

[1] George Brager, "The Indigenous Worker: A New Approach to the Social Work Technician," *Social Work*, Vol. 10, No. 2 (April 1965), p. 37.

[2] Felice Perlmutter and Dorothy Durham, "Using Teen-Agers to Supplement Casework Service," *Social Work*, Vol. 10, No. 2 (April 1965), pp. 41–46.

where be used on juvenile juries were recruited to work with younger children who were in special need of a helpful relationship with an older young person. High school seniors were trained to work in a "pal" or "big brother" type of relationship with children who were in need of such friendship because of personal or family inadequacies. As contrasted with service on a juvenile jury, this kind of experience gave the high school student a chance to have actual training in social work concepts, to have the experience of understanding a youngster's problem instead of acting peremptorily on the basis of the surface aspects in the episode of the moment. The student was given opportunity for growth through a sustained relationship with a youngster whose problems could become understood in some depth and whose need for the helping person would be very evident.

THE FORMER DELINQUENT AS A MODEL

Although the program in Champaign is not concerned with delinquents it involves a principle which is applicable for our purposes and which is being experimented with increasingly in correctional social work practice. Now that workers are getting over their instinctive objection to letting probationers or parolees associate with each other, and now that group work practice has actually brought clients together as a part of the treatment effort, the way has been opened to the next step of deliberately using clients as active agents in the treatment processes for other offenders.

That step has been taken in some instances as part of a structured program which recruits, trains, and employs suitable clients as assistants in regular helping processes. In others, there are highly informal adaptations of a treatment plan to the availability of some suitable client-helper of the moment. An example of the technique developing from this kind of serendipity is the case of Jerry Riley, a probationer in St. Paul, Minnesota. The probation office had been disconcerted to learn that Jerry, an inveterate petty offender, was being placed on probation after a stay in the workhouse. Jerry's Irish temper had kept him in trouble constantly until no one in the city was better known to the police. He was a good worker at his trade of painting, but he drank too much and his hefty physique made him a terror when anyone irritated him. He piled up a long record of convictions for disorderly conduct, assault, drunk driving, leaving the scene of an accident, resisting arrest.

He was just thirty-two years old when one wild episode brought him into court with a series of charges that earned him a total sentence of 240 days. After about 120 days were served the judge decided to suspend the rest and try Jerry on probation.

To the mild surprise of the probation office Jerry had been sufficiently sobered by his workhouse stay so that he actually managed to avoid more trouble for several weeks. When he had been on probation for about a month someone in the probation office who was working with a teen-age boy got to wondering if Jerry could be helpful. The boy was difficult to reach and seemed to be developing the same kind of behavior pattern that had been Jerry's problem. The officer was brash enough to try the idea and called up Jerry to ask him if he would be willing to help give probation supervision to the boy. Jerry was understandably startled by the suggestion that *he* could help someone else keep out of trouble and replied that he would have to think it over. But on thinking it over he decided to try it, and he did, in fact, essentially take over the probation supervision entirely.

After several months of progress the probation office felt that the boy's case was handled with more success than they might have expected without Jerry's help, and they made their appreciation clear to him by asking his help with other individually selected cases. Jerry became caught up in the work and took an aggressive interest in keeping his charges straight. When any boy assigned to him had a court appearance Jerry was right there with him and was probably at his best in the courtroom. He had the advantage of firsthand experience in courtrooms and did not in the least stand in awe of court processes. His experience had also given him an appreciation of the feelings of the young defendant in the courtroom and he could consequently gain tremendously in his rapport with his "probationer" when he stood by him and spoke for him in court. Jerry had an unabashed way of going to the bench and talking turkey with the judge, and had the personality to get away with it.

In due time Jerry was discharged from probation with no new offenses having occurred and with much tangible evidence of improvement. He had become active in Alcoholics Anonymous and had shown on several occasions a remarkable new restraint of temper in provocative situations. He still carries one or two cases at a time for the juvenile division of the probation office.

Generally the cases referred to Jerry are boys who are older teen-agers and the more sophisticated and hostile of delinquents. In the assigning of cases it is necessary that the parents be able to tolerate the plan. This is not always easy, for Jerry's name and record are well known and parents have a natural aversion to the implications of their son's being assigned to such a character. However, Jerry's utter dedication to any case he works with, particularly his practical helpfulness in difficult situations, invariably wins the support of parents. The support of the police has been harder to accomplish, although they have relaxed from their initial shock since they have seen the vast improvement that has been accomplished in Jerry himself when he came to feel a sense of usefulness to others. Newspaper publicity briefly jeopardized the arrangement, and social workers in other agencies were highly critical of it, but the fact that Jerry could ride out these episodes of turmoil and not betray either himself or his assigned cases is still more testimony to the potential that this technique may have.

The experience with this client as an aide to the probation office is similar to the experience of agencies in New York City that have used indigenous workers as homemakers to train overburdened clients in better home management. Jerry had a breezy, informal directness with his boys and their families. It contrasted sharply with the more self-consciously professional demeanor of the probation officers, but it quickly won the loyalty of his "clients." In a similar way the homemakers recruited from the same social strata as their clients were also refreshingly direct and practical. They won the good feeling and cooperation of their clients quickly by their direct attack on ostensible external problems and in this way proved a valuable supplement to the professional workers, who guided the management of the case with concern for the more basic problems involved.[3]

The use of the former client in these ways is an asset not only because of his ability to communicate with clients from similar backgrounds but also because of what he represents in his personal self. He is proof to other clients of the reality of upward social mobility. In hiring staff the administrators of character-building organizations and correctional agencies have typically kept in mind the desirability of finding men and women who would serve as good examples for young people to emulate. While the value of this has not been proved it would have to be said

[3] Gertrude Goldberg, "Untrained Neighborhood Workers in a Social Work Program," Chapter 7 in *New Careers for the Poor* by Arthur Pearl and Frank Reissman (New York: Free Press, 1965).

that with our belief in the usefulness of relationship as a major rehabilitative tool, we would have to believe too in the value of the therapist's presenting a good image. Where strong relationship exists there is likely to be imitation.

However, like so many aspects of correctional efforts, this measure may work best for the person who is in little or no need of the treatment. The boy from a good middle-class home who goes to camp and finds his hero of the moment in his camp counselor is easily capable of having this experience contribute further to his normal social growth if the counselor is a fine example of masculine virtues. But for a deprived, hostile, and delinquent boy the presence in his life of this role model, no matter how excellent, is not likely to have as much impact. The normal boy could look at his handsome, athletic, likable camp counselor and aspire to be like him some day, for there is not a substantial difference between what this adult is and what this boy can reasonably hope to be. The deprived and delinquent boy, looking at the same model, and instinctively aware of the social distance between them, assumes without even thinking about it that his world is a different one from the world of this adult and that he not only cannot reach it, but is not at all sure he wants to. Accordingly, in his case there is need for an additional ingredient in his relationship with the role model. He needs a model who demonstrates the actuality of progress from a disadvantaged condition to a better one. A program that has attempted to exploit this concept is the score program which has been used in Cambridge, Massachusetts, New York City, and Syracuse. Charles W. Slack, who developed it, comments, "Notice that it is not sufficient to bring the delinquent in contact with an individual who can demonstrate the *desired behavior.* We must bring him into contact with an individual who can demonstrate the desired *behavior change.*" [4]

There are many variations possible in applying this principle and each community would need to find its own adaptation according to the diverse kinds of neighborhood problems and kinds of resources available. In the score projects three types of persons are involved. There are, of course, the delinquents who are the objects of the program. A second type of participant is a former delinquent or an ex-convict who has matured and stabilized to the extent of now serving as a model

[4] Charles W. Slack, Unpublished Report to the Ford Foundation on the score Project, Part II, April 1, 1964, p. 24.

of behavior change. The third is a more conventional behavior model, a young man of the typical, conventional middle class, a well-adjusted and successful young businessman. Usually in the SCORE projects this role is played by members of the Jaycees, and the Jaycee organization carries much responsibility for support of the program.

The SCORE program uses a technique which is known as "operant conditioning," a theory of which is that random behavior is observed until some specific desirable bit of behavior occurs and the subject is then promptly rewarded. By consistent and persistent repetition of this the person's pattern of behavior can be modified.

This treatment approach also includes the concept (see Chapter 2) that the confirmed delinquent who is well identified with a delinquent street culture will not respond to a therapist-patient relationship but will accept an employer-employee relationship. The "employment" can be any of a variety of activities concerned with learning about delinquency or learning how to control delinquency or crime. The SCORE program utilizes a number of the principles already mentioned in this or preceding chapters: boys are paid for the work they do, i.e., coming to meetings to discuss the problem of delinquency; boys are rewarded unexpectedly for extra performance; boys are exposed to the behavior model (Jaycee) and the behavior change model (ex-convict); boys are treated as much as possible as equals by all persons involved in the program; boys are paid promptly in cash each time when the work is done; the functioning of the project centers on some type of delinquency research that is likely to be frequently revised to avoid loss of interest by the boys; and when a goal is established for the group it is limited, achievable, and realistic.

In addition to the three types of people mentioned it is necessary to have one staff or professional person. In fact, the continuation of the program depends on this person who coordinates the efforts and furnishes the project's motive power by devising the research or whatever other activity it is that forms the basis of effort and interaction by the component members. But the other persons also serve highly important purposes. The lay members are needed for their help in financing the program but are needed equally for their presence in the meetings. They join in the discussions in an unpatronizing, elbow-rubbing way with the delinquents, participating honestly with them in exploring the subject of the moment. For the delinquents this makes their first opportunity to mix with the remote, law-abiding business world on a man-to-man basis. Any such experience can help to give them a little better image of themselves. The former delinquent, or ex-convict, serves as a link between the laymen and the delinquents, for he is a model to both, an interpreter of either to the other, and, especially, a person who can help the delinquents to articulate their feelings.

When we talk about the score projects in connection with using the client as staff we may be talking about either the former delinquent who enters the project as the behavior change model or the delinquents themselves. For even the delinquents who are the focus of the helping process are received into the project as employees and are, in effect, paid to find their own means of improvement. A typical goal for the project to attack would be a simple reduction in arrests or negative police contacts. The boys may start out with discussions of why they seem to be having their particular brand of trouble — car thefts, fights, or whatever. The discussion has an extra quality of seriousness about it which derives from the fact that they have all been paid to come to the meeting as expert consultants to help the staff person do his research on why boys are delinquent. From this discussion they may go on to explore ideas on how arrests could be reduced. This in turn leads to experimentation with the ideas suggested, and involves keeping score for arrests during an experimental period which can be compared with a former period.

The persons who plan, organize, finance, and direct such a project focus their efforts ostensibly only on the accomplishment of external change. Not the least suggestion is made to the boys that they are being "treated" or "helped." If any change is proposed it is only in respect to statistics, such as the simple reduction in the number of police contacts per month. But experience has shown that outward change does not occur on a sustained basis without some degree of inner and more basic change being likely. Even if nothing does change except the outward behavior this would seem to be a very worthy accomplishment in view of the resulting reduction of offenses. In an appraisal of the New York City score program it was found that "During the first month (February 1963) there were nearly one hundred police contacts, i.e., on the average each of the boys had either three police contacts that month or spent three days in jail. In the month of April there were less than ten negative police contacts and during July when New York City was extremely hot and unpleasant, there were no police incidents or incarcerations of these thirty-four 'worst' boys." [5]

This kind of program is not found within the administration of a probation or parole service. A principle reason is that the funds involved are spent in unconventional ways that would be painful to the auditors who must police the spending in governmental agencies. Money is paid directly to the delinquents themselves and furthermore is paid out on a highly flexible basis with the treatment needs of the moment being more important than penny-by-penny accounting processes. However, it should not be impossible for correctional field services to adapt such techniques, and some probation and parole offices have made moves in this direction. Until the day when governmental agencies can be more flexible with their expenditures, it should be possible to combine public agency staff and private financing for program expenses. If there is an organization or a foundation to pay the direct program expenses, and if the agency does not balk at having some non-probationers in the program, then there should be no serious impediment to the operation of such a program by a correctional agency. St. Paul's Jerry Riley is the obvious type to function as the former delinquent, and probably any large probation office would have Jerry's counterpart who could be persuaded to help with such an endeavor and in doing so would find his own means to improvement.

ADAPTABILITY AS A PROGRAM ASSET

The SCORE idea, obviously, is meant to be extremely fluid. Unlike a more conventional community program which remains fairly fixed while the clients come and go according to their fleeting interests, SCORE attempts to adapt continually to the clients in order to keep them involved and have the maximum possible impact on them. A somewhat more fixed type of program that still tries to adapt to and hold the persons in it was tried in Washington, D.C. A program was developed in 1964 which attempted to utilize disadvantaged young people as leaders in social services with families like their own. The persons involved were not primarily offenders, although arrest records were a part of the evidence of their disadvantaged condition and a reduction of such trouble was part of the evidence of their improvement. The Community Appren-

[5] *Correctional Research*, a publication of the United Prison Association of Massachusetts, Bulletin No. 14, November 1964, p. 38.

tice Program, operated by the Center for Youth and Community Studies of Howard University, simply advertised that jobs were available for young people from sixteen to twenty-one years old who were out of school and who did not at the moment have any pending arrest or sentence.

After extensive interviews and physical examinations ten boys and girls were selected, most of whom had records of delinquency and backgrounds of family breakdown. Employment for them was planned in areas of child care, recreation, and social research, preceded by twelve weeks of training. The training consisted of almost daily group discussions plus meetings with experts who talked with them on various social problem topics. "Starting from their own experiences, the members of the core group were encouraged to examine the process of adolescence, and the problems of living in a poor area of the city. As the group progressed, it drew upon experts to discuss and examine with them areas of knowledge of human services common to all." [6]

This program, supported in part by federal grants, demonstrated some of the problems in developing clients as staff, as well as some of the dividends. Here, the apprentice applicants were brought into an already structured program, and since it was not something that had been engendered by these young people themselves they did not feel a sense of commitment to it. This points up the value of the SCORE approach in which the delinquents have a fairly free-wheeling opportunity to let their own group discussions determine the shape and direction of their endeavors, and so they give themselves more genuinely to the activity. In the Community Apprentice Program it was noticed that the group members were able to avoid responsibility for the outcome of the program and could even feel content with any signs of its failure because that would just reinforce their alien feeling toward the middle-class world.

The Community Apprentice Program nevertheless achieved a satisfying measure of success which perhaps is all the more impressive in view of its initial built-in handicaps. All ten of the apprentices stayed through the training and remained with the subsequent employment satisfactorily. They performed adequately in their work and made notable progress in their own socialization. The improvement was partly in

[6] Mimeographed report of the Community Service Program, Center for Youth and Community Studies, Howard University, Washington, D.C., March 1965, p. 22.

specific skills: "Although the procedures used were not rigorous or stringent, it was clear that the youths' ability to use language had increased
prodigiously. On entering the program, the youth had found it difficult
to perform reading and writing assignments. As they gained more experience in the program, however, they became increasingly competent and confident in their ability to handle these assignments. Since very
little specific remedial instruction was included in the program, the
increased skill might be attributed to a change in self-esteem. That is,
through continued reinforcements of various kinds, the youth had been
convinced prior to the program that they could not perform reading and
writing assignments. However, through engaging in successful nonthreatening and rewarding experiences, their underlying skills may have
become manifest."[7] There was also improvement in general social functioning. "The 'therapeutic process' essentially focuses around ego issues
involving identity, the relationship of the individual and group to meaningful work, a stake in the social system, and that other hallmark of
adolescence — 'action.'"[8]

THERAPISTS ON PAROLE

In the probation setting, or in the general community, it is obvious
that the use of clients as staff can be attempted in many different ways,
and that a high order of flexible ingenuity is called for in seducing the
clients into the program and holding them in it. The fact that probationers can be ordered into an activity has no application here, for this
type of endeavor must be clearly voluntary if it is to have the slightest
effectiveness.

But in regard to parole there is a slightly different condition. Volun-
tariness is important there too, but we are presented with the fact that
before a man becomes a parolee he is involuntarily incarcerated for a
period of time that permits us to expose him to a substantial amount of
training in the guise, perhaps, of group therapy, whether or not he feels
inclined to involve himself in it. If such treatment in the institution
proves effective the prisoner may be ready to work in some helping capacity on being paroled and to do so not only voluntarily but with eagerness.

An exciting experiment and certainly one of the most courageous

[7] *Ibid.*, p. 62.
[8] *Ibid.*, p. 89.

ones has been tried in a unique prison camp near Chapel Hill, North Carolina. As the program started in May 1964, it was a camp for young felons transferred from the state penitentiary, and it was staffed entirely by parolees! This kind of staffing was partly a matter of expediency rather than altogether the original intention, but it produced an experimental program that was a splendid contribution to correctional experience.

The program, known as Chydaru (Chapel Hill Youth Development and Research Unit), was the result of cooperative planning between California and North Carolina corrections officials who wanted to try the use of the therapeutic community with selected first-time offenders. The intent was to operate a small open prison camp with an appropriately experienced professional as superintendent who was to direct the group therapy process. His other staff members would be "culture carriers" — former inmates who had gone through the intensive group process themselves in a therapeutic community setting.

The theory was that inmates who are experienced in the kind of group therapy used at the California Institution for Men at Chino (see Chapter 3) sometimes develop the kind of skill needed for initiating others in the process. Some inmates gain considerably in their maturity and stability; they gain an appreciation of the potency of the group therapy method and develop skill in using the events of the day as content for the discussion sessions. The idea that took form in North Carolina was that men of this kind who had been truly helped might be used as particularly effective staff members in bringing the same helping process to other clients. Hardly less important was the recognition that in this situation the therapist may himself be substantially helped.

The North Carolina prison system acquired a small camp a short distance from the university at Chapel Hill. This semi-rural acreage, with a few simple wooden frame buildings and nothing else but woods, became the prison camp with a capacity of twenty. The staff members were selected from among parolees in California who had been on parole without new trouble for six months to a year and who had shown marked progress in their personal maturation and in their skill with the group therapy process. Six of them accepted the jobs offered them in North Carolina and were transferred there under the usual provisions of the interstate compact on parole. Since no professional had been found for the superintendent's position, one of the parolees was designated superintendent while the search for a professional continued.

The enterprise was backed by the governor of North Carolina as well as the prison director, and it was considered a joint venture of the Prison Department and the Institute of Government at the University of North Carolina. The camp superintendent was administratively responsible to the prison director but the whole project received close professional supervision from the Institute of Government. The prisoners selected to be residents of the camp were young adult felons who were serving first sentences. They were selected jointly by the prison administration and by clinicians from the Institute of Government.

The atmosphere at the camp was utterly unlike any conventional prison setting. Reversing the usual pattern of extreme regimentation, the camp had no daily schedule or any planned and imposed work programs. Each day it was left to the residents themselves to decide what work needed to be done around the camp and to organize and do the job. This created an atmosphere of freedom and brightness that was an impressive departure from the usual tense and repressive mood of prisons. A visitor coming on the grounds would be greeted cordially by a friendly group of young men among whom the staff and residents were indistinguishable from each other. They obviously felt under no pressure and yet it was evident from the projects completed that work was getting done. Furthermore, there was pride in the work accomplished. No one who has been acquainted with prison atmosphere could avoid feeling deeply gratified to find a group of prisoners in a setting where obviously there could be so much more healthful preparation for return to normal community living. And, what is more related to the focus of this book, it was equally gratifying for such a visitor to see a group of parolees functioning with a sense of importance and mission, in a fully genuine situation of responsibility, and with a sense of pride in having a peculiar skill and so a peculiar opportunity to be important. For the staff members were not just holding the camp together; they were actively conducting a therapy program. Every night of the week the staff, all of whom were housed on the grounds, would conduct group discussion meetings, teaching their clients the technique they had learned in their own prison experience.

In addition to the nightly group therapy sessions there were other, smaller group meetings in the afternoons for the discussion of work projects and problems or other special matters. There were also daily meetings of staff with clinicians from the Institute of Government for the discussion of any kind of administrative or treatment issues.

But, of course, the program was not all cheerfulness and promise. Something so radical and so loaded with men with problems is certain to have its daily frictions and potential dangers. One problem with new residents was the convincing they required that the staff members could not be manipulated. There was an understandable assumption on the part of any new resident that the ex-convict staff would naturally be on the side of the inmate in any mischief; so the staff had a constant problem in having to reject firmly the role of fellow convict and to insist strongly on being "staff" in a true sense.

A more persistent problem was the anxiety-provoking nature of so much freedom within the camp. The well-adapted convict has a great appreciation of rules and schedules. This does not mean that he respects them or feels conscientious about abiding by the rules. It does mean that he wants to know exactly what is expected of him and exactly what will occur when he either obeys or disobeys the rules. That way he can decide when it is worth the gamble to defy a rule covertly, and he knows — or thinks he knows — just what objective criteria will be considered when he meets the parole board. But when he is put in a setting with no rules and not even a daily work schedule, and nevertheless knows he has the parole board to face ultimately, the effect is potentially very provocative. How will the parole board know that he has been obeying the rules if there are no rules to obey? How can he know what to do to present himself in a good light if there are no structured and highly specific norms for what constitutes a good record in this kind of place? Because of fears like this some of the residents became too uncomfortable and requested return to the main prison. This too was a challenge to the parolee staff but presumably they would have a special appreciation of the feeling and unusual ability to handle the residents' anxiety in this area.

Although a professional for the superintendent's job was sought throughout the life of the project, no suitable person was found and so the parolee first designated carried that responsibility during the full thirteen months that the camp operated. It was closed in June 1965 because of failure of the state legislature to appropriate funds for its continuance.

For the most part the use of the parolee staff was highly satisfactory, although the experience showed that the steadying influence and close supervision of a professional superintendent was clearly needed. As the group therapy process begins to take hold in such a situation the intensity of the feelings developed calls for not only skill but very dependable emotional stability on the part of the staff. This was a severe test for the parolee therapists and the frustrations developed in them by the impact of the intensifying experience tended to emerge as some potentially dangerous acting-out behavior, both within the camp and in the community. Fortunately no serious problem behavior occurred and no parolee staff member violated parole. It did become necessary, however, to make some reassignments of duties and three of the parolees returned to other jobs in California.

During the latter months of the Chydaru program graduate students from the university were used as replacements for the parolee staff members who left and this seemed to be satisfactory during the short time that it operated this way. The general feeling was that with strong and close professional supervision on the job the parolee therapists could have been quite successful and that this staffing could have been entirely feasible in a permanent program. It is a tribute, finally, to the value of this technique that the parolee who carried the superintendent's role throughout the experiment was subsequently hired as the assistant superintendent of the Southfields Residential Group Center in Jefferson County, Kentucky.

In Reno, Nevada, the Synanon Foundation assists with a unique prison camp which is like the camp at Chapel Hill, North Carolina, in the sense that it is a small open facility with much of the program being presented by persons who are themselves former inmates. Beyond that, however, there are substantial differences.

Nevada's camp on Peavine Mountain north of Reno is an outgrowth of a Synanon program at the main prison in Carson City. The prison warden had invited Synanon to work with inmates in the prison and had been much impressed with the results. The Peavine camp had been operating as an honor camp under the penitentiary administration but it had not had a distinguished career. Anyone looking at the camp would hardly find this surprising. It was a minimal facility consisting of a quonset hut and three trailers. One trailer housed the kitchen and the other two contained bunks for a total capacity of about twenty. The

215

quonset hut doubled as the eating and indoor recreation room. Around this cluster of drab and cheerless accommodations was an equally drab landscape, devoid of anything but sagebrush. There was not even a well on the property, so water had to be trucked in from Reno.

The Synanon group, after having shown its effectiveness in the prison, was invited to participate in the program at the camp and also to advise the institutional classification committee in the selection of inmates for transfer to it. At the camp the twenty inmates are assigned daily to work with other state agencies, going without guard to conservation or forestry projects over a wide area. Three times a week the Synanon group visits the camp in the evenings to conduct discussion sessions or to participate in recreation for the men. The Synanon Foundation maintains a house in Reno from which members go both to Peavine and to the main prison at Carson City to carry on their programs for inmates.

It is a deeply satisfying experience to see such high morale as exists in this inmate group, housed in a physical setting so abjectly poor as the one on Peavine Mountain. There has been almost no problem of escapes, fights, or other prison abuses. The camp has no custodial features at all and the one unarmed guard who is posted there takes no part in the program but acts mainly as a custody representative of the prison.

The significant thing about this for the purposes of our discussion here is that essentially all the persons who conduct program activities at the camp are themselves former institution inmates. Most of them have served sentences for narcotics offenses and, most remarkable, one of the Synanon members who goes daily to the prison and is in charge of the Synanon program there is himself a parolee from that same prison. Unlike the North Carolina experiment, these men are not state employees, and the relationship between them and the prison is only cooperative and quite informal. Nevertheless, the project gives every appearance of being highly successful.

The Peavine camp was the first major instance of Synanon's helping offenders generally instead of limiting itself to addicts. As indicated in the preceding chapter the developing belief of Synanon leaders is that addiction is only a symptom and that Synanon can attack the basic immaturity that leads, in one instance, to narcotics use and, in other instances, to quite different kinds of antisocial behavior. Some of the inmates transferred to Peavine are addicts but usually most of them are not.

While Peavine and Chapel Hill are vastly different from each other in character they both have made a significant contribution to the concept of helping offenders by use of people who themselves have been helped. They both are tributes to the courage of prison administrators who were willing to take a chance on a bold and untried scheme. The fact that the two camps have both shown such potential even with their many differences makes it clear that the concept is a potent and adaptable one.

PRE-PAROLE TRAINING FOR SOCIAL SERVICE

As an example of more deliberate and structured planning for the hiring of parolees there is the New Careers Development Project based at the California Medical Facility, a reformatory at Vacaville, California. This project, financed by a National Institute of Mental Health grant, was set up originally to train selected inmates from various correctional institutions who were transferred to Vacaville for the program. They were to be prepared for eventual work in social service jobs by four months of training while in the institution and a similar period of training on the job after being paroled.

The assumption is that some of the young men in the prison population have had much natural contact with the world of the poor and so have a greater sense of comfort and a greater communicative ability in dealing with poor people. If such inmates have shown improvement under the therapeutic programs offered them in the prison, and if their records do not include alcoholism, use of narcotics, mental illness, or severe offenses against the person, they may be suitable candidates for training as "change and development agents." If they perform satisfactorily through the training period they are paroled to jobs wherein, as employees of the state, they are engaged in social research or other kinds of social service among disadvantaged families.

The training process includes instruction that will give the inmate background information in a wide variety of social problems. Lectures and discussions have included such subjects as the dynamics of current social forces, the effects of automation, the effects of the current population trends, the dynamics of group therapy, mental retardation, cybernetics, the civil rights movement, and the nature of governmental social programs. The men at Vacaville who are in this training program have much more freedom in their institutional schedules than the other inmates. They are much less regimented in their movements about the building and they are free to stay up at night as late as they want. They have classwork each day in the form of seminars and discussions for which they are expected to do a substantial amount of reading. They are provided with plenty of sociology texts and they obviously delve into the material with great interest. Much of the learning process is accomplished with techniques that cause the men to raise their own questions and then search for their own answers. Sample projects are devised in which the men must gather and analyze data, write a report, and present the report for class discussion. Frequent group discussions and role-playing sessions are used.

In this program the inmate is trained to work as a member of a team consisting of at least one parolee and one professional, the latter usually being a graduate student, who enters the program in partial fulfillment of his work toward a graduate degree. The students participate in the training on a part-time basis and later, when the inmates are paroled, it is hoped the team that has thus been developed will continue to function.

The team is seen as having particular usefulness because it cannot be expected that either the professional or the parolee will have a facility for all the types of communication involved. The indigenous worker will communicate well with the disadvantaged families being worked with, but he may not be able to deal easily with government officials, community leaders, and others who must be involved in a social service program. But if the team members who work together have close rapport they, collectively, have a very wide range of effective communication at their disposal.

Although the team idea was an important part of the original planning, it is not being adhered to exclusively. The administrators of the program are careful to be adaptive and flexible in order to exploit their growing experience and to take advantage of any new ways that appear for using these parolees. In a number of instances the change and development agents are working in single assignments and more uses for them are appearing. The executive office of the state has urged the use of more and more inmates trained for social service functions, and the State Bureau of Vocational Rehabilitation has asked to be supplied with such personnel in quantity.

But while there is this good response on the part of governmental units generally there has not been similar good response from the correctional agencies. It is not surprising that correctional institution staff members would take a cautious view of such a program. The inmates in training for this program enjoy a special status in the institution and as evidence of the heresy in the whole scheme, the inmates are granted an easy familiarity on a casual first-name basis with the professional staff members who direct the project. Furthermore, the free-wheeling discussions and the introspective processes of the group permit the inmates to analyze institutional staff and staff-inmate relationships. This can be a deeply unsettling specter for correctional institution officials and it helps to explain why the growing demand for these inmate trainees is coming from outside, rather than inside, the correctional bureaucracy.

In New York the State Division for Youth has also been experimenting with hiring former wards for social service work. With the help of a foundation grant the division has created a special aftercare service for boys released from its START centers (see Chapter 5). In addition to giving the usual intensive counseling services to help the boys make the transition to community living, the project selects and trains a few boys to serve as assistant boys' supervisors. It is hoped that the employment of such boys will help convince the other boys of the genuine regard the state has for them, and of the fact that they actually can aspire to important professional work.

The boys receive training in interviewing techniques, in using community resources, in making observations, and in writing reports. They are paid by the hour and may work part time while attending school. In fact, it is hoped that this kind of employment will give them positive encouragement to pursue further education. As assistant boys' supervisors they are not considered social workers and do not carry responsibility for counseling. Their major contribution is in the process of reciprocal interpretation and data-gathering for research. They are expected to ". . . visit various graduates' neighborhoods, go into their homes, and gather data used in the research study. They talk with the other graduates about employment, school, and community interests. This information, so often guarded and withheld from adults by adolescents, is then shared with the project supervisor. In essence, the two new boy supervisors demonstrate positive models to which other graduates may aspire in their own communities." [9]

In the first year of experimentation with this program the Division for Youth had much reason to feel encouraged. Six boys were trained and hired. The worst that happened in the first year was that two of these left because of their lack of interest. The others were proving to be both useful and interested.

The administrators have been coming to feel that the boys selected for this work should be out of the START center and back in the community for some months of successful living before being chosen and put into this kind of job. A successful period of adjustment makes them a better risk and gives the boy himself the added strength and status that comes from knowing that he really can make the grade as a parolee — just as he must help others to do. This is similar to the situation in the Chydaru camp project, where the employees were parolees who had been out on parole for a few months before being hired to work in the camp. In the Vacaville program, on the other hand, the change and development agents are selected while they are in the institution, and are prepared to start work immediately upon release and without a testing period in the community first. This is an interesting difference. The Vacaville system provokes arguments from those who believe that a parolee should be hired only after he has been out long enough to show some ability to adjust successfully in the community.

The use of clients in sociological research is spreading and is being tried in a number of prisons as well as in field services. Another area in which clients can be used is in teaching, and this has been subject to some experimentation in California with the help of a grant from the Office of Economic Opportunity. In one experiment during the summer of 1965 a number of assistant teachers were recruited from among housewives, high school students, and school dropouts, all from the disadvantaged areas where the schools were. Some were probationers assigned to the project. With four assistants assigned to each classroom, the effectiveness of the teaching was greatly increased. "The assistant teachers were especially adept at enhancing communication with the children, as many of them grew up in the area and knew the ways of the children and their families. They served as translators or 'linkers' be-

[9] *Youth Service News* (New York State Division for Youth, Albany, New York), Vol. 15, No. 3 (Winter 1964–1965), p. 4.

tween children and families, between teacher and families, and between children and teacher. The teacher could take on a new role. She or he was no longer seen as a disciplinarian and did not have to be overly concerned with control problems in a large, overcrowded room of physically active children . . . The assistant teachers visited the homes, helped the families to understand the purposes of school and to encourage rather than minimize the child's participation in learning. They brought back to the teacher and to the daily discussion groups significant information from the home and community to help understand each child's unique approach to the classroom." [10]

But while the increased effectiveness of the teaching process was important, we are more concerned here with the effect on the indigenous assistant teachers. "Many of the staff were persons who had worked hard at menial labor most of their lives — many looked tired when they began the project. Others detested work or obligations, and had been driven to impulse-seeking activities; four were on probation to the project for the summer. During the course of the project, their physical appearances changed, along with their manner of approach to people and to life situations. Many became excited over learning, more thoughtful, creative, and enthusiastic over relations with children, some after nearly a lifetime of tragic economic and social disadvantage." [11]

The experiences in this instance have impressive implications for a vital cooperative effort between correctional programs and school programs.

[10] "Job and Career Development for the Poor," preliminary draft of a report prepared for the California Office of Economic Opportunity by the New Careers Development Project, October 1, 1965, p. 15.

[11] *Ibid.*, p. 16.

8

The Halfway House

An outstanding development in the correctional field in recent years has been the great new interest and wide experimentation in residential programs that might serve in one way or another to help the offender avoid going to or staying longer in a penal institution. The trend provides a distinctly new dimension in the correctional field which had always before offered just two housing choices — the custodial institution or home (probation or parole). It includes an element that has been familiar in other countries but not so well known in the United States: the use of a private agency in the service of the correctional field, often with some kind of subsidy from the state. The best known form of this new correctional facility is the halfway house, often run by private eleemosynary organizations but serving and working closely with governmental agencies.

The halfway house is so well established now that it is easy to forget that it came on the scene very recently, having started in America only during the 1950's. The idea has caught on rapidly, and halfway houses have made their appearance in all parts of the country. It is not surprising that the philosophy, goals, function, and organizational format of halfway houses have been varied and confused. Actually the differences are a healthy sign, for if this type of service is to be of maximum benefit to the correctional field it must present a variety of facilities to serve what is, after all, a highly varied clientele. Variety is also useful by way of testing the different approaches to this kind of community work with the offender and to determine just what are the best characteristics of the halfway house. It is to be hoped that confusion in the philosophical concepts can be reduced as the various facilities learn by doing.

At present the functional characteristics that seem to be common to most halfway houses for adults are the following: (1) to provide permissive but supportive housing to the person who must leave a correctional institution without a suitable job or home, or both; and (2) to give some degree of personal help to the resident in getting him properly adjusted to free society again.

The first purpose is standard among all such facilities and in some instances is extended to include probationers as well as parolees. The second is standard in a general sense, but there is great variation in its application, for halfway houses are widely divergent in their beliefs on how far they should go in actively providing control or counseling to the resident. A halfway house program may be highly structured, with required participation in various elements of it, or program as such may be nearly undetectable in a very casual and permissive facility. This will depend largely on the philosophy of the organizational or denominational background which supports and guides the administration of the house. While the kinds of programs that are appropriate to the halfway house setting will be discussed here, it seems logical first to consider the administrative conditions under which they operate.

ADMINISTRATIVE BASES OF HALFWAY HOUSES

Privately operated Dismas House, the first widely known facility of this kind, was organized in St. Louis in 1959 when Father Charles Dismas Clark, with funds contributed from a Jewish friend, bought an old school building in which the service was established and still operates. Dismas House is organized as a foundation and is dependent entirely upon private contributions plus fees from the residents. Roncalli House in Minneapolis, a much smaller operation, is similarly operated as an independent Catholic facility. The American Friends Service Committee is another religiously motivated group that has moved into this kind of work. Its Crenshaw House in Los Angeles was one of the first halfway houses, created in 1958 upon the urging of Kenyon Scudder. (He had first enlisted the Friends' cooperation in establishing a prison visiting program for men at Chino who had no visitors.) The Crenshaw House director was responsible to a governing board known as the Crenshaw House Committee, and it is of significant interest to note that at least two former residents were appointed to this committee. Crenshaw House eventually closed when its director moved to another job. More recently the Friends have established another, similarly administered house in San Francisco, known as Austin MacCormick House. Still another denominational house that has become well known is St. Leonard's House in Chicago, which is operated by Episcopal clergy who are responsible to a board with mostly Episcopal members.

Though houses like these ordinarily are not official instruments of the church, they do operate with the advantage of support and prestige that stems from a great denomination. On the other hand, it is possible for a facility to get its start and continuing impetus from nothing more than the energy of one person, and this was essentially true of the William C. Harness House in Stockton, California. Though it has a lay citizen board, it was solely the idea of Mrs. Alice Harness who wanted to do something for former prisoners and so started a house named after her son, a World War II military casualty. Without broad support and without experienced or professional direction, however, Harness House has had an uncertain existence. Its ability to survive and to continue to be useful is a tribute to the dedication and perseverance of Mrs. Harness, who functions as the director.

In substantial contrast to these administrative arrangements there are several halfway houses that have the ample sponsorship and financing of the United States Government. It could be argued on a technicality that these are not properly included among halfway houses, but they do serve the same basic purpose and so in this sense belong to this discussion. These are the federal prerelease guidance centers, and, as the name implies, they are used for men who actually have not yet been paroled. Customarily, when the release plan for a federal prisoner includes placement at one of the centers he is sent there after having been approved for parole and with a future parole date set. In most cases the men have from three to four months left to serve when they are transferred to the prerelease guidance center, so they still are in a prisoner status, even though they begin to enjoy the relative freedom of what is essentially a halfway house.

The six centers, located in New York City, Washington, D.C., Chicago, Detroit, Kansas City, Missouri, and Los Angeles, are all operated by or for the Federal Bureau of Prisons as an integral part of the bureau's services. The center in Detroit is operated under a contractual arrangement with the state of Michigan so that it may be used jointly for state and federal cases. For the purposes of the Michigan Parole Board the center is identified as a state penal facility so that the state may transfer men to it before parole just as the Federal Bureau of Prisons does. The arrangement is a sensible one; it suggests a way for such a facility to be maintained in a locale where there is need for it, but not enough need if it must be solely for state or solely for federal cases. In this instance it is the federal government which operates the center, with the state contracting to pay a sum per diem for each man it places there. The state also provides one staff member, the employment counselor. The prerelease guidance center in New York City departs from the usual administrative pattern by being operated by Springfield College on contract to serve the Bureau of Prisons.

Contrary to the ideas of Father Clark, who was opposed to governmentally operated halfway houses ("If you let the state in, they'll ruin everything"),[1] there is an increasing trend on the part of state governments to develop their own community residential centers or to partially subsidize the operation of private ones. In Delaware a house known by its address, "308 West Residence" (Wilmington), is operated by the Correctional Council of Delaware (a prisoners' aid agency) but in a house owned by the state. Since the state makes the property available at no cost, this constitutes a material support of the project in itself. In addition now the state makes a direct grant in aid each year and the county of New Castle also appropriates funds for the operation of the residence.

In California a challenging new trend was established with the Community Correctional Center located in Oakland and opened in 1965. It is an all-purpose facility administered by the Parole and Community Services Division of the Department of Corrections. In addition to housing parolees as in a typical halfway house, it is also headquarters

[1] William Krasner, "Hoodlum Priest and Respectable Convicts," *Harper's*, Vol. 222, No. 1329 (February 1961), p. 61.

for all the parole officers in that region, and is used as a center for recreation, counseling, and group meetings for any clients, whether or not they are residents. California is planning to develop more such centers.

An even more recent development of this kind is found in the several Community Correctional Centers in Kentucky. These are being developed with special emphasis on vocational training as a service to the many men from rural areas who emerge from prison with almost no job skills. The first center, located in Harlan, opened in September 1965 and is the first of several to be operated with financial support from the Economic Opportunity Act and administered by the Kentucky Department of Corrections.

In juvenile work one of the first state-operated facilities was the Riverside Group Home in Tacoma, opened in 1962. The Washington State Department of Institutions, which operates this home for boys who are leaving state training schools, has been sufficiently gratified by the results to open another such home more recently in Seattle.

Michigan has become more heavily involved in halfway houses for juveniles than most other states. The state experimented first with use of one cottage on the grounds of the training school in Lansing, and then an appropriation was made to establish several separate houses. These were started in 1964 and within a year there were in operation five houses for boys and one for girls.

In Los Angeles halfway houses for teen-agers have been tried mainly as private endeavors, but in New York similar programs are state operated. Typical is the New York State Group Residence for Girls, located in a building owned by the state in Manhattan and operated to serve girls being released from the girls' institution at Hudson. Also owned and operated by the state is Seaman House, which is a New York City facility serving boys being released from state institutions. The Group Residence for Girls serves only the girls' training school at Hudson and so is administered by that institution as an extension of its own program. Seaman House, however, serves several institutions in the eastern part of the state and so is operated by the Home Service Bureau of the State Department of Social Welfare.

Halfway house administration has shown the pattern of development that has been seen in other areas of correctional history in which private or denominational sponsorship has taken the lead and governmental support has followed. It seems likely that governmental involvement will become more and more the rule. There probably will always be certain well-known and successful facilities that will remain purely private, but already it is evident that many privately sponsored halfway houses falter soon after getting started because they lack the financial backing or administrative resources necessary to keep them going. Even when a house is adequately supported and directed it may suddenly close if the director leaves for another job and no replacement is available. Finding the right person to run the house is at once the most difficult part of its operation and the most crucial element in its quality. The private organization that attempts to operate a halfway house may have considerable difficulty in locating a director who has the special qualities of personality and temperament needed for this demanding job, and this points up the advantage that a governmental operation has. The governmentally operated house is likely to be a part of a large correctional program in which experienced persons can be found for promotion or transfer when a sudden vacancy occurs. Father Clark had a point in arguing for the qualities of personal dedication that motivate the private operation, but in the long run a sizable proportion of halfway houses will need to be operated by government agencies for the sake of the dependability of their staffing and financing.

The movement of government into the halfway house programs in very recent years is also part of a swing away from massive penal institutions. That is, it represents more than just a means of helping a man who has left the institution; it is beginning to serve as an experiment in ways to reduce the use of prisons in the first place. This, of course, is a noble motive but, typically, the impetus comes first from quite practical considerations. With their rapid population growth many states have been faced with having to build enormously expensive additions to their penal facilities unless more reasonable alternatives can be found. The halfway house presents an appealing device for easing the situation, although such houses will have to be provided in far greater quantity before they will help substantially in reducing the pressure on prisons and training schools. However, as experience is gained with them their other assets become evident and argue further for their use. They provide a measure of control and supervision that is much greater than the usual parole supervision for the man not yet ready for the latter, while at the same time they involve the resident in community employment and social life, in contrast to the artificial and regimented life of the prison.

One argument for the halfway house is the often underrated problem of overdue parolees. It is seldom realized how many prisoner days are added to the cost of the average institution by the difficulties in making plans for home and job in cases in which parole is otherwise approved. An indication of this is seen in a study done in the Federal Reformatory at Chillicothe, Ohio, for the year 1958.[2] There were 398 men released on parole that year and 172 of them were overdue. Of these, 31.5 percent were overdue more than 20 days. In that one prison in that one year there was a total of 3923 overdue man days. Lack of employment was the major reason for the delay, although it is ironical that half of those who were delayed for lack of employment were finally released without a job anyway. Altogether, 87 percent of the delays were due either to lack of employment or to lack of a suitable home plan, both of which are problems that would have been answered by the availability of halfway house facilities. "Most correctional officers will agree that the presence of an abundance of overdue parolees may have a demoralizing effect upon the inmate population and the parolee himself. Overdue cases also hamper the efficient operations of correctional administration, both in the institution and in the parole and probation offices. In addition, of course, unnecessarily overdue parolees constitute some economic waste due to the cost of their additional confinement."[3]

It has been traditional with parole boards not to release a prisoner until he has a job. There is sound basis for putting great emphasis on employment, but there are also times to make exceptions. A strict adherence to the rule leads to solutions that are not really solutions. The parole officer in desperation gets the promise of a job for the inmate, but without achieving any real appropriateness in the job selection. It gets the man out, but it does not serve the intended purpose otherwise, since a discontented parolee on an unwelcome job is a poorer risk than a parolee who has a few days of unemployment while looking for a job that he wants.

A recent development in New York State shows that parolees released to jobs they themselves found have a distinctly better success

[2] Bruce K. Eckland, "Overdue Parolees in a Federal Reformatory," *Progress Report* (U.S. Bureau of Prisons, Washington, D.C.), Vol. 8, No. 1 (January–March 1960), pp. 5–14.
[3] *Ibid.*, p. 5.

rate than parolees released to jobs found by parole officers. The group of men released without a job at all, but on reasonable assurance that with the parole officer's help a job could soon be found, also had a better success rate than the parolees who went directly to jobs found by the parole officers.[4]

This strongly suggests the great usefulness of the halfway house which can help get men out without delays beyond the parole date and can give the parolee close supportive supervision while he finds his own employment.

PHYSICAL PLANS AND LOCATIONS

As halfway houses have started they have had to grope for answers to such questions as the kinds of neighborhoods to locate in, the kinds of buildings to use, and the ways to make peace with neighbors. A variety of neighborhoods have been used without the issue of which is best being settled. St. Leonard's House in Chicago and Dismas House in St. Louis have been located in blighted areas that have high delinquency rates. While they can theorize that their residents feel more comfortable in surroundings such as many of them came from anyway, they cannot feel certain that this is the final answer. Just one thing is fairly certain and that is that in such neighborhoods there is less objection from neighbors.

However, this too is not an absolute. When the Friends set out to establish Crenshaw House in Los Angeles they wanted to avoid any location that would suggest a downgrading of the residents, and preferred something that might be a modest step up instead. Accordingly, they picked an old house in good repair, located in a reasonably quiet, respectable, and stable neighborhood. They saw it as important for the neighborhood to be well integrated and for the house to be close to public transportation. The same conditions apply to their other house, Austin MacCormick, in San Francisco. Before opening Crenshaw House, members of the Friends Service Committee visited all the homes in the neighborhood to interpret the proposed program and test the sentiment. They found no opposition at all, and the local advisory committee which they appointed to deal with community relationships had very little work to do.

[4] John M. Stanton, "Is It Safe to Parole Inmates without Jobs?" *Crime and Delinquency*, Vol. 12, No. 2 (April 1966), p. 150.

Most halfway houses have found that the old house, built fifty years or so ago, with its two and one-half or three stories, big rooms, and average neighborhood has been the best facility available. Not every time, however, does such a choice meet with neighborhood acceptance. One example of the fierce resistance that sometimes arises has been the vehement and sustained reaction of the neighbors of Daytop Lodge (see Chapter 6) on Staten Island. Not quite a usual halfway house, Daytop invited the intense opposition because of its location in a particularly conservative residential area, and because of serving drug addicts, a group that tends to be frightening to the average person. Whether the neighborhood is inimical or not, there is a tendency to feel now that in opening a new house it is best just to move in and start up without advance preparation of the neighborhood, but with subsequent courting of neighborhood acceptance to whatever extent the circumstances suggest.

It is rare to find a halfway house occupying a building that is designed and newly constructed for that specific purpose, but one instance of this is the new one for boys built by Washington State near Seattle. Boys who were already living in the Tacoma Riverside Group Home (an old but comfortable frame house) were consulted to get their ideas on how it should be designed. They specified, for instance, that it should be a two-story house (like home) and that instead of either single rooms or large dormitories the sleeping rooms should accommodate three or four boys each.

Church property has occasionally been adapted for halfway house use. The federal prerelease center in Los Angeles has leased a former Baptist church and seminary, and with a nominal amount of remodeling has made it very appropriate to its new use. It is located in a lower economic but fairly well-preserved residential area that offers the advantage of good accessibility to jobs and transportation, but the disadvantage of a high incidence of narcotics use nearby. The Detroit prerelease center is in a church parish hall that had become unused in a transition neighborhood, and the center in New York City also uses church property of this kind. A departure from the usual housing arrangement is the Chicago prerelease center which is located in a portion of a downtown Y.M.C.A. residence. It is a multi-story, hotel-like building in which a block of rooms has been leased to the Bureau of Prisons. Space for administrative offices is included so that it is all an integrated unit on the fifth floor. The newest prerelease center is also in a Y.M.C.A.

residence building, occupying the third floor of an unattractive, out-worn Y.M.C.A. in an older part of Washington, D.C.

Location of a residence in a neighborhood of good quality might lead to local opposition to the facility, but whether the neighbors fight it or only politely ignore it the result may be some feeling of isolation for the halfway house. In New York City, Hudson's Group Residence for Girls is in a building that had previously housed a private residential pro-gram. They find that they have no problem with the neighbors, but neither do they have any useful rapport with the middle-class neighbor-hood, in which the girls are not entirely comfortable. This tends to force the girls' continuing association with their former neighborhoods.

In looking at the range of possibilities and experience it would seem that as long as there is reasonable neighborhood toleration, the halfway house can be operated successfully in either a deteriorated neighbor-hood or in a much better area, but that the best choice is probably an area that is as high as or somewhat higher than the average level in back-grounds of the halfway house residents. It is evident too, that the loca-tion is not as important as the quality of the staff and the atmosphere of the living situation that they create.

There have been interesting experiments with housing halfway house programs in already existing facilities for housing and feeding indigents. In Los Angeles, the Midway Center, operated by the Volunteers of America, was housed in the Clifton Hotel, a residence largely devoted to serving homeless men, principally alcoholics. While this offered housing that could easily be adapted to the use of ex-prisoners without neigh-borhood objection, it proved to be a partial handicap too. The name of the hotel was a little too well known and its association with alcoholism made it difficult for men to get jobs while having to give that address.

However, experience elsewhere suggests that this handicap can be avoided. In Minneapolis, Roncalli House operates as part of the larger House of Charity which includes a residence for alcoholics and a large daily free meal service for indigents. This halfway house program is operated in the same building with the residence program for alcoholics, and a certain amount of mixing between the two kinds of residents occurs. However, the fact that the two operate under different names, even though housed in the same building, has helped to keep any stigma from transferring from one program to another.

A similar background is found in the St. Joseph's House of Hospitality, operated by the St. Vincent de Paul Society in Pittsburgh. This was a charitable housing and feeding program operated for indigents, and in 1961 a halfway house feature was incorporated into it. A Penal Committee of the St. Vincent de Paul Society was formed to govern the new program which was carefully geared to the needs and requirements of the Pennsylvania Parole Board.

In discussing this aspect of halfway houses a type of facility should be mentioned that is very close to the halfway house idea and sometimes is confused with it. This is the preparole or prerelease center that is sometimes developed as part of a correctional system. Michigan, Wisconsin, and Colorado have well-known centers of this type. In one sense they can be considered halfway houses — that is, they are separate from the prison, they serve inmates who are approaching their parole or release dates, and they provide new freedom and training for the inmate. However, unlike the usual halfway house, these centers do not involve community living. The men in them are still inmates and they do not have jobs in the community. Another sharp difference is that such centers, with their populations of 50 to 300 men, are massive in size compared with the typical halfway house population of a dozen or less.

Colorado's Pre-Parole Release Center, which is considered "minimum custody," is located six miles from the State Penitentiary at Canon City. The program provides much less regimentation than the prison and there are daily class sessions to reacquaint men with the business of living on the outside. Outside speakers are scheduled to talk to the men about seeking and holding employment, about parole regulations, automobile operation, budgeting and wardrobe tips, plus many other topics. Many educational movies are shown.

In Wisconsin the Walworth Pre-Release Center performs a similar function for men transferred to it from three different penal institutions. Walworth makes a little more attempt to get the men into the community on a limited basis, as the inmates may at times go out for some recreational activities or for drivers' license examinations.

The Michigan Parole Camp, with a similar intensive educational program, is on property adjacent to the Jackson Prison and has a capacity of 160 men in its wooden barracks set in a camplike wooded area.

All these facilities work hard at the task of preparing inmates for their return to outside competitive living, and they seem to be having some effect in reducing the return rate. They serve a distinctly useful purpose, but the inmate who needs a halfway house placement on his release still has need of such placement even though he has gone through a prerelease center. The prerelease center is not located where the man will be going to live and work, it does not get him started in an actual outside job, and because it is a large facility and an integral part of a state correctional system it has the prison culture about it instead of the more normal community-living character that a small halfway house strives to provide.

PROGRAM

One professional person in the business is fond of remarking that "A halfway house without a program is just a flop house." After viewing a number of such facilities any observer is likely to agree. However, it is not always easy to define the program, for a good halfway house tends to have some of the qualities of family living, and how can we ever define "program" as we find it in a family? An ordinary family is likely to have no program at all in the usual institutional sense, and yet the close relationships and constant informal business of family living may be the most richly satisfying program to be found.

It is in respect to program that differing philosophies of halfway house operation reveal themselves most. A halfway house may be established with the clear purpose of being helpful to the residents in an active personal treatment sense. If so, the facility is likely to have counselors on the staff who help with job finding, who conduct group discussions, or who provide personal casework help. Attendance at group discussions or educational sessions may be required.

In other facilities the philosophy may be to provide only a shelter while the resident finds his own means to survival in the community. In some such houses no employment counseling is provided and it is left entirely to each man to find his own job. But, if so, it is not a matter of the house having no concern with these personal problem areas. Usually a house, such as Dismas, which does not provide casework service, for instance, will have an understanding with an appropriate local agency to which residents are sent for counseling as needed.

As an example of the effort to provide aggressively active help to its residents, 308 West Residence in Wilmington, Delaware, includes on its staff two caseworkers plus part-time consultants in psychiatry, psychol-

ogy, and group therapy. Each resident has regularly scheduled interviews with an assigned caseworker and is expected to attend the two
group meetings each week when personal adjustment problems are discussed. The residence attempts to get the men actively involved in
community life through the use of volunteers who come regularly and
sponsor such activities as Great Books discussions, woodworking projects, church attendance, Alcoholics Anonymous membership, and participant sports like bowling and baseball.

Differing philosophies will also be reflected in the kinds of rules that
govern a halfway house program. In general the halfway houses try to
avoid the prison atmosphere of regimentation by giving the residents a
chance to use real freedom. The federal prerelease guidance centers are
probably the most controlling in this respect, since their residents are
still in a prisoner status. This means that rules about coming and going
must be fairly exacting; residents must sign out when leaving the building and must keep the center advised where they are at all times. In
leaving the premises evenings or weekends residents must have passes
which are subject to exacting time rules.

When a man is released from prison to a federal prerelease center he
travels by bus to the center by himself despite being still in a technical
status as a prisoner. There is usually little difficulty about the men arriving satisfactorily. Any absconding is likely to come later.

Curfews are common in most halfway houses, with 10 P.M. or 11 P.M.
being usual on week nights. The problem is in deciding what to do
when a resident returns later than curfew time. In a few of the houses
the door is locked at curfew time and any resident returning too late is
simply refused entrance and is on his own. More likely, though, he is
given a chance to explain and is admitted if there is a reasonable excuse
for the lateness. St. Leonard's House, because of its location in a high
delinquency area, keeps its doors locked all the time and at curfew time
each night the cylinders in the locks are changed. In some houses the
door is not locked at any time and if there is any understood curfew
time this is enforced mainly by letting the residents handle it in their
group discussions.

Fairly typical of house rules were those of Crenshaw House which
were simply no liquor, no women in bedrooms, no illegal activities. At
Austin MacCormick House rules are even less apparent. According to
its director, ". . . we have no rules or regulations as such, i.e. nothing

written down. We proceed on the assumption that a man coming here knows adult responsibility; conversations are held with him to hopefully alleviate the need for the difficulties . . . there is perhaps a greater amount of freedom here than in many other halfway houses and . . . so far, we seem to feel that it is working rather well on the whole. There seems to be a better than average concern and sense of responsibility one for another than we could have anticipated. For example, one resident in recent weeks had been using liquor more increasingly (he has subsided in the last few days) and the other residents helped on several occasions to bring him back home from downtown bars, help him to bed, counsel with him, etc."[5]

The absence of rules tends to suggest that there will accordingly be some freedoms that have special appeal to the newly released parolee. If there is no rule against raiding the refrigerator, for instance, there is likely to be an expectation that residents may indulge in snacks when they wish. At the Los Angeles federal prerelease center the refrigerator is kept well stocked and it is understood that residents may help themselves for snacks when they come in from work or during the evening. Food is of immense psychological importance and this privilege not only can be a calming and satisfying factor, but can also reduce pilfering and the strains that it causes in the house.

At 308 West Residence the residents are free to take what they want from refrigerator and pantry and to make their own lunches to carry to work. At Shaw House in Washington, D.C., however, the experience was that when the refrigerator was so freely available at all times it tended to interfere with proper meals. The men would revert to old habits and eat snacks when they wanted to instead of showing up for meals. This also had the effect of reducing attendance at the evening discussion groups. So in order to get all the men to meals together with the advantage of greater "family" feeling the practice was started of locking the kitchen immediately after supper was served every day. At Shaw House this seems to be a useful and effective procedure.

Whatever the kind of rules, the halfway house setting will provide the resident with a much less regimented life than the one he was accustomed to in the institution. The halfway house director will have to be prepared for the difficulties this can produce. Sometimes a prison inmate may be granted a parole fairly promptly on the basis of a good

[5] Stanley Epstein, in a letter to the author, May 18, 1965.

apparent adjustment as seen in his general obedience to the rules, but he may be a conformist who can adapt to the prison regimentation when necessary to suit his own purposes, though without any real inner improvement. On release to a halfway house such a person may be a surprise because of constant misconduct, in contrast to his behavior in prison. In the atmosphere of greater freedom he loses the exacting guideposts that surrounded him in prison and he shows that he has learned nothing about developing his own inner controls for handling his freedom.

Some halfway houses may assume that such a resident is out of place in such a facility, since they make little pretense of trying, in the short time they have, to do a character-building job on persons who are not yet ready to use the halfway house. But a few of the houses may utilize their active group discussion program to accomplish a treatment effect with this problem resident. This is more likely to be true of the specialized houses which function as part of a treatment continuum for certain types of offenders. An example that may be cited is the East Los Angeles Halfway House which is a state facility for paroled narcotics addicts.

The most usual specific program feature in halfway houses is the use of group discussions. This will vary from a once-a-week "house meeting" to an intensive group therapy practice with meetings up to five times a week or more. The simple house meeting may be little more than a gripe session wherein residents argue over rules and procedures and try to work out their immediate surface problems of adjustment to the residence. The more therapeutically conducted sessions will be held oftener in order to have maximum impact during the brief time the men are in the program. In the East Los Angeles Halfway House where the length of stay averages three months, the group therapy sessions are held every evening. In this facility the resident does not just leave when he has a job and feels ready to go on his own. He leaves only with permission granted as a joint staff and group decision. So the nightly group sessions are conducted as in the Highfields programs, with emphasis upon self-examination and group responsibility for all members.

In addition to the free-ranging group discussions there are sometimes other kinds of group activities of a specific educational nature. The federal centers, for instance, arrange weekly meetings on various subjects regarding employment or other specific aspects of socialization. These group discussions can also be as ineffectual as petty gripe sessions or a vital process in making a cohesive family atmosphere with high morale. The difference is an indefinable one that is likely to reflect the skill of the staff. An interesting example of what this can lead to occurred in Crenshaw House where the residents developed a strong group feeling and even a sense of responsibility toward other men who are yet to be paroled.

In the Crenshaw House group meetings the idea grew that in addition to a halfway *residence,* many men needed a halfway *job.* This would be a temporary job placement of a low-pressure sort that would give a man some immediate work and pay while he got accustomed to working again and while he looked for a more permanent job. The men reasoned that no one would be in a better position to understand and help the new parolee in such a situation than other parolees, so they proceeded to plan a "halfway job" program.

One of the men was a sign painter with skill in silk-screen work and all aspects of poster painting and display work. He suggested that in that kind of work there were jobs at various levels of skill, making it a suitable business for unskilled men to work in temporarily. The residents agreed and so the painter resigned from his job to set up a business in sign painting and silk-screen work. Without leaving their own jobs eight other residents joined the venture by contributing all the spare cash they could get together for capital, and by working evenings and weekends to fix up the store building they rented and later by helping with the sign painting. Their hope was that once the business was operating successfully they could regularly offer temporary jobs to men who had no employment prospects at the time of parole eligibility.

It was a noble experiment and it deserved a better fate than it received. To be effective, of course, it had to have the sanction of the state correctional authorities so that the parole board could properly grant parole with such a job plan. But a large bureaucracy moves ponderously, while the parolees themselves are impatient; so the business and the dream ended after nine months of working unsuccessfully to achieve financial security and state recognition.

While some halfway houses simply provide a home for a man while he looks for his own job, the new Community Correctional Centers in Kentucky offer a sharp contrast to this. These, in effect, are special-purpose halfway houses that seek to meet the needs of men under age twenty-five who have little education and no job skills. The centers represent a synchronization with related programs that goes far beyond the independent functioning of most halfway houses. Because they are operated by the same governmental department that operates the prisons they can provide a continuum of training from the institution to the halfway house. While he is in the prison the inmate can be given a start in his vocational training and then be granted early parole for placement in a Community Correctional Center. There he continues his training in a program that is identical not only to the institutional vocational training program that he has come from, but also to the training in the state vocational schools, so he may transfer to one of these later with no loss of academic progress. The early parole is a fairly essential part of the process since it is otherwise difficult and sometimes impossible to get a man to accept placement in a Community Correctional Center when it is not in his home community.

The Community Correctional Centers, as the name is meant to imply, are also available to the local courts as temporary placements for diagnostic purposes. The centers include on their staffs a psychologist and a vocational guidance counselor in addition to the director and the kitchen and maintenance staff. The centers, which are initially financed by federal grants, are somewhat larger than the usual halfway house, for they may accommodate up to twenty-five residents each.

Recognition of the crucial nature of the employment problem is a primary aspect of the program in any halfway house even though most of them are not giving vocational training such as that offered in Kentucky. The smaller houses make no special staff assignment for employment assistance, but those that are larger tend to consider the employment counselor a highly important staff position. As a partial deviation from this view, Shaw House has two caseworkers and no employment counselor. Their belief is that the caseworker should give the whole range of personal counseling service, so each resident deals with his assigned caseworker regarding employment or any other personal problem areas.

The importance of employment is also a prime factor in the location of a halfway house. Since most of the residents will not have cars while they are still in residence, it becomes important to them for the house to be located conveniently close to public transportation routes and not too far from major job areas.

HOUSE MANAGEMENT PRACTICES

A problem faced by nearly every halfway house is the collection of board and room charges. Operation of such a facility requires a budget that will permit the housing and feeding of any resident without charge until he begins to work and have an income. In several instances it is forbidden for the new resident even to look for work during the first few days. Roncalli House, for instance, requires a new resident to remain in the house and work on housekeeping jobs for two weeks before looking for or taking a regular job. They consider this a helpful step in getting the resident gradually accustomed to his new situation.

The federal prerelease centers are about the only ones for adults that make no charge for board and room even when the resident is working. This relates to the fact of the resident's technical status as a prisoner and the traditional assumption that the prisoner does not pay for his care. They do, however, actively counsel with the resident regarding the handling of his money and they insist on a certain amount being saved regularly. In other houses the charges vary from $15 to $25 per week, and at Dismas House, if the man has paid dependably, a percentage of all he has paid is returned to him when he leaves the house. This grows out of Father Clark's original reluctance to charge at all. He was persuaded to make charges for the sake of encouraging a sense of responsibility in the clients, so this partial refund is the compromise.

In one house the resident is expected to pay for board and room beginning immediately with his arrival at the house, and whether or not he has a job. Either he must use for this any money he had on discharge or else he is expected to pay the arrearages he has accumulated when he does get work. Residents at Dismas House who are unemployable not only are not charged, but may be paid $5 per day for work within the residence.

Collection of the board charges is a continuing problem in most houses. Collections range anywhere from 50 to 98 percent of amounts owed, depending on the general climate of the house, type of residents, and the collection technique used. It is easy to suspect, too, that the percentage will depend to some extent on the basic financing of the house, for the director who knows that he has fairly secure financial backing will have less motivation to put insistent pressure on the residents to pay regularly.

Whatever the collection rate the halfway house cannot hope to recover a large percentage of its costs ·through the charges to the residents. While the financing will vary greatly, an indication of what to expect is given in the income figures of 308 West Residence in Wilmington. This halfway house, which charges residents $15 per week and also asks them to work two and one-half hours per week in the house, had income of $37,718 in 1964. Of this amount only $1650 came from rent collected from residents. The following year the rent collections increased for reasons which the director describes as follows in a 1965 report: "The heartening increase in rental income is due almost entirely to our improved rental collection techniques, administered by Mr. Green. Every Friday night Mr. Green has a rent conference with each resident, at which time the resident has the opportunity of paying or arranging housework for his room and board."

Another aspect of house management that has been of concern to administrators is the question of what categories of offenders should be accepted and which, if any, rejected. It has been common to find that such categories as sex offenders, homosexuals, narcotic addicts, and flat-time dischargees have been barred from halfway house admission. These restrictions have perhaps been characteristic of the early, groping period of halfway house operation and a proper aspect of the caution that is wise in starting an untried kind of program. Some of the houses that have started with such restrictions have since shown an encouraging tendency to try any type of person who seems to need what a halfway house has to offer. Father Clark had a mildly surprising intake restriction in the early days of Dismas House. "Not many first-timers — they're not the best risks — too many of them still think they can make that one big strike." [6]

Even though most halfway houses have now had the courage to try accepting any type of offender, there is still a need to exercise skill in selection, as there is value in having a balanced variety. This problem is seen in one of the halfway houses which has a very noticeable carry-over of the prison culture in it, with cliques that form and align themselves against the staff. There is an instinctive avoidance of visitors, an air of distrust, and wherever there are locks on doors, cabinets, or desks there are surrounding jimmy marks. A major reason for this seems to be that this house accepts men exclusively from only one institution, a reformatory. For that reason all the residents are young men in their early twenties at most and they have known each other before in the institution. Halfway house operators seem to agree generally that the younger men are more rebellious and that several of them together will often become a clique in which each strengthens the rebellion of the others. To have exclusively young men, and then to have them all coming from one institution, bringing a common culture with them, is a situation that makes a substantial handicap for the staff.

Accordingly, a house will be more fortunate if it can draw from several different institutions and can achieve a variety of ages and types of offenders. One house, Austin MacCormick, has even tried the unique practice of mixing in a few persons who are not offenders at all. In the original concept of the house it was thought that the quality of the experience for the residents would be improved if there could always be one or two persons, such as students, staying there and living as any other residents. Theoretically it would make the house even more truly a step into normal society for the parolees. The experience with this idea has been too slight as yet to indicate how successful it may be. A somewhat similar arrangement has been in effect at the Blackfriars Settlement in London where ex-prisoners are given residential facilities as in a halfway house. These facilities are often shared by graduate students from the Institute of Criminology at Cambridge.

STAFFING THE HALFWAY HOUSE

The kind and amount of staff in a halfway house will first be shaped by the character of the sponsoring agency. The federal prerelease centers, being integral units of the Bureau of Prisons, will naturally have civil service personnel drawn from other assignments in the bureau and so usually experienced in prison work. A typical staffing pattern in the prerelease centers is a director, caseworker, employment counselor, and three or four correctional counselors. These latter are subprofessional persons who help in general supervision of the residents, and at times assist the casework staff in making home visits and other community contacts on behalf of the residents. Though this may seem like a more than adequate staff size for a small facility, the fact of day and night operation, seven days a week, means that no more than one correctional counselor is likely to be available at a time. In addition to these staff members the prerelease center that has its own kitchen and dining facilities must have a cook. A secretary and night student supervisors will also be usual. In at least one instance the cook is actually an inmate from a nearby federal institution, placed in the center as his regular work assignment, rather than being there as one of the regular residents.

Generally, the denominational sponsors follow a more flexible and informal staffing pattern in their facilities. Dismas House, headed by a Catholic priest, operates as far as possible with staff persons who themselves are former residents. Dismas, with a capacity of sixty men, is probably the largest facility of this type in the country, and much of the housekeeping and maintenance work on its aging physical plant is handled by current residents who are not easily employable elsewhere.

The American Friends Service Committee, in setting up Crenshaw House and Austin MacCormick House, has been somewhat exceptional in hiring a male director whose wife would also be closely involved in the operation. This effort to contribute to the family feeling of the facility by having "parents" in charge has been effective in these two homes with populations of only about ten men each. Contributing to the quality of such an operation is the very careful selection process conducted by the Friends. Applicants for the director position are screened minutely, with the process including the use of projective psychological tests. The emphasis has been on finding persons who are very normal, natural, warm, and dedicated.

Shaw House, run by the Bureau of Rehabilitation (a prisoner's aid agency) in Washington, D.C., uses about half the time of the agency's director and in addition has a program supervisor and two caseworkers, all of whom are trained social workers. Also full-time employees are a secretary and a cook. The latter is another person who should be carefully selected; the Shaw House experience is fairly typical in finding that the cook is in a natural position to be one of the influential and stabilizing persons in the house.

The halfway house presents the same staff dilemma as is common in the training schools for juvenile delinquents. If the staff lives in there can be more of the warm family feeling in the living situation, but at the same time this is harder on the staff and it is difficult to get staff members to do it. Crenshaw House, with a husband and wife staff living in at first, next door later, was a good example of the positive qualities this brings. But when that husband and wife left, the house had to close.

In Delaware the Prisoner's Aid operated 308 West Residence during its first few years with a director who was a bachelor, and, until he later married, he lived in an upstairs apartment in the house. It was felt that this added a good quality of feeling to the house, but again, this was an arrangement which was related to the person of the moment and it cannot be sustained if a change in personnel occurs. For the most part, the halfway houses have recognized the impracticality of finding staff people who will immerse their personal lives fully in the job, and so staff members generally live off premises and report to work as they would in any other agency.

OTHER TYPES OF RESIDENTIAL PROGRAMS

In an article on the subject of halfway houses Robert Meiners speculates on the possibility of operating such a program without a residence.[7] Perhaps it could be done by a central office which would utilize apartments, rooming houses, and a variety of other housing resources. There are some aspects of the idea that have appeal, such as the fact that it would more quickly get the clients out into the workaday community while still giving them active help; it would permit the giving of help on an equal basis to men and women; it would avoid the administrative problems of running a house; it would permit a wider variety of solutions for the wide variety of clients that need to be served.

An adaptation of this idea is found in the informal cooperative arrangement between the state parole agent and the Salvation Army in Sioux City, Iowa. The Salvation Army has a men's residence with well-designed and well-maintained dormitories for temporary use of any homeless men. The state parole agent regularly uses this resource for any parolee who needs a halfway house type of placement. The parolee is mixed among the other residents as if he were not different at all, and he is not identified in any way to the other residents as a parolee. The parole agent and the Salvation Army staff work together to provide the client with the employment counseling and other kinds of help he may need. The arrangement seems to work to the genuine satisfaction of both the parole office and the Salvation Army, and it is a sensible solution in this moderate-sized community that could hardly support a regular halfway house. In a few other cities, especially in California, similar use is being made of Salvation Army centers.

Elsewhere experience is being gained with combining "detached"

[7] Robert G. Meiners, "A Halfway House for Parolees," *Federal Probation*, Vol. 29, No. 2 (June 1965), p. 51.

service with an established halfway house. Dismas House, with no facilities for women, gives help to women by making arrangements for them in other residential resources. St. Leonard's House also has always maintained a nonresidential service for women, and in fact this kind of auxiliary service is almost all that has been available to women during the brief history of halfway houses. The only established facility of this kind for women has been the Isaac T. Hopper Home in New York City. Actually, this home is only part of a private casework agency which is over a hundred years old. It accepts from any court or correctional institution referrals of any women, sixteen or older, who need help with job placements, with housing, with medical or psychiatric treatment, or who need any other variety of either practical help or counseling service. Residential care may or may not be involved. An ancient but well-maintained and comfortable house near the Bowery houses the agency staff and the residential facilities, which can accommodate nine women. Most residents remain less than a month.

Any halfway house for women will inevitably have to decide whether to serve pregnant women. In view of the homes already available to serve unmarried mothers, it is likely that halfway houses for women will decide, as has the Isaac T. Hopper Home, not to accept these cases.

A more fully detached program, and a well-organized one, was the Resident Home Program which was begun in August 1960 by the Youth Division of the Michigan Department of Corrections. The particular focus of this program, which was supported by a foundation grant, was to recruit foster homes as temporary placements for youthful parolees. The arrangement, as in the usual boardinghome program, was to pay each home a per diem allowance for each person placed there. The operation of the whole program was directed by a specially assigned agent from the parole system. The homes were recruited in a variety of ways and preference was given to homes that were typical of normal, conventional, well adjusted family living. As their experience developed, however, the staff found that there could often be more success with families that had had to cope with various forms of family disability, for these seemed to have a more ready acceptance of the parolee and a better capacity to make him comfortable. Later it appeared that there might be still more gain in some cases by using established boardinghouses instead of foster homes. Boardinghouse operators were experienced in dealing with all types of people and could take the parolee in just like anyone else; altogether such a placement presented a particularly nonthreatening situation for the client.

A program like this tends to be different from the usual halfway house situation because of a characteristic that is common to all foster home programs. In the cases that have particular need for the service and are fortunate to get suitable placements the arrangement tends to become relatively permanent. So the client who would stay in a halfway house for a matter of weeks before going out on his own might stay in the foster home for months or even years if it has been a comfortable placement that meets his needs. This has happened a few times and probably the only negative aspect of this is that it removes the home from the pool of available placements.

The two-year financing for the Resident Home Program enabled the state to pay a home $17.50 per week for the man's board and room until he could become employed and assume the payments himself. The supervising agent held weekly group counseling sessions for the parolees at a Y.M.C.A. and while these were found to be useful, they did not have the effectiveness that can be achieved when the men in the group are all living under one roof. Although the program was tried for only a limited time, in a limited area (Grand Rapids), it proved to be a method that has potential value as a means of accommodating a wider variety of persons than could successfully be put under one roof. It can be equally useful for male and female parolees, for instance, and if developed over a wide area it could avoid the fixed geographical limitation of the halfway residence.

FACILITIES FOR JUVENILES

The halfway houses designed for juveniles are not materially different from those operated for adults, but there are substantially fewer of them. Michigan is one of the exceptional states that now has set up such facilities. Starting in 1964 six homes were developed, one of them being for girls. They are administered under the State Department of Social Services which administers aftercare field services. These homes are in urban areas and they are established in large old houses. Acceptance by the surrounding neighborhoods has been no problem; a much more important concern has been cultivating a cooperative attitude on the part of the schools.

The staffing of one typical house, with a capacity of twelve boys, includes a "boys' supervisor" who functions as the house manager, three other boys' supervisors, one of whom works at night, and one cook. It has been usual for the night man to sleep during the late night hours, but there has been a certain amount of stealing among the boys and it is thought that it may be better to have the night man on duty awake all night.

Because the residents are juveniles and many are in school, there is no expectation that they will pay room and board. Those boys who have jobs handle their own money and may give it to the house director to save for them if they wish. The staff finds that a difficult and continuing problem is to help those boys who are not in school to find jobs.

In general the living situation for these boys has worked rather well. They are jealous of their clothing and much concerned about protecting clothes from loss or theft. An allowance given to the non-working boys helps to reduce, but does not eliminate, stealing. This is a problem that varies as the character of the group in the home changes from time to time. There has been very little tendency toward fighting.

It is the practice to require all the boys to do a scheduled and apportioned amount of housekeeping around the premises, and if it is necessary to ask any boy to do more than his regular assignment in this work he is paid for it. An important element in the administration of the facility is the availability of a petty cash fund for a wide variety of special needs including allowances.

The privilege of going out in the evenings is limited. The boys must have special permission and must be in by 10 P.M. on week nights or 11 P.M. on weekends. Girl friends may be entertained in the living room. One evening each week (Friday) the boys all go together to some form of recreation such as to a movie, bowling alley, or swimming pool. The previous evening the boys meet and decide what the excursion will be, then on Friday evening they all participate. The transportation and admission costs for these recreational evenings are met entirely by the state.

Unlike halfway houses for adults where the length of stay is a short period while the resident gets established in a job, the house operated for juveniles will find that turnover has to be much slower. When Washington started its Riverside Group Home in Tacoma in 1962 it planned a stay of about six months for each boy, but this limitation was not feasible. A boy just could not properly be pushed out after some arbitrary period of time, so it became the practice to let the boy stay until he is emancipated sufficiently to handle himself outside. Some boys have stayed at Riverside as long as two years.

Unlike the Michigan facilities, Riverside has on the staff one woman whose duties include sewing and the supervision of housekeeping. Other staff members find that much of their usefulness is in transporting the boys to jobs, for most of them work at a variety of neighborhood jobs after school. From their earnings they pay their own school expenses and dental bills, and buy their own clothes. The ability to hold a good job and manage money competently is a major basis of status among the boys in the home. The boys also pay 10 percent of their earnings into a house fund that is used for recreational supplies and repairs and improvements around the house. An interesting experience has been that some of the boys have found foster home placements for themselves as a result of the close relationships they have developed with employers. This has been considered a good outcome, for it gets the boy into a home of his own choosing and opens a place for another boy in the residence.

Rules about smoking, dating, and housekeeping activities are kept as simple and few as possible, and are carried out essentially as they would be in a family home. It is found that the boys do not gang up as a total group in any negative sense; they have a mutually supportive feeling but they do not become a cohesive group otherwise. They develop their own individual interests and go their own ways to a considerable extent. It is interesting to note that they object to the use of the term "halfway house" for their residence, for this would imply that they are still partly in institutional status. They insist that they are all the way out instead of just halfway. The boys at Riverside are not alone in this feeling and for this reason the term "halfway house," for all its usefulness in general discussion of this type of facility, is almost never used as part of the actual name of any such residence.

A sort of cousin to the halfway house idea is the group home program that is being used in some areas. Some of these programs have started accidentally rather than deliberately, and, in fact, some of the best such homes have brought themselves into being, so to speak, rather than being administratively recruited and developed. In one instance a foster home in Humboldt County, California, started serving the local welfare department in 1961 with a license to take five children. The foster parents soon showed both the skill and the interest to deal with more children and older children, so the home was soon taking boys on probation, with its capacity increased to fifteen. In this instance the foster father gives essentially all of his time to the operation of the home, as does his wife. It is the sort of resource that is a tremendous asset in the county, and the local court depends heavily upon it as an answer to those cases that need noninstitutional placements. At the same time it places the court in the position of becoming dependent upon a resource that might disappear as quickly and as easily as it appeared if the foster parents for any reason had to discontinue the use of their own home for this purpose.

A similar foster home has developed to serve the court in St. Paul, and this one has an unusual feature that provides extra program value. A local couple who operate an Italian restaurant became interested in helping delinquent boys, and their attempts with one or two boys grew into a virtual career in operating a large-sized group foster home. Again, this is the unusual couple that has the rare knack of being able to live with a group of boys in their own home and to give all of them the warm acceptance that enables them to stabilize and mature. This they accomplish even though there are usually ten to fourteen boys at a time in the home.

The juvenile court in St. Paul uses this home for boys who are sixteen or older and who may be able to survive on probation if they can get out of their own homes and into a strongly supportive foster home. All the boys are in school and most of them have part-time jobs. The county welfare department pays the usual daily rate to the home for each boy, but by special agreement with the court it is the probation office that supervises.

The extra feature in this facility is the restaurant operated by the foster father. Any of his boys who needs and wants a job can work in the restaurant. The boy who does take such work must start first in the kitchen on menial assignments to see how serious he is about wanting to work and to accept the discipline of a job. The next step is to move into the dining room as a waiter and this he can do whenever his kitchen performance seems to suggest that he is ready for the promotion. No other waiters or waitresses are hired in the restaurant; waiting service is handled exclusively by the boys in the home, each working a few hours each day without interfering with school homework that must be done. The restaurant work is an opportunity for the boys to earn money and to learn work habits under the immediate supervision of the man who knows them best. It also adds to this foster father's opportunity to develop close rapport with his boys through the hours of associating with them on the job.

Boys stay in this home until they graduate from high school or become eighteen. Because they are older teen-agers and because they are a fairly large group it is found that to a large degree a subculture develops similar to that in the Highfields programs. The foster parents encourage a strong group feeling with group responsibility for standards of conduct, and this group culture is highly effective as long as boys leave and are replaced one at a time. Since this measure of control is quite effective, the probation office leaves the active supervision to the foster parents. All the boys placed in this home are on the caseload of one probation officer, but though he visits in the home with some frequency he does not maintain active contacts with individual boys in the customary sense of probation supervision as long as any problems in the cases seem to be under adequate control by the group and the foster parents. He intervenes actively in a case only when asked to do so by the foster father. The effect of this is that the boys generally are much less aware of being on probation than would be usually true and this makes it more tolerable for them to be on probation for the fairly lengthy periods of time necessary for them to remain in the home until graduation from high school.

It may be true that by putting a dozen or more in one home the lines of relationship between foster parents and children are weakened, but we see in the home described above the substitution of a different element that can be equally as effective — the support and control of the group. Though the younger child in a foster home ordinarily needs a close relationship with the foster parents, the older teen-ager is beginning to reach for emancipation from adult domination and for him the support of his peers may be the more effective factor, if a strong adult is just near enough to give assurance of control and support when the group has trouble in handling its own problems.

It may or may not be true that the large group home is less desirable for younger children. Child welfare workers tend to think of foster homes having not more than three or four children, that is, not more than the parents can relate to closely. Foster homes for delinquents as young as eight or nine are sometimes needed, and children of such age as yet need the support of strong relationships with parent figures or other adults. But there are exceptions here too, for there are times when even the young child cannot tolerate a close relationship with a substitute parent. The child welfare worker often faces a dilemma when he has a child whose own home is too deteriorated and damaging for him to remain in it longer, but when the child nevertheless has a very strong feeling for his mother. When he is placed in a foster home and is confronted by a substitute mother who invites his love, the internal emotional conflict can be severe. The more successful the foster mother is in kindling a loving response from such a child the more guilty the child may feel for betraying his own mother in this way, and the resulting discomfort erupts in symptoms such as runaway behavior. In such cases the group home may be a more successful placement since the relationship with the foster parents is diluted by the fact of more children being involved. Whatever the number of children, however, the real factor of success is the capacity of the foster parent to give love with an understanding of the child's need: requiring no more response to that love than the child is ready to give.

In the state of Wisconsin the use of group homes for delinquents has reached a considerable degree of refinement, aided by the fact that the state correctional services are administered within the same department as state welfare services. The Wisconsin practice is to have the group homes take from four to eight children each, these being children who have been committed to the state as delinquent and who need such placements either instead of or after going to a correctional institution. The state spends money on this group home program rather generously in the belief that if it is going to work it will need to be supported fully and that at its most expensive, the group home is still cheaper than the institution.

The financial arrangements reflect the philosophy involved and give a suggestion of the elaborate administrative planning and organization required for a successful program of this kind. After a prospective home is thoroughly investigated and found to meet health and safety requirements, the home is licensed and children are placed in it under the active supervision of the state probation and parole agent serving that district. The agent is expected to give close supportive counseling to the foster parents as well as active supervision of the wards in placement there. These homes are paid on a subsidy basis, with a standard monthly allotment for each bed available, whether or not it is in use at the moment. The basic board rate paid for each child is increased after the home has been in satisfactory use for a year. A higher rate may be paid to a home that is asked to take a child with special problems, such as enuresis or difficult dietary requirements. As a recognition of the exhausting nature of this twenty-four-hour job, an allowance is now made to foster parents so that they can employ substitutes occasionally and get away for a vacation.

In addition to the basic board rate foster parents are reimbursed for expenses such as clothing, school supplies, and transportation to hospital or doctor. Medical, dental, and psychiatric care costs are also authorized as needed. A monthly personal allowance for each child is available.

A big city adaptation of the group home plan is represented by the Apartment Home Complex operated by New York's Division for Youth. In 1965 the division inaugurated the plan with three separate facilities in the Bronx, each of which can take about seven boys. These boys are not severely delinquent but are likely to be the kind that have come to juvenile court because of truancy and incorrigibility. They have been found to be reacting in such ways to emotional pressures in their homes and are clearly in need of removal from home though not in need of institutional placement.

As one typical arrangement, for instance, the division for youth has rented two contiguous apartments on the fourth floor of an ordinary large apartment house. A door was cut between the two apartments, making them, in effect, one large living area with six bedrooms. The staff consists mainly of just the houseparents, a husband and wife who are hired to serve as full-time parents to the boys and to provide them with a family setting in as normal a way as possible. The houseparents live in the apartment and are on duty twenty-four hours per day, five days per week. The man may have a regular job elsewhere even as a natural father does. The woman does all the cooking and housekeeping. They are likely to maintain a separate domicile of their own that they can go to on their two days off. Relief personnel are provided to serve in all three apartment centers when the houseparents have their time off.

In these apartment facilities the emphasis is on encouraging the boys to live as normally and responsibly as would any apartment dweller who must live in peace with his neighbors. Nearly all the boys are in school and in most instances they will be remaining in this group facility until they can emancipate themselves. An observer is certain to be impressed with the good quality of family living that develops in such a program as the boys relax when the home pressures that have plagued them no longer are present.

A similar program has been developed by Children's Village, a private institution which has recently started three group homes in the New York City area for boys being released from that institution but unable to return to their own homes. In many respects these are like the Wisconsin group homes except for the very urban locations and the fact that the foster parents are hired. One of these homes, for example, consists of a duplex of two attached houses. Doors cut through from one side to the other make it all one house that provides a room and bath for houseparents plus rooms and a bath for eight boys. Here too, the house is leased by the agency and the houseparents are hired to be on duty day and night for five days per week. Unlike the house fathers in the Apartment Home Complex, the fathers in the Children's Village homes are not expected to work elsewhere. The work in the home and the liaison with the parent institution seem to require the full time of both parents. Here again, an unregimented natural family living quality is the goal, with the agency furnishing clothes, weekly allowances, and all other physical needs for the boys. This situation also attempts to avoid a problem that sometimes occurs with the ordinary foster home. Foster parents, being quite human themselves, will at times lose patience with a certain child and ask for his removal, an action they are in a position to require since it is their own home. But where the foster parents are employees, and the agency is in command of placements and removals, the child has more protection.

Even so, the essential element in any kind of foster home program is still the quality of personal warmth and skill in the foster parents. It is the need for this factor that makes any variety of these foster home services uncertain and constantly changing as good parents inevitably come and go. A foster home either has the spark of genius for helping children, or it does not, and if it does not, no amount of money can buy it. But when truly good foster parents can be found they are a very valuable asset to the state, and a proper reimbursement for their service will be an economy if it helps to sustain, for a maximum period of time, their availability to children who need them so crucially.

9 --

Community Involvement in Corrections

Among all the imaginative new techniques being developed and applied within the correctional field, not the least significant is the vital effort to involve the lay citizen's interest and participation in correctional programs. Heretofore the layman has been more than content to leave this grubby field to those public servants who care to work in it, and usually those public servants have been equally satisfied to be left alone. There still is, on the part of some correctional administrators, an anxious resistance to the idea of letting lay people take a hand in corrections in any way, but the realization is rapidly spreading that a systematic and genuinely active involvement of lay citizens can help bring to a correctional program the sort of support that the administrators will find wonderfully effective.

Such participation and support can take many forms and will need to be adapted very differently to different programs and even to different geographical locales. In the large cities there can now be found extensive and sophisticated programs for involving lay citizens in corrections work, but small towns and rural areas can do fully as well, depending upon the resourcefulness of the leadership available. Sioux City, Iowa, for example, a city of 91,000, has for several years been quietly supporting a

253

home-grown project known as the Restoration Club, which brings parolees and a number of average townspeople into folksy and useful contact with each other.

The Restoration Club is the beneficiary of no government or foundation grants. It is not accompanied by any research and it is not conceived or directed by any well-trained professional. It is the product of the good will and imagination of the local parole officer who has an eighth-grade education and had many years' experience in police work before taking the parole job with the state.

A major asset of the project is the attack it makes on the problem of social distance between parolees and ordinary citizens. Experience leads us to believe that the apathy of the client about working to improve himself is often related to his sense of hopeless distance from the conventional middle-class community. At the same time the apathy of the community toward the general crime problem is related to the average person's remoteness from and complete lack of acquaintance with any real people in correctional caseloads. The Restoration Club attempts in a natural and informal way to reduce this distance and provide this acquaintance. It works because the parole officer is a man who has the necessary enthusiasm for the idea and the personal qualities needed to enlist the enthusiasm of other people.

The simple idea is that the Restoration Club is an organization in the town to which anyone can belong who is interested in probation or parole. The parole officer is the organizer and general sparkplug of the club and he lets his parolees know that he sees it as important for them to belong. Wives or husbands are also urged to attend. Equally important is the membership of some merchants, lawyers, ministers, and other average citizens who have become interested because they know the parole officer, respect him, and have become infected by his contagious interest in his work. Once a month the club holds a meeting in the local Y.M.C.A. with the parolees, their spouses, and the lay citizens mingling familiarly on a first-name basis. Part of the evening is taken up with a formal business meeting in which there is the usual reading of the minutes, old business, new business, election of officers, etc., etc. It is an opportunity for the parolees to have an experience in the sort of things that average, middle-class people do, and to see themselves with some satisfaction in that role. For the citizen members it is an opportunity to get to know a number of parolees on a friendly man-to-man basis and to discover the problems they have and the human qualities they bring to the solving of them. Between meetings there may be contacts also as a parolee may go to one of the citizen members of the club for some help or advice.

A California experiment in using local businessmen to help probationers find jobs showed the same happy results from getting easy rapport established between the two kinds of people. "The interviewers, most of whom are local businessmen, have many things to offer the probationer. First, as representatives of the community, they can give the probationers a sense of belonging. Where many probationers have felt like 'outsiders looking in,' they now have, perhaps for the first time, someone who represents the middle-class business community expressing enough concern to sit down with and try to help them." [1]

The value of this kind of community involvement is difficult to prove even though any reasonable person would immediately recognize its probable usefulness. As compared with other Iowa parole districts, the area served by the Sioux City parole officer has had a lower rate of parole violations, though this could easily be due to the personal qualities he brings to his job aside from the use of the Restoration Club. But even if not one parole violation has been avoided as a result of the club there is still an important purpose that it serves. We have seen in recent years the general and immense gains made in respect to mental health and the problem of retardation because of a more enlightened public attitude. The most important issue has not been whether a citizen volunteer could go into a hospital and directly contribute to the recovery of a mental patient; the bigger gain has been that the improved understanding of the general public has provided a supportive context in which services to the mentally afflicted could be vastly improved. A better public attitude has produced more funds, both public and private, for research which has led to better treatment. More patients can be released early from hospitals and families today are more willing to take them home again.

Public ignorance of a social problem leads to public rejection of the people who personify that problem. This has been the condition of the public's relationship to crime and delinquency, and until we bring the public into a far more intimate acquaintance with it the new techniques

---

[1] David P. Macpherson, "Community Action for Employment of Probationers," *Crime and Delinquency*, Vol. 10, No. 1 (January 1964), p. 41.

we professionals develop will not achieve their full potential. The parole officer in Sioux City has an idea that should be taken to heart by many correctional programs that could be doing much more to create a community climate that would make their expensive professional operations more effective.

An example of the more sophisticated program involving lay persons is the SCORE program, which has already been discussed in Chapter 7. This program takes advantage of a community group, the Jaycees, that is already formed, instead of assembling a new group of individually recruited persons as the Restoration Club does. So the young men who become involved in SCORE are already organized to provide community services; they have some financial resources to contribute; and they are persons who have the advantage of youthful energy now and the prospect of being community leaders in a few years. With regard both to the present and the future this makes them an excellent group to be impregnated with knowledge and concern about delinquency and its treatment.

Of course civic clubs have always sponsored service projects, but the uniqueness of the marriage of SCORE and the Jaycees is that SCORE, by its essential nature, makes it imperative that the members of this organization become personally active in it. Nor is this just to save money by avoiding salary costs; but the active and very real participation of the Jaycee member himself is an integral part of the technique, and he knows that the project needs his personal activity and would not work with hired staff in his place. It is consequently one of the most honest devices for lay involvement that is presently in use.

PUBLIC PARTICIPATION BECOMES PUBLIC SUPPORT

In an earlier chapter it has been mentioned that professionals in probation and parole tend to be fearful of any suggestion that they try working with their clients in groups. In view of this it is especially interesting that there is fairly extensive experience with using lay persons from the community to conduct group discussions. Michigan has been doing this since 1954 when lay persons were invited to visit and become acquainted with one of the state's penal camps. Some of the visitors were interested enough to want to help the program in a specific and personal way, so a lay group counseling program gradually evolved. It was given particular impetus when Camp Pugsley, a "probation" camp, was opened in 1956. Camp Pugsley was intended as a forestry camp setting for older teen-age boys who needed to be placed away from their own homes for a period of time but without commitment to the conventional training school. So it was envisaged as an open camp in which boys on probation might live. It would be hard to prove that the character of the institutional experience at Camp Pugsley is substantially different from that at many regular forestry camps to which boys are committed, but the volunteer counselors there give it a link with the community that is unusual in correctional programs.

When the camp was opened in its fairly remote rural area there were no nearby big cities or colleges to provide part-time professionals who could help with the counseling, so some businessmen from the nearest town, Traverse City, were enlisted as group leaders.

Although the plan originally grew out of an effort to acquaint the general public with correctional programs, it has become a means of obtaining actual service from lay people to an extent that once would not have been thought possible. Not only to Camp Pugsley, but to most of the correctional institutions in the state, the volunteers now come weekly and each meets with a group of eight to ten persons for an hour to an hour and one-half. Following the group session the volunteers stay for a session with staff members who review with them the dynamics of what seems to be happening in each group, and give them suggestions on technique. The group leaders are encouraged to work in pairs as co-leaders so that the group can be more certain of meeting every week even though one leader may have to be absent.

Obviously, the use of this kind of leadership means that group therapy in the professionally sophisticated sense is not being attempted. But there are plenty of areas of discussion that the lay leader can handle adequately. The inmates in his group will someday return to the outside where they must find a job and in various other ways deal with the business world. The group leader, a man from the outside business world, can talk with them about job finding and job holding, the use of credit, and many other practical matters that will be crucial to the men when they leave, and, of course, these are subjects that the professional staff could not handle so well as these volunteers can. But also, there is real value in the mere fact of the businessman being present in the institution in this way. It reduces the inmate's feeling of rejection and increases his sense of belonging to the outside world if he can become comfortably acquainted with an average, everyday sort of person who comes to the institution week after week for no other reason than his genuine interest in being useful to persons he regards as human beings notwithstanding their incarceration.

Although the volunteer group leader will start his group counseling experience by keeping to safe and practical topics of discussion, it may, or course, lead to discussions in more depth. In some instances strong rapport will develop between the leader and his group, and if he is a perceptive and interested person he will learn much about counseling techniques from his experience and from the training sessions with the staff. So at times the counseling may become more personal and intensive. The experience in Michigan suggests that the feared dangers in this have not been as real as were supposed, and that the process can be kept in adequate control through competent supervision of the volunteers.

Most programs for the use of volunteers are, like this one, promoted and guided by the professionals who staff or administer correctional services. An exception was an unusual program in Toronto which was formed by several lay persons as an effort to help the parolee feel at home in the community. A group of citizens conceived the idea of having an apartment that could serve as a meeting and lounging spot for parolees and for volunteers interested in being useful to them. There was one social worker on the board that was formed to operate the project and an apartment was rented in the same building where she lived so that she could give it her frequent attention. There was no attempt to provide any structured program other than to get word to any parolees being released to that area that they could drop in at the apartment at any time. Interested volunteers were on hand in the evenings to greet any parolees who came and to help them, without pressure, to feel comfortable and to meet new friends. It was conceived as a very concrete way to make the parolee feel wanted and accepted in the community. The volunteers kept the refrigerator stocked and encouraged visitors to have snacks at any time. Some parolees occasionally cooked meals for themselves there, and sometimes a group of them would have a meal or a party. To a certain extent they talked about personal problems with volunteer counselors who were available, though more of the activity was social or concerned with practical personal matters. "One came regularly twice a week — one night to play chess with a volunteer and the other to study with his help. One came for Sunday dinner only; some to watch television. Some learned to dance there with the help of enthusiastic volunteers, others to play bridge or scrabble. Some have found it helpful for laundry purposes or for a shower. One boy, without his own home since infancy, cooked all his meals in the flat but slept elsewhere. One man, for whom a sewing machine was rented, altered suits for several others. While it has not been satisfactory to have anyone living in the flat for long periods, since this limits its usefulness to others, it has been invaluable for a few days on release from prison or at times of illness or emergency." [2]

Obviously it becomes important to select with care the volunteers for a project like this and one of the factors in selection that was originally underestimated was age. The majority of the parolees were young men and they showed a better responsiveness to volunteers who were near their own age than to those in the thirty to forty age group. This required selection of men who had the advantage of youth but also perceptiveness and dependably good judgment. The older volunteers continued to be fully useful but in more specialized ways rather than in general socializing.

The cost of operating the apartment varied from about $3000 to $4800 per year, depending on rent levels and the amount of use; and the board seemed to have little difficulty in meeting this expense through solicitation of cash contributions in the community. Though it was felt that the project was highly worth while it was discontinued pending reappraisal after two and one-half years.

The board's concept of the rationale for this type of service is a well-expressed bit of philosophy that is not only supportive of the apartment idea, but is also pertinent to the whole process of helping offenders: "Most people involved in crime have lacked a steady home background. They are making mistakes as adults which more fortunate people made as children, but with a striking difference. When children from happy homes make mistakes they learn through the wise handling of the situation by their parents. They also take it for granted, when being disciplined, that the parent is there and will be there, still caring, when the discipline is over. The person involved in crime, however, who did not

[2] Sophie Boyd, "Report of a Volunteer Project to Assist in the Social Adjustment of Persons Released from Prison," *Canadian Journal of Corrections*, Vol. 7, No. 4 (1965), p. 397.

learn as a child and who, as an adult, is making the same mistakes, is disciplined by a prison sentence and there is often no parent figure there and no continuing relationship with someone who cares and who will help him learn from his mistakes. If this point of view is valid, then the apartment (which in a sense has been a home base giving 'parenting') can provide this continuing relationship." [3]

VOLUNTEER PROBATION OFFICERS

The Toronto apartment was a fine joint effort by a sincere group of lay people, but often any noteworthy program for involving lay people in direct service to clients grows from and is dependent upon the special personality qualities of just one dynamic person who assumes the leadership. Bureaucracies, too, should deliberately structure and promote plans for community involvement but it is likely instead that any efforts of this kind are originated by an individual, such as the Sioux City parole officer, who develops and sells the program through the force of his own personality.

It is an understandable tendency. The successful marshaling of a number of volunteers to work in an area of social service that is seldom popular calls for a unique combination of personal gifts. Invariably the leaders of such programs are characterized by ebullient personalities, exceptionally wide acquaintance with useful people in the community, and a knack of getting other people to catch the spark of enthusiasm. This indispensable combination of qualities is at once a boon and a bane. It is important to the successful initiation of a good volunteer program, but it can also mean that the program is so much one man's operation that it may not survive that man's departure — or even his continued presence. It may be that this is a condition that is more characteristic now in the field's early experience with volunteer programs and will not be so usual a few years later when we learn to teach community organization methods to more people coming into corrections.

One energetic volunteer program has been created by the judge of Michigan's Royal Oak Municipal Court. On being newly elected in 1959 he started what has become perhaps the most noticed probation volunteer program in the country. A particularly gratifying aspect of this program is that it is conducted in a court dealing with misdemeanants.

[3] *Ibid.*, p. 399.

Generally the courts at the municipal level represent a vast wasteland of inadequate or nearly nonexistent social services and it is especially heartening to find a major effort in this area such as this court is making.

Royal Oak, a city of 90,000 population, is adjacent to Detroit and is predominantly a middle-class suburb. The new judge found that he had no probation service at all attached to his court and only token service, in effect, available from a county probation office. The judge proceeded to enlist the help of some of his friends who were willing to supervise probationers, and gradually a sizable group of volunteer probation officers was developed.

Inevitably such an effort begins to be strangled by its own success. Administrative chores become demanding and it is found that there is a limit to the number of volunteers that can be enlisted successfully without paid professional direction. The court in Royal Oak, faced with these problems, began to acquire some paid staff although it still operates with a surprising minimum of such.

The essential professional staff consists of nine counselors, each of whom works for the court only about five hours per week. They all have specialized training in various disciplines such as social work, psychology, or guidance counseling, and they all have full-time jobs elsewhere. Most of the defendants who are placed on probation are assigned to these counselors, who carry about twenty-five cases each. However, most of the cases so assigned are then also assigned to volunteers. After six years of development there were about seventy-five volunteers active in the program and it was hoped that this number might be doubled eventually. Each volunteer carries only one case at a time and he is not asked to assume the authoritative role that is usually expected of the probation officer. His role is essentially described in the explanation that he is to be a friend to the probationer. He is to inspire the psychological lift that comes to a probationer who sees a person giving without pay of his time and effort only because of his genuine interest. He may be in a good position to provide help with job finding or with some of the other practical problems that present such frustrations to this kind of clientele. The philosophy which the judge himself holds in regard to this may or may not agree with concepts of volunteer court services elsewhere. "The concern which the judge feels for the probationers must be expressed vicariously. To the vast majority of them, the court purposely remains aloof and punitive. To only a very few can the court speak informally and with compassion. Thus, the volunteer can fulfill a role of a friend and companion of the probationer. It would be a fatal error for the court to try to fulfill this role. It is also wrong for the volunteer to act like a judge. You do not have to be judgmental, you do not have to be authoritative, you do not have to be concerned with punishment. You are relieved of this duty. You must be a friend. Let the court represent authority. You represent acceptance, understanding, affection and concern." [4]

For reasons that are not too clearly advanced, the counselor remains active with the case even though he has enlisted a volunteer to work with it. Both the counselor and the volunteer expect to see the probationer at least once a month. The volunteer is to give the counselor a very brief written report monthly about the number of contacts he has had, but there is little demand for any qualitative reporting of his work. There is no concern on the part of the staff about the dual relationship with the clients, and instead it is supposed that the counselor and the volunteer are carrying somewhat different functions that probably could not be combined in one kind of worker. There has been a trend toward letting the volunteer carry more of the case responsibility by himself, but this is not so much because of a changing concept of technique as it is a matter of yielding to the pressures of increasing caseloads.

The Royal Oak volunteer plan is actually seen to operate with pronounced limitations when scrutinized closely. Not only does the volunteer not carry the authoritative character of a probation officer, but he is restricted in the kinds of cases assigned to him. Volunteers are not given cases of persons over twenty-two years of age and they are not given cases of persons who appear to be emotionally disturbed, or who are sex offenders or alcoholics. Such cases are usually assigned to the counselors only.

To handle the growing administrative demands as the volunteer program built up, the court recruited a retired businessman as administrator of the whole effort. Later two other retired men were added, one as an assistant administrator and one as a presentence investigator. These three are paid from the very limited funds now being furnished by the city of Royal Oak, but they are paid only token salaries. All three are receiving their Social Security retirement benefits and they are paid no

[4] Keith J. Leenhouts, Fifth Annual Report of the Probation Department of the Royal Oak Municipal Court, August 1, 1965, p. 18 of exhibits.

more than they are allowed to earn without jeopardizing those payments. They have no clearly required number of hours to work but as a simple matter of interest in what they are doing they are working essentially full time. The administrator and his assistant carry their own caseloads, usually taking the kinds of cases, such as alcoholics, that are not assigned to volunteers. As of the end of 1965 there were about 400 active probation cases. With fewer than 100 of these being carried by volunteers it is evident that the various part-time staff members are still carrying the major burden of work.

A somewhat surprising fact is that there is no paid clerical staff for this program. The administrator has a list of women in the community who are available to give occasional help and these are called upon from time to time to work for a day or so. They get to the job at their own expense and put in a full day with no compensation at all.

One feature of this program that has little to do with volunteers except that it too costs the city no money is a Saturday work program in lieu of conviction. The idea is a simple one and seems to have much to commend it even though there has been no systematic evaluation of it. The philosophy has been that young men with no previous criminal record should be spared the handicap of such a record if they can "learn their lesson" without the adjudication process. It is also felt, however, that in avoiding the criminal record there should not also be avoidance of punishment. So the court has used its "work detail" as a way of imposing a penalty without incurring a record of conviction for the defendant. By arrangement with the Royal Oak Department of Public Works, the court may allow a young defendant to work for the city for a prescribed number of Saturdays while his case is continued on the court calendar. The defendant is told that if he wishes to avoid having a record he may elect to do this weekly work, and for this privilege he must pay $48 per month. If he is interested in knowing what his sentence would otherwise be before he decides which alternative to take, he is told that he must decide without any such information or promises. All he can be assured of is that after completing the prescribed weeks of Saturday work he will have to return to court and if his work has been satisfactory his case may then be dismissed with no court record having been put on the books. If he does not choose this course the court then proceeds to dispose of the case in the conventional manner.

In the usual case the Saturday work is specified to extend for a period from one to three months and occasionally more. The defendant must fill out and submit a formal application for the program and pay his $38 in advance each month. These men work in groups of five to seven under the direction of one of the regular city employees. For this extra Saturday work the work supervisor must be paid time and one half, and this is the principal cost being met by the fee charged to each defendant. After some initial apprehension the unions accepted the plan since it does provide extra employment for a few of the Public Works employees and it is understood that the work done by the court groups is work that otherwise would not be done. Much of it is a matter of cleaning up parks or cleaning park equipment.

In most cases these men must accept informal probation supervision along with their work assignments. If they fail to show up or do not work satisfactorily each Saturday they may be returned to court and have their assigned Saturdays extended or else have the plan terminated with the court then making a conventional disposition of the case.

The work detail plan is conducted as a truly humane way of dealing with certain misdemeanant cases and has the additional appeal of remarkable economy. The combination of the work detail feature and the volunteer sponsors provides Royal Oak with services which are substantially better than those of most courts serving misdemeanant cases. Furthermore, the enlistment of the volunteers has made many important people in the community aware of and closely acquainted with the court processes for misdemeanants, and this is a unique and valuable accomplishment.

Certain values demonstrated by the Royal Oak volunteer program have significance for other courts that might be interested in trying this approach to improvement of services:

1. The idea of building a service composed wholly of volunteers is workable as an initial effort but not as a permanent arrangement. The fact is that a volunteer service needs good administration as much as any other kind of organized activity does. It will survive in its initial stages without professional leadership while it enjoys the fresh energies and enthusiasm of the leader and the early recruits; but as it grows in size and settles down for the long haul there must be strong, skilled, full-time executive direction.

2. A volunteer program can get services started where funds for paid services could never be obtained initially. Particularly at the misdemean-

ant level it is extremely difficult to get appropriations for adequate probation service, but when a sizable and influential segment of the community is enthusiastic about a program, and when the program's value has thus been demonstrated, the public funds begin to be available to put the work on a properly supported basis.

3. The personality of the leader, usually the judge, is critical as an essential factor in the program's success, and it also has critical potential for later handicapping the program severely. Contributing time, energy, and money to the assistance of criminal offenders is not one of the popular causes. It can seldom compete with causes that involve the poignant problems of distressed children, for instance. So volunteers are not going to respond spontaneously to the cause of the adult criminal. They will respond to the personality of a leader, however, and the initiation of a volunteer probation service will need such potent leadership in its early stages. The risk is that some leaders do not have the ego strength to give up the spotlight when the initial impetus is gained and the time comes for administrative organization to replace the sole reliance on the personality of the leader. If the leader must keep the controls to himself the program becomes administratively hollow as it gets larger, and if the leader departs for any reason, or if his capacity to lead falters, the program can wither.

Fortunately, the Royal Oak program in its fifth year of operation was beginning to show signs of transition to administrative system. It is a program that deserves permanency and though its existence is a tribute to the leadership of the judge, it will survive and continue to honor the vision of its initiator only if it can eventually become independent of his daily and personal direction.

LEADERSHIP ESSENTIAL TO VOLUNTEER PROGRAM

The Royal Oak experience points up the fact that a volunteer sponsor program has a better chance when confined to a limited geographical area. When it serves one city or county it gains momentum from the context of local civic pride in which it operates, and the leadership can have greater effect as the person who directs the program can make an immediate and continuing impact on the townspeople who volunteer. By contrast, the federal probation system has for several decades used volunteer parole sponsors, but, with the program spread thinly over a whole country, no leader in Washington, no matter how dynamic, can accomplish any truly infectious influence over volunteers so far removed both from him and from each other. And a volunteer program, lacking, as it does, the motive power of the payroll, must draw its fuel from the ever-fresh enthusiasm of close-at-hand leadership.

This does not mean that a volunteer program can work only at a local level. It means only that efforts of similar quality will show a greater effectiveness at the local level than at a state or federal level. One example of a state-wide volunteer program is found in Connecticut where a private agency, the Connecticut Prison Association, operates a program that provides sponsors within the adult correctional system. Though this volunteer program seems to be working well at the state level, Connecticut is a very compact state in which it would be rare for a sponsor to have to travel more than sixty miles from his home to any institution or to any meeting of sponsors.

This sponsor program, being under a private agency, is, of course, administratively separate from the correctional system and is offered to the latter on a cooperative basis. So in this program the sponsor is not carrying official responsibility for cases; this remains in the hands of the institutional staff or the parole officers. The sponsor supplements the regular services by being available as a friend to the client. The casework staff in any institution may ask the Prison Association to assign a sponsor to any inmate who has no family or whose family is failing to meet the person's emotional need. Or a sponsor may be assigned because there are special practical problems in the case with which a lay person might particularly help. In some instances inmates themselves ask for sponsors, and, of course, their motives are not necessarily pure. But the ulterior motive is not important if the inmate is otherwise a person who is in need of the help that a sponsor can give.

The practice is to get the sponsor assigned six or more months in advance of the inmate's parole date, and the sponsor is then expected to visit his parolee once or twice a month. This period of time provides opportunity to develop a good relationship so that when the inmate leaves the prison and is no longer a "captive case" it is hoped that he will, as a parolee, still make use of the sponsor's friendship. Actually, the client's acceptance of a sponsor is fully voluntary and the arrangement can be terminated any time by either party. Although the program has some of the appearance of a "prison visiting" program it is more concerned with preparation for a successful parole experience in which the sponsor will be even more actively involved. A sponsor is assigned only one case at a time.

The Connecticut Prison Association has directed this program through the services of a social worker from another agency who has been employed to give about twelve hours per week of his extra time to the recruitment, training, and supervision of the sponsors, of whom there were about one hundred active at the end of 1965. Recruitment of sponsors is accomplished largely by stirring up interest through speaking engagements, in addition to the usual word-of-mouth advertising that any such program gets.

As an orientation procedure a number of new sponsors are asked to attend at least three meetings which are set at times convenient to them. These include thorough discussion of parole supervision so that the sponsor will not confuse his role with that of the parole officer. In subsequent meetings discussions are led by prison administrators and criminologists. A final meeting is held at one of the institutions. On a continuing basis there are monthly training meetings for all sponsors.

A program of this kind can expect to meet resistance initially, as the institutional administrators cannot be expected to welcome a radical new idea that someone else thought of. Even though a façade of cooperation may exist there will be need for patience in working out the many little ways in which the institutional world and the volunteer program have to adjust to each other. For instance, the institutions, which restrict each inmate to a limited few visits each month, were inclined to count the visit of the sponsor just as any other. For the success of the program it was essential that the sponsor's visit not be charged against the inmate's monthly quota, and this impediment had to be patiently worked on and eliminated.

At the end of four years of experience with the program the Prison Association is satisfied that the program is worthwhile even though a systematic evaluation has not been done. It is felt that its effectiveness lies in producing greater community awareness of correctional programs and consequent greater support for them.

In Perth, Australia, there is an example of the kind of volunteer program that achieves active community involvement under well-organized professional administration. The Child Welfare Department of Western Australia uses volunteers extensively to help with the supervision of delinquents who are placed on probation to that department by children's courts. Unlike Royal Oak, where the selection and instruction of volunteers is quite informal, the Perth volunteers are recruited systematically, screened, and trained elaborately. Much of the recruiting is done by advertisements in various public information media and then questionnaires are sent to all persons who respond. Detailed information is requested about their life history, education, and work record. An applicant's work history is relied upon as a major indicator of his stability.

Invariably the use of public information media for recruitment of volunteers produces far more responses than are usable, for this brings out persons whose reasons for volunteering are superficial, or suspect in various other ways. A quick and sweeping elimination process is therefore the first step. In one recruiting campaign in Perth 420 persons initially applied. Through scrutiny of the questionnaires these were screened to 80, and subsequent interviews left just 20 persons who were usable. As items of objective criteria it is required that volunteers (1) have at least a high school education; (2) preferably be married — no unmarried man over age 28 is accepted; (3) be in good health; (4) show good job stability; (5) have some hobby interests; (6) not be involved in too many extra activities.

In the interviews some more subjective criteria can be checked, such as kind and degree of motivation and balanced, healthy quality of religious interest. The volunteer must be willing and available to attend training sessions that are scheduled for twice a week, these usually being held in the mornings for women and in the evenings for the men. Staff persons from the Education Department of Western Australia either give lectures themselves or engage other persons locally to speak to the volunteers on subjects such as child welfare laws, development and use of case histories, preparation of reports, child psychology, causes and treatment of delinquency, human development and behavior. Each session is three hours, with one and one-half hours devoted to each of two subjects.

These training sessions have been supplemented by Saturday afternoon visits to training schools where the volunteers have a chance to help staff members handle groups of boys or girls. These visits provide actual contacts with children; they give more meaning to the content of the training sessions and they keep the volunteers content to stay with the long period of training. Even so, the original six-month period of training was found to be too long, for the volunteers were likely to fret about the delay in getting into actual case handling. The general practice has been to give the volunteers cases at the point that probation supervision begins; they do not do the initial investigations. Originally they were given the more tractable cases, but this was unsatisfactory, for they were bored with them. Consequently, the volunteers now receive more difficult cases, and sometimes even those that need intensive help. They may be assigned up to three cases each. Furthermore, the volunteer carries the case responsibility in a true sense; it is not also carried by one of the professionals.

As would be expected, the Child Welfare Department finds that such a program must include the three basic essentials of careful selection, thorough initial training, continuing supervision. Their sixty or so volunteers are under the full-time supervision of one staff member who allocates cases, reviews case records, and discusses them with the individual volunteers. There are also monthly meetings in which the volunteers as a group can talk over case management and techniques with the staff supervisor.

Ordinarily a volunteer program is assumed to mean that the workers receive no pay at all, but in the Perth experience it has been found desirable to make a small payment that will at least reimburse the volunteers for any of their out-of-pocket expenses. So each is paid about $45 (American) annually, and whether or not this meets the worker's expenses, the department feels that this gives it a much clearer right to require standards of performance and to terminate the service of any unsatisfactory person. There is no assumption that this is a cheap program. It does provide probation supervision at less expense than a fully staffed service, but the cost is not negligible. The selection process includes advertising costs and a considerable amount of expensive staff time in the interviewing and psychological testing. Though the Education Department organizes the training course, it bills the Child Welfare Department for the lecturers' fees. In general, that department is well pleased with the plan as being an economy measure to a limited extent and as being constantly valuable for public relations purposes.

Even though the correctional field seems to have an increasing interest in this use of volunteers, there is some ambivalence about it, with signs that it is even a declining practice in certain areas. Some European observers are tending to give less encouragement to volunteer programs as more people are available who have professional training and as more specialized techniques are developed.

Japan has used volunteers extensively and still is quite reliant on them, but officials there note that with the increased urbanization people have less personal interest in others and the lay citizens consequently do not respond as well to the volunteer probation work. Nevertheless, Japan does still make copious use of volunteers. The Japanese probation system recruits and selects them through its regional Probation-Parole Supervision Offices, where selection committees screen the volunteers for financial stability, motivation, and good standing in the community. The volunteers are formally appointed to two-year terms by the minister of justice and while they receive no salary they are reimbursed for any expenses and are compensated for any accidents incurred in this service. The Japanese government estimates that about 47,000 volunteers were active in adult probation work in 1965 and in regard to their usefulness they make the reasonable comment that "Probation is a treatment method to rehabilitate an offender in his community. Therefore, the understanding and cooperation of the community is indispensable."[5]

For volunteer services to juveniles there is a national coordinating council in Japan that fosters 730 Women's Rehabilitation Aid associations. These are less concerned with direct supervision of individual children than with supplementing state services by operating shelters, supplying medical care, clothing, or money, or arranging employment.[6]

Sweden is another country that has made the use of volunteers an integral part of its probation and parole services. In a major address at the Third United Nations Congress on the Prevention of Crime and the Treatment of Offenders, held in Stockholm in 1965, Sweden's minister of justice spoke of the many advantages of a volunteer program, including its value for good public relations, and mentioned that sometimes budgets for the Swedish correctional system have moved more successfully through Parliament because of the extra sympathetic support of members who themselves have served as volunteers in corrections. This suggests the wide range of kinds of people who respond to the volunteer program in Sweden, and the fact that this service has status enough to attract volunteers of substantial position and ability. Ordinarily a

[5] *Adult Probation and Other Non-Institutional Measures in Japan,* pamphlet published by Ministry of Justice, Japan, 1965, p. 13.
[6] *The Present State of Juvenile Delinquency and Counter-Measures in Japan,* pamphlet published by Ministry of Justice, Japan, 1965, p. 26.

staff person does the presentence investigation for the court, and if probation is granted the defendant is placed under supervision of a volunteer already selected by the staff person who investigated. Swedish volunteers are paid a token amount very much the same as the rate used in Perth. And like the experience in Japan, Sweden finds that volunteer probation officers in small towns and rural areas function well enough, but the impersonal bustle of the big cities tends to defeat the interest and the effectiveness of the volunteers.

England has traditionally used volunteers for prison visiting, and in one program, operated out of the Blackfriars Settlement in London, extensive training is given to volunteers, including regular visits to the prisons being served by the aftercare program. The professional staff person in charge of the volunteer program is thus given an opportunity to observe the way the volunteers handle themselves in relation to the prisoners. This provides a testing for the volunteers and gives them an opportunity to begin their acquaintance with the correctional program and the process of helping its clients. No pay is given these volunteers.

In Denmark, where probation and parole services are provided on a national basis by the Danish Welfare Society, the use of volunteers is a well-established practice. Over 800 volunteers are actively supervising probationers or parolees. A few of these carry as many as twenty or thirty cases each, but the majority of the volunteers have only from one to five cases. The practice is for all cases to be the responsibility of the regular professional workers who themselves supervise the more difficult ones, while about three-fourths of the cases on each caseload are assigned to volunteers. These volunteers come from a great variety of professions and are paid a fee of about $3.00 per month for each case they carry. They must provide the professional staff with regular case progress reports and are expected to call on the professional worker for assistance when problems of more than a routine nature arise.

THE COMMITTEE

There are some potential volunteers who may have little inclination for or skill in working directly with cases, but who can be useful to courts or correctional agencies in other ways. Offering such people committee membership may sound like an unexciting substitute for work with cases, but if it is cleverly conceived, committee work can be both effective and satisfying.

One of the better known practices of this kind is the appointment of an advisory committee, to a juvenile court, for instance. It is usually expected that the committee will advise mainly in respect to the probation services, and it is generally assumed that the creation of such a committee is, categorically, a good thing to do. But it should be recognized that although it can indeed be a good thing to do, it can also be a mistake. Some of the factors which determine which it will be are clear-cut and objective, while others are very subtle.

The subjective feelings with which a judge approaches the concept of an advisory committee may lead him to reject the idea if he is troubled by a sense of insecurity, or he may be led to try the idea — for the same reason. That is, his reaction may be that he needs no committee to tell him what to do, for he is the judge and he is the boss. Or he may decide that a committee of townspeople who become, in effect, his claque, will reflect his eminence, and so he looks for ego support in the committee device.

The person with the more secure personality will recognize that an advisory committee is never in a position to usurp or interfere with a judge's prerogatives unless the judge himself is weak and indecisive. He also recognizes that if sensible, responsible townspeople are put on such a committee any action they take will ordinarily be for the same eventual goal that the judge has, the improvement of his court and its services. He will also recognize that these goals are not jeopardized by the possibility of occasional disagreement between him and his committee. If the committee is going to have the prestige to be really helpful to the court it will have to have strong individuals on it, and an inherent feature of such strength is independent thinking.

So it is fairly obvious that the first important factor in the success of an advisory committee is the nature of the motivation of the judge or administrator who chooses to appoint such a committee. It would be too naive to assume that advisory committees are always appointed by people who are truly looking for advice. The appointing authority may see a committee as a practical political move in view of coming elections, for instance. Sometimes the committee is not expected to advise the court on what to do, but only to agree with something the court has already decided on and to help accomplish it. This in itself can be either a worthy or an unworthy motive. If a judge has a specific and subjective goal in mind and asks only that a committee echo his demands for what he has already decided upon, this is not in accord with the usual advisory committee concept and it may lead to disillusionment all around. This does not mean that a citizens' committee must in all instances formulate its own concept of its goal. Sometimes, as a result of a professionally done survey, or because of some amply self-evident condition, there is, properly enough, a predetermined action to be accomplished. In such a case a committee may be appointed and, with no loss of integrity, it may set out to accomplish a goal that has already been objectively determined. But this would be an action committee more than an advisory committee, and if the purpose for its creation has been honestly conceived and honestly presented to the committee it is a fully valid procedure.

However, for a truly advisory committee it is ordinarily essential to give the committee an honest charge to look at a proposal and to recommend or act according to the committee's own independent judgment. Not incompatible with this concept is the situation in which a committee is asked to help accomplish a goal stated in general terms, leaving the committee to determine and act on the specifics. As an illustration of this, one juvenile court judge was handicapped by having to work in quarters which were the shabby and cramped remnants of some city-owned facilities provided by the uninterested city council. The judge was unable to get any attention for his protests about the gross unsuitability of the space and nothing was accomplished until he appointed an advisory committee to the court. This is the kind of situation that calls for sensitive handling on the part of the judge, who should have good awareness of his own motives. In this instance the judge did have in mind a general goal for his new committee: to help him improve the working conditions of his court; but he did not dictate the specific form of that goal. He pointed the committee's attention toward the entirely self-evident problem in the court's physical setting and let the committee take it from there in its own way. It was left to the committee members to determine through their own study what was needed and what would be the best way to get it. The result was that these lay people presented to the city council not just a demand, but a plan. They had located a building, developed a design for remodeling, and mustered some broader community interest in and support for the idea. In due time the court moved into its new quarters, an abandoned fire department station which was completely rebuilt to provide probation offices, waiting rooms, courtroom, and judge's chambers, all of it modern, attractively impressive, and spacious. The committee had been used honestly and skillfully, and it did a fine job for the court.

An example of the action type of committee also comes from a juvenile court setting. In one major city there never had been a detention facility for juveniles and the necessity of jailing the children along with adult prisoners was a situation that was clearly bad. It was not necessary to have an advisory committee decide whether or not there should be a separate facility. It was only a matter of having a committee that would get action. To make the matter still more certain, consultants from the National Council on Crime and Delinquency had studied the situation, had recommended strongly that a detention facility be built, and had determined the size it should be. The facility still was not being built because the county board of supervisors was not feeling the necessary urgency about spending public moneys in this way.

At the court's request, the Community Welfare Council appointed a committee that was solely for the purpose of getting this one job done. Fifteen persons were recruited for the committee, and not one of them had any professional connection with social work, courts, or corrections. If they had any real knowledge of the operation of a juvenile court or detention facility it was only incidental. But this reflected the skill in their selection, for their job was not to appraise the need for or the use of such a facility; that had already been done by the professionals. Their job was to mobilize the power structure of the community to get the necessary final action taken. To this end, the members appointed were representatives of several of the biggest businesses in the city, and representatives of various organizations that were prestigious and influential. And in most instances these representatives were not just lower echelon personnel; they were the very top managers.

This central committee, used for its power and prestige, was then given the technical help it needed by the appointment of an auxiliary committee of experts, who became, in effect, an advisory committee to the action committee. Members on this subsidiary committee were social workers, police, agency executives and persons working in various capacities with delinquents. They met with the main committee but sat apart and had no voice or vote in the main committee's deliberations. They were there only to make their knowledge available to the committee members as needed.

The action committee designated subcommittees to explore such questions as the type of building needed, the site to be used, and the best method of financing. It took the committee a relatively short time to formulate its recommendations and to present them with effective publicity to the governing body of the county. When resulting action was taken by that body to go ahead with the project the committee was through.

Even if there is the soundest kind of motivation in the appointment of a committee it may be either a disappointing venture or a successful one depending upon the kind of people appointed and the kinds of assignments they are given. Too often, for instance, such committees have been put to work on a permanent basis when there is not a permanent job to be done; and this is one of the most common and more serious errors. If an advisory committee is intended to be permanent it requires work, imagination, and perseverance on the part of the judge or administrator whom it serves. It also requires skill and devotion on the part of some staff person who works with the committee. It can be a fatal error to suppose that an advisory committee can be appointed and sustained without any continuing investment of staff time. There is both professional and clerical time involved in feeding information and ideas to the committee members, in arranging fact-finding experiences for them, in arranging meetings, keeping records, and dealing with the endless questions and individual problems that a really active and useful committee can produce. The amount of work and the requirements of diplomacy that are involved are nicely suggested by a member of one such committee, writing about the staff members who "either know the answers to our questions or can get them posthaste — at the other end of the phone, as well as by mail. Besides, they have genuine political acumen; and they do not have the holier-than-thou attitude that is often encountered in 'trained' social workers who do not realize that most of us are 'trained' in something — if only life!" [7]

A committee does not live and function without something to do, and an agency is wise not to set up a continuing advisory committee unless it has a supply of tasks worthy of the committee's attention, and is prepared to provide the staff time necessary. Otherwise, it is likely that after an initial experience of dealing with some specific tasks, and

[7] Mrs. Edmund P. Williams, "Citizen Action Program in Texas," *N.P.P.A. News*, Vol. 38, No. 3 (May 1959), p. 2.

perhaps quite successfully, the committee is called together less and less often, then finally not at all. Or if the agency loses interest and offers less and less real work for the committee to do, the members make little effort to get to the meetings and the committee is then, for all practical purposes, dead. It may never really be recognized as defunct, but is just allowed to wither and cease functioning without any act of termination. This can hardly be called tragic, but it does leave those committee members less satisfied with their experience and so not quite such boosters for the court or agency as they should be.

It is for this reason that there is much argument in favor of the ad hoc committee such as the one described above that gave the final push to the detention home construction. A committee that is formed to give its attention to just one specific problem offers the advantage that committee members can be selected who are peculiarly appropriate to the task at hand; and it is possible to offer them definite release from the committee work as soon as the specific task is completed. This limited term of service also means that it is possible to get particularly high caliber and busy people who would not be able to accept membership on a continuing or permanent committee.

It is fairly natural for an agency to think of appointing an advisory committee and putting on it the educators, clergymen, social workers and others who have the kind of knowledge and concern that is related to the function of the agency they are to advise. This is fully appropriate if the committee is truly to be used for generating professional advice and guidance on some aspect of the agency's program. But when such people are appointed to a committee that may be more of a multi-purpose committee, such as a permanent advisory committee is certain to be, it will be found that the experts have limited usefulness on the committee and may even be a handicap to it.

In one instance a group of high school and junior high principals was deeply concerned about the need for a new facility for delinquent girls and was offering its services to the juvenile court to help get authorization for such a facility. When a study and action committee was appointed to promote the needed facility the principals were disappointed that their proffered help was not being used; no representative from their group was on the committee. The simple reason was that a high school principal, like any other professional who is working close to the problem, is not a suitable person for a committee that eventually has to influence the body of elected officials who must appropriate the money if the hoped-for project is accomplished. The politicians are superbly practical by necessity; they know that such a professional pays an infinitesimal fraction of the taxes that would be involved and he influences no block of votes. A labor union representative might know much less than the school principal about the character of the problem being considered, but if he is briefed on the proposed project and is sold on it he is a far more effective committee member, for his good will is going to be of importance to the members of the appropriating body at the next election. In the same way, the president of a large business concern will be of substantial influence because he represents an important part of the tax source from which the proposed project will be financed.

It becomes obvious that a major part of the art in using citizen committees lies in the sensitive selection of the right people for the right job, and then in giving them only that job to do. Persons of prestige and power in the community are usually gracious about helping an important social service project by accepting a committee assignment. But such people cannot give their time for an indefinite period and they will not be happy or useful if asked to do a job which is beneath their level of ability. This is not snobbery but only the fully practical concern of good use of their time. They are busy people, making important contributions in the business world, and their time should not be drawn upon for committee work unless it is for a task that challenges their capacity and offers them a chance to apply their talents and weight appropriately.

The most noteworthy application of the power-packed study and action committee in corrections is the Citizen Action Program which was developed by the National Probation and Parole Association (now National Council on Crime and Delinquency) in 1955 with an initial grant of $600,000 from the Ford Foundation. The technique was developed in eight states where the program was initially tried and by the end of 1965 there were eighteen states using this device to upgrade correctional services. Some highly satisfying progress had been made in most instances.

The typical procedure is to provide first a professional staff person, and a secretary, and then to start searching for names of suitable council members. This leads to an extremely large number of interviews as suggestions are solicited in conversations with many knowledgeable people. Council members are sought from among the highest level business executives in the state, from presidents of the largest and most influential organizations, or from among outstanding professional persons. As suitable names are acquired and screened the staff proceeds to get appointments to talk with these prospects. This is a crucial step, for it may be almost as much a matter of talking the prospect out of the assignment as of talking him into it. That is, he must be given the sales pitch that will get him interested, but at the same time he must not be oversold. In fact, he must be faced very realistically with the realities of the task, principally the amount of work involved. While it is hoped that he will join the council, he should not agree to do so, nor would he be accepted, if he cannot be a working member. Big-name people are sought for council membership, but no one is wanted just for his name. Each member must be willing and able to get to most of the monthly meetings and must be ready in other ways to help prepare the council's reports or carry its influence to the public or to the legislature. With candid, hardheaded recruitment like this the states have usually been able to put together councils that have great potential for accomplishing concrete improvement in correctional programs. Council members receive no compensation for their time and they pay their own expenses to meetings. This is part of the quality of objectivity and independence that characterizes these councils and that contributes so much to their effectiveness.

In keeping with the initial premise of a truly working council, the members are expected to work from their own knowledge of correctional problems rather than just supporting the views fed to them by professionals. So the first months in the experience of any citizen council are occupied in studying the whole correctional system in the state. In many states council members have visited jails, been locked in cells in reformatories, eaten in prison mess halls, been assigned one by one to spend a day with a parole agent, observed parole board hearings, toured juvenile training schools. From these observations they have been able to assign priorities to the needs of correctional services and have worked energetically to bring to the public more information than it has ever had before about the problems of the state correctional programs. The councils also work directly to influence legislation, but usually they find it essential first to educate the general public, for increased budgets and improved programs can best be accomplished when public concern is aroused.

Some of the significant programs discussed in the preceding chapters were created as a result of Citizen Action Programs. Altogether they have provided a splendid demonstration of the concept that not only can a lay person be highly effective in a professional field, but also the top-level business executive will give his attention, time, and energy to a volunteer effort like this if the effort is intelligently organized and if the issues present a challenge commensurate with the level of executive time and ability being expended.

For the professional agency executive who seeks to influence community attitudes, strengthen correctional resources, or just get larger budgets for his own operation, the skillful enlistment of lay citizens can be a vital factor in progress toward such goals. But he will also need a store of patience, for the public moves ponderously even though the man with the problem yearns for action now. This is true despite the fact that sociological changes are more rapid and profound with every year that comes. We can exploit the climate of change, and should do so whenever it will serve the purpose of local needs, but we must be prepared also for stubborn resistance to change. One author has commented that "Inertia, no less than social change, is a basic characteristic of human society." [8]

This is very true, but the persistence of the inertia we meet will be cracked most effectively by those professionals who learn how to enlist lay persons who, though they start with no technical knowledge of our work, have the energy and influence to generate fresh enthusiasm and perspective. To an increasing extent the significant progress to be made in probation and parole will be accomplished by this combined effort of the interested citizen and the correctional administrator who brings to his job a measure of what we might call practical imagination.

[8] Wayne McMillen, *Community Organization for Social Welfare* (Chicago: University of Chicago Press, 1945), p. 35.

BIBLIOGRAPHY AND INDEX

Bibliography

CASEWORK PHILOSOPHY AND METHOD

Aptekar, Herbert H. *Basic Concepts in Social Casework*. Chapel Hill, N.C.: University of North Carolina Press, 1941.

Bindra, Dalbir. *Motivation: A Systematic Reinterpretation*. New York: Ronald Press, 1959.

Chwast, Jacob. "A Small Goal Is Big Enough," *Crime and Delinquency*, Vol. 9, No. 2 (April 1963), pp. 158–162.

———. "Control, the Key to Offender Treatment," *American Journal of Psychotherapy*, Vol. 19, No. 1 (January 1965), pp. 116–125.

Clegg, Reed K. *Probation and Parole*. Springfield, Ill.: Charles C. Thomas, 1964.

Cloward, Richard A., and Lloyd E. Ohlin. *Delinquency and Opportunity*. Glencoe, Ill.: Free Press, 1960.

Glasser, William. "Reality Therapy," *Crime and Delinquency*, Vol. 10, No. 2 (April 1964), pp. 135–144.

———. *Reality Therapy*. New York: Harper and Row, 1965.

Grant, Marguerite Q., and Martin Warren. "Alternates to Institutionalization," *Children*, Vol. 10, No. 4 (July–August 1963), pp. 147–152.

Haley, Jay. *Strategies of Psychotherapy*. New York: Grune and Stratton, 1963.

Halleck, Seymore L. "The Impact of Professional Dishonesty on Behavior of Disturbed Adolescents," *Social Work*, Vol. 8, No. 2 (April 1963), pp. 48–55.

Hamilton, Gordon. *Theory and Practice of Social Casework*. New York: Columbia University Press, 1951.

Hardman, Dale. "The Function of the Probation Officer," *Federal Probation*, Vol. 24, No. 3 (September 1960), pp. 3–10.

Kahn, Alfred J. *A Court for Children*. New York: Columbia University Press, 1953.

Keve, Paul W. "Jail Can be Useful," *N.P.P.A. News*, Vol. 35, No. 5 (November 1956), p. 1.

283

Konopka, Gisela. "Adolescent Delinquent Girls," *Children*, Vol. 11, No. 1 (January–February 1964), pp. 21–26.
Lykke, Arthur F. *Parolees and Payrolls.* Springfield, Ill.: Charles C. Thomas, 1957.
Lytle, Milford B. "The Unpromising Client," *Crime and Delinquency*, Vol. 10, No. 2 (April 1964), pp. 130–134.
MacGregor, Robert, *et al. Multiple Impact Therapy with Families.* New York: McGraw-Hill, 1964.
Martin, John B. "The Saginaw Project," *Crime and Delinquency*, Vol. 6, No. 4 (October 1960), pp. 357–364.
Massimo, Joseph L., and Milton F. Shore. "A Comprehensive, Vocationally Oriented Psychotherapeutic Program for Delinquent Boys," *American Journal of Orthopsychiatry*, Vol. 33, No. 4 (July 1963), pp. 634–642.
Neisser, Marianne. "Judgments and the Nonjudgmental Attitude in Therapeutic Relationships," *Social Casework*, Vol. 46, No. 5 (May 1965), pp. 278–282.
Newman, Edward S. "An Experiment in Intensive Probation with Boys," *Crime and Delinquency*, Vol. 8, No. 2 (April 1962), pp. 151–160.
Overton, Alice. "Establishing the Relationship," *Crime and Delinquency*, Vol. 11, No. 3 (July 1965), pp. 229–238.
Parad, Howard J., and Roger R. Miller, eds. *Ego-Oriented Casework: Problems and Perspectives.* New York: Family Service Association of America, 1963.
Peck, Harris B., and Virginia Bellsmith. *Treatment of the Delinquent Adolescent.* New York: Family Service Association of America, 1954.
Rogers, Carl R. *The Clinical Treatment of the Problem Child.* Boston: Houghton Mifflin, 1939.
Rumney, Jay, and Joseph P. Murphy. *Probation and Social Adjustment.* New Brunswick, N.J.: Rutgers University Press, 1952.
Saginaw Probation Demonstration Project, The. Printed report of the Michigan Crime and Delinquency Council, 1963.
Schwitzgebel, Ralph R. *Street Corner Research.* Cambridge, Mass.: Harvard University Press, 1964.
Slack, Charles W. "Experimenter-Subject Psychotherapy: A New Method of Introducing Intensive Office Treatment for Unreachable Cases," *Mental Hygiene*, Vol. 44, No. 2 (April 1960), pp. 238–256.
"Survey of Supervision Practices of Probation Offices in the United States District Courts, A." Mimeographed report by the Federal Probation Training Center, Chicago, Ill., 1964.
Wallace, John A. "A Fresh Look at Old Probation Standards," *Crime and Delinquency*, Vol. 10, No. 2 (April 1964), pp. 124–129.
Warren, Marguerite Q. "An Experiment in Alternatives to Incarceration for Delinquent Youth," in *Correction in the Community — Alternatives to Incarceration.* Monograph No. 4, Board of Corrections, California, June 1964.
Young, Pauline V. *Social Treatment in Probation and Delinquency.* New York: McGraw-Hill, 1952.

GROUP PROGRAMS

Ackerman, Nathan W. *The Psychodynamics of Family Life, Diagnosis and Treatment of Family Relationships.* New York: Basic Books, 1958.
Bell, John Elderkin. *Family Group Therapy.* Public Health Monograph No. 64, U.S. Public Health Service, U.S. Department of Health, Education, and Welfare, 1961.
Bixby, F. Lovell, and Lloyd W. McCorkle. "Guided Group Interaction in Correctional Work," *American Sociological Review*, Vol. 16, No. 4 (August 1951), pp. 455–461.
Casey, Barbara. "Delinquent Parents Anonymous," *Focus*, Vol. 32, No. 6 (November 1953), pp. 178–182.

BIBLIOGRAPHY

Crites, Mark M. "Group Counseling for Probationers and Staff," *Crime and Delinquency*, Vol. 11, No. 4 (October 1965), pp. 355–359.

Durkin, Helen E. *Group Therapy for Mothers of Disturbed Children.* Springfield, Ill.: Charles C. Thomas, 1954.

Faust, Frederick L. "Group Counseling with Juveniles – by Staff without Professional Training in Groupwork," *Crime and Delinquency*, Vol. 11, No. 4 (October 1965), pp. 349–354.

Fenton, Norman, ed. *Explorations in the Use of Group Counseling in the County Correctional Program.* Palo Alto, Calif.: Pacific Books, 1962.

Fenton, Norman, and Kermit T. Wiltse. *Group Methods in the Public Welfare Program.* Palo Alto, Calif.: Pacific Books, 1963.

Irwin, Olive T. "Group Reporting in Juvenile Probation," *Crime and Delinquency*, Vol. 11, No. 4 (October 1965), pp. 341–348.

Jones, Maxwell. *Social Psychiatry.* Springfield, Ill.: Charles C. Thomas, 1962.

———. *The Therapeutic Community.* New York: Basic Books, 1953.

Klaw, Spencer. "Inside a T-Group," *Think* (publication of I.B.M. Co.), Vol. 31, No. 6 (November–December 1965), p. 26.

Konopka, Gisela. *Therapeutic Group Work with Children.* Minneapolis: University of Minnesota Press, 1949.

———. *Social Group Work: A Helping Process.* Engelwood Cliffs, N.Y.: Prentice-Hall, 1963.

———. "Adolescent Delinquent Girls," *Children*, Vol. 11, No. 1 (January–February 1964), pp. 21–26.

Luger, Milton. "Launching a New Program: Problems and Progress," *Syracuse Law Review*, Vol. 15, No. 4 (Summer 1964), pp. 693–703.

Mandel, Nathan Gary, and William H. Parsonage. "An Experiment in Adult 'Group-Parole' Supervision," *Crime and Delinquency*, Vol. 11, No. 4 (October 1965), pp. 313–325.

Middleman, Ruth, and Frank Seever. "Short-Term Camping for Boys with Behavior Problems," *Social Work*, Vol. 8, No. 2 (April 1963), pp. 88–95.

Miller, Michael M. "Psychodrama in the Treatment Program of a Juvenile Court," *Journal of Criminal Law, Criminology and Police Science*, Vol. 50, No. 5 (January–February 1960), p. 453.

Keve, Paul W., and John J. Fallon. "Sending Them Down the River," *Children*, Vol. 11, No. 5 (September–October 1964), pp. 174–178.

Primer of Short-Term Group Counseling, A. Pamphlet issued by Philadelphia Youth Study Center, September 1, 1962.

Rosenbaum, Max, and Milton Berger, eds. *Group Psychotherapy and Group Function.* New York: Basic Books, 1963.

Sarri, Rosemary C., and Robert D. Vinter. "Group Treatment Strategies in Juvenile Correctional Programs," *Crime and Delinquency*, Vol. 11, No. 4 (October 1965), pp. 326–340.

Slavson, S. R. *An Introduction to Group Therapy.* New York: International Universities Press, 1952.

Taylor, Charles W. "An Experiment in Group Counseling with Juvenile Parolees," *Crime and Delinquency*, Vol. 7, No. 4 (October 1961), pp. 329–336.

Wall, John, Jr., and June Ellis. "Group Treatment of Adolescent Males in a Juvenile Court Setting," *Federal Probation*, Vol. 21, No. 2 (June 1957), pp. 18–22.

Weeks, H. Ashley. *Youthful Offenders at Highfields.* Ann Arbor: The University of Michigan Press, 1958.

THE PROBLEM OF THE ADDICT

Brill, Leon. "Preliminary Experience of a Pilot Project in Drug Addiction," *Social Casework*, Vol. 42, No. 1 (January 1961), pp. 28–32.

IMAGINATIVE PROGRAMMING IN PROBATION AND PAROLE

Brown, Thorvald T. *The Enigma of Drug Addiction.* Springfield, Ill.: Charles C. Thomas, 1961.

————. "Narcotics and Nalline: Six Years of Testing," *Federal Probation,* Vol. 27, No. 2 (June 1963), pp. 27–32.

Celler, Emanuel. "An Alternative Proposal for Dealing with Drug Addiction," *Federal Probation,* Vol. 27, No. 2 (June 1963), pp. 24–26.

Chein, Isidor. "Narcotics Use among Juveniles," *Social Work,* Vol. 1, No. 2 (April 1956), pp. 50–60.

————, et al. *The Road to H.* New York: Basic Books, 1964.

Control and Treatment of Narcotic Use, The. Publication No. VII by National Parole Institutes of National Council on Crime and Delinquency, New York, September 1964.

Diskind, Meyer H. "New Horizons in the Treatment of Narcotic Addiction," *Federal Probation,* Vol. 24, No. 4 (December 1960), pp. 56–63.

Frazier, Thomas L. "Treating Young Drug Users: A Casework Approach," *Social Work,* Vol. 7, No. 3 (July 1962), pp. 94–101.

Harms, Ernest, ed. *Drug Addiction in Youth.* Long Island, N.Y.: Pergamon Press, 1965.

Klonsky, George. "Extended Supervision for Discharged Addict-Parolees," *Federal Probation,* Vol. 29, No. 1 (March 1965), pp. 39–44.

Kolb, Lawrence. *Drug Addiction.* Springfield, Ill.: Charles C. Thomas, 1962.

Lowry, James V. "Hospital Treatment of the Narcotics Addict," *Federal Probation,* Vol. 20, No. 4 (December 1956), pp. 42–51.

Maurer, David W., and Victor H. Vogel. *Narcotics and Narcotic Addiction.* Springfield, Ill.: Charles C. Thomas, 1954.

Narcotic Drug Addiction. Mental Health Monograph No. 2, U.S. Department of Health, Education, and Welfare. Washington, D.C.: U.S. Government Printing Office, 1963.

Narcotics Law Violations, a Policy Statement. Advisory Council of Judges, National Council on Crime and Delinquency, 1964.

Nyswanger, Marie. *The Drug Addict as a Patient.* New York: Grune and Stratton, 1956.

President's Advisory Commission on Narcotic and Drug Abuse. *Final Report.* Washington, D.C.: U.S. Government Printing Office, November 1963.

Proceedings, White House Conference on Narcotic and Drug Abuse, Sept. 27, 28, 1962. Washington, D.C.: U.S. Government Printing Office, 1962.

Rehabilitation in Drug Addiction. Mental Health Monograph No. 3. U.S. Department of Health, Education, and Welfare. Washington, D.C.: U.S. Government Printing Office, May 1963.

Schnur, Edwin M. *Narcotic Addiction in Britain and America.* Bloomington: Indiana University Press, 1962.

Shelley, Joseph. "Probation for the Drug Addict," *Focus,* Vol. 31, No. 1 (January 1952), pp. 1–6.

————, and Alexander Bassin. "Daytop Lodge: Halfway House for Drug Addicts," *Federal Probation,* Vol. 28, No. 4 (December 1964), pp. 46–54.

Wilner, Daniel M., and Gene G. Kassebaum, eds. *Narcotics.* New York: McGraw-Hill, 1965.

Wolk, Robert L., and Meyer H. Diskind. "Personality Dynamics of Mothers and Wives of Drug Addicts," *Crime and Delinquency,* Vol. 7, No. 2 (April 1961), pp. 148–152.

THE INDIGENOUS WORKER

Brager, George. "The Indigenous Worker: A New Approach to the Social Work Technician," *Social Work,* Vol. 10, No. 2 (April 1965), pp. 33–40.

BIBLIOGRAPHY

Briggs, Dennie L. "Convicted Felons as Social Therapists," *Corrective Psychiatry and Journal of Social Therapy*, Vol. 9, No. 3 (1963), pp. 122–127.

Cressey, Donald R. "Social Psychological Foundations for Using Criminals in the Rehabilitation of Criminals," *Journal of Research in Crime and Delinquency*, Vol. 2, No. 2 (July 1965), pp. 49–59.

Mogulof, Melvin B. "Involving Low-Income Neighborhoods in Antidelinquency Programs," *Social Work*, Vol. 10, No. 4 (October 1965), pp. 51–57.

Pearl, Arthur, and Frank Riessman. *New Careers for the Poor*. New York: Free Press, 1965.

Perlmutter, Felise, and Dorothy Durham. "Using Teenagers to Supplement Casework Service," *Social Work*, Vol. 10, No. 2 (April 1965), pp. 41–46.

Riessman, Frank. "The 'Helper' Therapy Principle," *Social Work*, Vol. 10, No. 2 (April 1965), pp. 27–32.

THE HALFWAY HOUSE AND THE GROUP HOME

Breslin, Maurice A., and Robert G. Crosswhite. "Residential Aftercare: An Indeterminate Step in the Correctional Process," *Federal Probation*, Vol. 27, No. 1 (March 1963), pp. 37–46.

Carpenter, Kenneth S. "Halfway Houses for Delinquent Youth," *Children*, Vol. 10, No. 6 (November–December 1963), pp. 224–229.

Kennedy, Robert F. "Halfway Houses Pay Off," *Crime and Delinquency*, Vol. 10, No. 1 (January 1964), pp. 1–7.

Krasner, William. "Hoodlum Priest and Respectable Convicts," *Harper's*, Vol. 222, No. 1329 (February 1961), pp. 57–62.

Meiners, Robert G. "A Halfway House for Parolees," *Federal Probation*, Vol. 29, No. 2 (June 1965), pp. 47–52.

Nice, Richard W. "Halfway House Aftercare for the Released Offender," *Crime and Delinquency*, Vol. 10, No. 1 (January 1964), pp. 8–14.

COMMUNITY ORGANIZATION

Boyd, Sophie. "Report of a Volunteer Project to Assist in the Social Adjustment of Persons Released from Prison," *Canadian Journal of Corrections*, Vol. 7, No. 4 (October 1965), pp. 394–405.

Green, Helen D. *Social Work Practice in Community Organization*. New York: Whiteside, 1954.

Leenhouts, Keith J. "The Volunteer's Role in Municipal Court Probation," *Crime and Delinquency*, Vol. 10, No. 1 (January 1964), pp. 29–37.

McDonald, Miles F. "Citizen Action: An Essential to Correctional Progress," *Crime and Delinquency*, Vol. 4, No. 4 (October 1958), pp. 356–364.

McMillen, Wayne. *Community Organization for Social Welfare*. Chicago: University of Chicago Press, 1945.

Macpherson, David P. "Community Action for Employment of Probationers," *Crime and Delinquency*, Vol. 10, No. 1 (January 1964), pp. 38–42.

Reed, Hugh P. "The Citizens' New Role in Combatting Crime," *Federal Probation*, Vol. 24, No. 4 (December 1960), pp. 31–36.

Ross, Murray G. *Community Organization; Theory and Principles*. New York: Harper and Row, 1955.

287

Index

Advisory committees, 272–277

Alabama Boys Industrial School, aftercare project, 56–57

Alameda County, Calif., program for drug addicts, 185–186

Alcoholics Anonymous, 190, 202, 234

Amenia, N.Y., START center, 164

American Friends Service Committee, halfway house program, 223–224, 229, 242

American Medical Association, 175

Apartment Home Complex (New York), 251–252

Auburn, N.Y., START center, 164

Austin MacCormick House (San Francisco), 224, 229, 234–235, 241–242

Australia, volunteer program in Perth, 267–269

Authority, function of helping process, 25–29

Base Expectancy Scoring Method, use in California, 40–43

Blackfriars Settlement (London), 241, 271

Boston, Citizenship Training Group, 108–110

Brentwood, N.Y., START center, 164

Brooklyn, N.Y.: use of programmed learning, 59–60; probation office residential program, 195

California: Special Service Unit, 10; use of Base Expectancy Scoring Method, 40–43; Intensive Parole Unit, 42; Community Treatment Project, 43–47; Community Delinquency Control Project, 55–56; group work training program for state parole officers, 66, 70–72; attitude of correctional system toward Synanon, 194; experiment with teacher helpers, 220–221; use of Salvation Army centers as halfway houses, 243; use of businessmen to help probationers, 255. *See also* Alameda County, Austin MacCormick House, Chino, Crenshaw House, East Los Angeles Halfway House, Humboldt County, Los Angeles, Oakland, Sacramento, San Francisco, Santa Monica, Stockton, Vacaville, William C. Harness House

California Department of Corrections: Special Service Unit, 10; Community Correctional Center, 225

California Institution for Men, *see* Chino

California Youth Authority, 43, 55, 56

288

INDEX

Maryland, *see* Montgomery County
Massachusetts, *see* Boston, Cambridge
Massimo, Joseph, research project, 12, 13, 19
Meiners, Robert, on halfway houses, 243
Methadone, use in addiction treatment, 178
Michigan: Saginaw Project, 54–55; halfway houses for juveniles, 226, 245–246; Parole Camp, 232; Resident Home Program, 244–245; Camp Pugsley, 256–258; use of laymen, 256–258; Royal Oak volunteer program, 260–265. *See also* Detroit
Middletown, N.Y., START center, 164
Midway Center (Los Angeles), 231
Minneapolis: first probation officer, 3; girls' discussion group, 77, 79; groups for divorced, 80; Weekend Ranch Program, 111–126; flying program, 128–130; hospital work program, 132; Restitutional Work Program, 134. *See also* Roncalli House
Minnesota, *see* Minneapolis, St. Paul
Minnesota Department of Corrections, group work research, 65, 77
Mississippi River, raft trip on, 116–121
Montgomery County, Md., use of psychodrama by juvenile court, 61

Nalline test, for narcotics use, 181, 185
Narcotics addicts, 19: relation of law enforcement to drug cost, 174–176; role of hospital, 176–179; community treatment programs, 179–188; use of self-help techniques (Synanon), 188–195; Daytop Lodge residential program, 195–200; East Los Angeles Halfway House, 236
National Academy of Sciences, 175
National Council on Crime and Delinquency, 274, 277
National Institute of Mental Health, 43–44, 179, 195, 217
National Probation and Parole Association, 277
Nevada, *see* Ely, Las Vegas, Reno
Nevada Youth Training Center, 127
New Careers Development Project (Vacaville, Calif.), 217–219, 220
New Jersey, *see* Highfields
New Jersey Narcotic Study Commission, 182
New Jersey State Department of Institu-

tions and Agencies, operates Highfields, 163
New Orleans: use of co-leader in group work, 77; terminus of raft trip, 118
New York City: parole surveillance unit, 10; case of parolee and black socks, 20; classification of parole cases, 40; drug cost in, 174–175; Washington Heights Rehabilitation Center, 179–181, 182; Special Narcotic Project, 182–184, 186–187; Synanon house, 193; Daytop Lodge, 195–200, 230; SCORE program, 206, 208–209; federal prerelease center, 225, 230; Seaman House, 226; Isaac T. Hopper Home, 244; Children's Village, 252
New York State: START centers, 164; parolees and jobs, 228–229. *See also* Brooklyn, Kings County, New York City, Syracuse
New York State Division for Youth: START centers, 164, 219–220; Apartment Home Complex, 251–252
New York State Division of Parole: surveillance unit, 10; classification of cases, 40; Special Narcotic Project, 182–184, 186–187
New York State Group Residence for Girls, 226, 231
Newark, N.J., Essexfields, 163–164, 169
North Carolina, *see* Chapel Hill

Oakland, Calif.: Community Delinquency Control Project, 55; Nalline testing by police, 181; Community Correctional Center, 225
O'Donnell, John A., on addicts, 177
Ohio, *see* Chillicothe, Cleveland, Hamilton County (Cincinnati)
One Hundred Dollar Misunderstanding (Robert Gover), 11–12
Oxford, N.J., Highfields program, 163, 165

Parents, group work with, 100–105
Peavine Mountain camp (Reno, Nev.), 215–217
Pennsylvania, *see* Philadelphia, Pittsburgh
Pennsylvania Parole Board, 232
Perth, Australia, volunteer program, 267–269
Philadelphia: group work by probation officers, 69, 70; use of puppets at Youth Study Center, 90
Pigeon, Helen, on reporting practice, 5, 6

291